# Ordo: Bath, Word, Prayer, Table

A Liturgical Primer in honor of Gordon W. Lathrop

Don

Many thanks for your support, friendship and guidance I have had for!

Every Blessing

Andy Lyons

# Ordo: Bath, Word, Prayer, Table

## A Liturgical Primer in honor of Gordon W. Lathrop

### Opening Essay by Edward Schillebeeckx

edited by

**Dirk G. Lange**

and

**Dwight W. Vogel**

OSL Publications
Akron, Ohio

# Ordo: Bath, Word, Prayer, Table
## A Liturgical Primer in honor of Gordon W. Lathrop

2005 by OSL Publications

ISBN 1-878009-52-4

This book is printed on acid-free paper that meets the
American National Standards Institute Z39.48 Standard

Produced and manufactured in the United States of America by
OSL PUBLICATIONS
*The publishing ministry of The Order of Saint Luke*
P. O. Box 22279
Akron Ohio 44302-0079

Cover art of the Torslunde Altarpiece is from the National Museum of Denmark
and used by permission.

All rights reserved. No part of this publication may be reproduced, stored in a retrieval system, or transmitted in any form or by any means, electronic, mechanical, photocopying, recording, or otherwise, without the prior permission of the copyright owner.

> The Order of Saint Luke is a religious order dedicated to sacramental and liturgical scholarship, education and practice. The purpose of the publishing ministry is to put into the hands of students and practitioners resources which have theological, historical, ecumenical and practical integrity.

*To the bath and the table,*

*To the prayer and the word,*

*I call every seeking soul.*

Inscription on a church bell at Hutchinson, Minnesota,
and later at West Denmark Lutheran Church
in Luck, Wisconsin

# Contents

Tribute ............................................................................................................................ xi
Preface ........................................................................................................................... xii

Introduction: Priming the Conversation on Liturgy ..................................................... 1

## TRAJECTORIES

1. Towards a Rediscovery of the Christian Sacraments: Ritualizing Religious Elements in Daily Life ......... 6
   *Edward Schillebeeckx*
   Introduction .............................................................................................................. 6
   Archaic Religious Images Deter Believers from Joining in Liturgical Celebrations ............. 7
   Reactions to the Breach between Anthropology and Theology
      in Traditional and Modern Sacramental Doctrine .................................................... 10
   Questions that are Inadequately Answered, and Pointless Questions that Need No Answers ..... 17
   Outline of a New View of Sacramental Liturgy, Theology and Pastoral Practice ................. 23

2. Liturgy and the Truth about Human Suffering ........................................................ 35
   *Don E. Saliers*
   Biblical Sourcing of the Church's Liturgical Life ....................................................... 37
   Human Suffering and the Dangerous Memory (*memoria passionis*) .......................... 40
   The Paradoxical Character of Liturgical Participation ............................................... 41
   Liturgy as a "School for Compassion" ...................................................................... 43
   The Limits of Liturgy in the Face of Suffering .......................................................... 44

## LITURGICAL ORDO

### 3. Gathering, Ordo, and Baptism .................................................................. 47
*Anita Stauffer and Dirk G. Lange*

    Part I - S. Anita Stauffer ................................................................................. 47

    Part II – Dirk G. Lange ................................................................................... 51

        Baptism: a Confrontation ........................................................................ 52

        Baptism and Faith .................................................................................. 54

### 4. Proclaiming and Preaching ................................................................... 58
*Samuel Torvend*

    Now You are the Body of Christ ...................................................................... 58

    The Needs of the Body .................................................................................. 59

    The Movement of the Body ........................................................................... 60

    The Body Breathing Out ................................................................................ 61

    The Movement of the Body ........................................................................... 63

    Nourishing the Body ..................................................................................... 65

    The Body Given Away .................................................................................. 66

### 5. Teach Us to Pray ................................................................................... 71
*Gail Ramshaw*

    Western Liturgical Prayer ............................................................................... 71

    The Prayer Jesus Taught ................................................................................ 73

    The Eucharistic Prayer ................................................................................... 75

    The Prayer of the Day .................................................................................... 77

    The Intercessions .......................................................................................... 78

### 6. Eating, Drinking, Sending: Reflections on the Juxtaposition of Law and Event in the Eucharist ......... 84
*Dirk G. Lange*

    Eucharist and Law ........................................................................................ 84

    Eucharist as Event ......................................................................................... 86

    Hermeneutics of Event .................................................................................. 91

    Eucharist and Sending ................................................................................... 96

## LITURGICAL RE-ORIENTATION

### 7. Liturgy: Praising God .................................................................................. 100
*Melva Wilson Costen*

Groaning In Praise .................................................................................. 100

Ancient Roots of Praise .......................................................................... 101

Hebrew Temple Praise ............................................................................ 101

Psalms in the Hebrew Assembly ............................................................. 103

Psalms in the Christian Assembly ........................................................... 105

Other Expressions of Praise .................................................................... 107

Praise in Twenty-First Century Liturgy ................................................... 111

Praise as Foundational to the Shape of the Liturgy ................................. 113

### 8. Liturgy: The *Ordo* of Liturgical Space ............................................... 118
*Gláucia Vasconcelos Wilkey*

Précis: A Church's Need of a House ....................................................... 118

A Metaphor from the World of Music ..................................................... 119

People and Place as One: A Theme Ancient and New ............................ 120

A Room for A View ................................................................................ 122

A Second Metaphor: *Semillas Besadas* ................................................. 127

Sunday: the *Dia da Festa* ...................................................................... 128

Epiphany: Theology, Culture and the Stars ............................................. 131

Everywhere This River Goes .................................................................. 134

### 9. Liturgy: The *Ordo* of Time ................................................................... 139
*Dwight W. Vogel*

Lord's Day .............................................................................................. 141

Daily Prayer ........................................................................................... 143

Liturgical Year: Times and Seasons in the Church's Life ....................... 156

10. LITURGY RESHAPING SOCIETY .................................................................................. 164
    *Cynthia D. Moe-Lobeda*
    The Question: Posed, Answered (Offensively), Posed Anew ............................................ 164
    A School for Morally Empowering Seeing ...................................................................... 166
    Eucharist as *Koinonia* .................................................................................................... 172
    Communion as *Eucharistia* and as True "Body and Blood of Christ" ......................... 177
    In Sum ............................................................................................................................. 179

11. VIOLENT DEATH, PUBLIC TRAGEDY, AND RITUALS OF LAMENT: AN INTERFAITH AGENDA ............................ 188
    *Herbert Anderson*
    The Proximity of Death without Meaning or Sense ....................................................... 188
    Public Tragedy and Communal Grief ............................................................................. 190
    Restorative Stories and Rituals ....................................................................................... 191
    Planning a Public Ritual Response to Public Tragedy ................................................... 192
    Rituals of Lament ............................................................................................................ 196

12. LITURGY: MANY BECOMING ONE ............................................................................. 201
    Liturgy: A Sign That Unites And Divides ...................................................................... 201
    Liturgical *Ordo*: A Road to Unity ................................................................................. 202
    Conclusion ....................................................................................................................... 213

## CONCLUSION

BATH, WORD, PRAYER, TABLE: REFLECTIONS ON DOING THE LITURGICAL *ORDO* IN A POSTMODERN TIME ........... 216
    *Gordon W. Lathrop*
    Postmodern challenges to an ecumenical *ordo* ............................................................. 218
    Misuses of the *Ordo* ...................................................................................................... 219
    The *Ordo* as Ordinary Life, Ritualized to Bear the Gospel .......................................... 221
    On Doing the *Ordo* in a Postmodern Time ................................................................... 224

CONTRIBUTORS ................................................................................................................ 229

PUBLICATIONS OF GORDON W. LATHROP ....................................................................... 231

# Introduction

## Priming the Conversation on Liturgy

*Dirk G. Lange*

Participating in an on-going conversation, as the various theologians do in this book, allows the opportunity for reflection. This is true for the writers represented here as they reflect on years of collegiality and conversation with Gordon Lathrop; it is also true for the reader, who is privileged not just to overhear the conversation but to be an active participant in that conversation through the vehicles of reading and reflection. This conversation is not a theological or even liturgical symposium offering us the opportunity to debate the "meaning" of the liturgy or aesthetics or desire, going our way confident in our position and in our (often categorical) assessment of our colleagues' viewpoints. Rather, participation and reflection in this sort of on-going conversation can return us to a beginning we may not have fully understood before.

What do I mean? Leaving the strictly liturgical domain, we may find a language from outside theology. Remember Socrates who, after having heard the many divergent speeches on eros, speaks himself about an encounter in his youth with Diotima? He returns to the beginnings of a conversation that has followed him throughout his life. This conversation marked Socrates profoundly. Many years later, in the *Symposium*, he returns to begin that conversation again. His reasons for returning and questioning remain unknown to us but here, in the on-going conversation of this book, something "returns" as well. In these chapters we return, in different ways, to our on-going conversations with Gordon W. Lathrop; we share those conversations and explore ways in which they might bear fruit for the ecumenical shape of the liturgy. But strangely, in that "returning," something also begins – something of which even the individual authors are not always fully aware.

This primer witnesses to a profound liturgical dynamic in its structure and in its content. The structure appears straightforward: a section dealing with the components of the *ordo* and a section of commentary on what that *ordo* means for individual lives, our society and our world. Yet that straightforward structure is strangely bracketed by two other sections, one that dares call itself "Trajectories" and the other "Conclusion." These two "strangely" bracket the main sections because the one, "Trajectories" questions those very directions and the second, "Conclusion," invites us to further exploration.

In the opening chapter of "Trajectories," Lathrop's doctoral advisor, Edward Schillebeeckx, returns to honor the work of his student. The reader will notice something peculiar with this chapter. It does not look back but looks forward by posing questions that shake the foundations of liturgical theology and practice, challenging theologians to develop questions pertinent for liturgical theology today.

Edward Schillebeeckx, in this magisterial chapter outlining his current thought on liturgical studies and hinting toward his future work, calls upon the words of a poet in speaking of "a vision distilled to ritual" (Schillebeeckx, page 24). Liturgy is the vision of God's dominion distilled into ritual and the rhythms of our daily lives. "In innumerable, decipherable, historical moments, in ordinary daily life among people in the *here and now*, we can discern sparks of the grace of God's kingdom which continually 'irrupts' into human history in and through our faithful commitment to the world's problems. We can share, experience and interpret those sparks of divine grace *in* our human behavior. As people, as believers, we also 'ritualize' it at appointed times, celebrating what happens and praising God" (Schillebeeckx, page 24).

Liturgy is the celebration of an irruption: God's irruption into our lives, a theme that will be pursued repeatedly by the authors of this primer. Liturgy is not simply the remembering of a past event but the distillation of that event as an irruption in the present moment. It is discovering the Cross present in the world today (see Lange, "Eating, Drinking, Sending: Reflections on the Juxtaposition of Law and Event in the Eucharist," page 84).

Schillebeeckx's appeal to the field of ritual studies comes with an admonition and a warning. We need to explore a language that comes from the outside, from beyond the boundaries of theological discourse, all the while remembering that every theory has a "hole." There is no decisive victor "in the battle for consensus on a conclusive theory of rituality" (Schillebeeckx, page 17). We are constantly challenged to negotiate the juxtaposition between *legomenon* and *dromenon,* the verbal and the physical. Schillebeeckx poses haunting questions: How do we revitalize lost meaning? How do we survive by way of ruptures?

Don Saliers understands this "vision distilled to ritual" in terms of welcome. The liturgy as ritualized irruption is transformative of irruption in our human experience. Liturgy is not an escape from the contradictions of human living, it is the welcome of everything human – joy and suffering. Christian liturgical life with "its own profound center in the passion, death and resurrection of Christ" (Saliers, page 41) places human experience in juxtaposition to the "truthfulness" of the divine engagement. In that juxtaposition, something new is said about suffering: the liturgy does not "save" us from suffering. It does not protect us but it gives us a vision for the world in which suffering and the whole stretch of human pathos is brought into a deeper, Gospel rhythm. With the irruptions of human living that are both suffering and joy, liturgy sings new song.

Gordon Lathrop echoes the brackets opened by Schillebeeckx and Saliers. Perhaps the reader should begin at the end, reading the last chapter first! The liturgy itself begins with an ending. Baptism (and in the remembrance of baptism) proclaims death, then life – immersion into the death and resurrection of Jesus Christ. In other words, the liturgy always points beyond itself. The underlying dynamic suggests that we cannot close the liturgical circle; we cannot definitively "define" what is happening.

Lathrop begins with a fiery irruption that silences the bell and, in that silence, questions the relevance of the *ordo* (Lathrop, page 216 - 217). This question makes explicit the questions throughout this primer. Each author asks about relevance and in that questioning breaks open the *ordo*, freeing the *ordo* from any enslavement to ideology. The *ordo* is not a "meta-narrative" (Lathrop, page 219). The *ordo* does not close down discussion, searching, life; it does not regress into liturgical unification or liturgical centralism (Lathrop, page 220). Much more, the *ordo* invites. It invites into "the pattern of these good things" (Justin Martyr, *Apology*). The *ordo* invites into a pattern that is curiously juxtaposed against itself – maintaining juxtaposition as its very structure. The "ecumenical *ordo*" (Lathrop, page 224) is this juxtaposition.

The ecumenical *ordo* is, first of all, a "critical conversation." This conversation is deeply engaged throughout this book. S. Anita Stauffer reminds us of the plurality of baptismal practices and baptismal metaphors and the challenge these pose to any easy conceptions of initiation we may have. Gail Ramshaw, examining the dynamics of different prayers forms (the Lord's prayer, prayer of the day, eucharistic prayer, and intercessions), focuses on our attempts to access a "power" beyond ourselves. But this power is none other than Jesus Christ who constitutes a connection between the divine and the human (Ramshaw, page 73). This power is none other than that person constituted by juxtaposition – Jesus and Christ – and so our prayer holds at least two things in tension, the already and the not yet. We, the praying assembly, become witnesses in our own lives to this juxtaposition. This connection is not to be sought far off nor isolated in particular liturgical acts or symbols but in and through the cries of a needy world – a world ever present in the eucharistic celebration. My chapter, "Eating, Drinking,

# Ordo: Bath, Word, Prayer, Table

Sending," focuses the eucharistic action on a dissemination of meaning. When we remember Jesus Christ, when we remember the cross, we are placed next to suffering in this world. Samuel Torvend summarizes the second section ('Liturgical *Ordo*') when he writes that preaching, placing word next to word, word next to body, moves us "toward the city" (Torvend, page 66). The juxtaposition within worship itself, including the juxtaposition of our bodies within the assembly, will send us to Christ in the city – Christ present as the useless, impure, hungry (Torvend, page 67).

The section entitled 'Liturgical Re-Orientation' addresses the question of worship's relationship to the world – to culture, society, religion. Melva Costen explores praise as an often "overlooked *anamnesis*" (Costen, page 100). Praise is expressed not only as exuberance but in deeds and actions (Costen, page 108). The whole body moves towards God, joining the rhythm of the universe in its joy and in its pain. This movement, this rhythm, is a deep irruption of the Holy Spirit through ritual action. Liturgical spaces sense this rhythm as Glaucia Vasconcelos-Wilkey demonstrates (see chapter 8). Our spaces need to give the Spirit room to irrupt. Our liturgical spaces need to give us a "room for a view:" a way of seeing, hearing, enacting, thanking God for mercy tasted in Christ (Vasconcelos-Wilkey, page 122). But this "room for a view," this liturgical space in which we encounter the Triune God, is not an isolated space: connected to the life around it, it re-orients the world. A space of prayer is a space that invites all into its pattern, especially the outcast and the "not-so-like-us " (Vasconcelos-Wilkey, page 126).

The house re-orienting us in space, enabling us to see and hear what our eyes and ears might miss, is echoed in a re-orientation of time. In liturgical time, as Dwight Vogel writes, "memory, mystery, and imagination all have appropriate roles to play" (Vogel, page 140). In a fine analysis of the history and structure of daily prayers, Vogel asserts that time itself is redefined through liturgical action. Yet even the *ordo* of daily prayer is not a fixed "order" but the Church's on-going experience of being formed into a deeper rhythm of liturgical, even Gospel, time. And this *ordo* of liturgical time is itself a witness to the "one great Paschal unity" (Vogel, page 159) placing the seasons in juxtaposition to Easter and the days of the week to the day of the Resurrection, the eighth day. Once again, even the rhythms of our lives are constantly opened to a deeper reality.

Cynthia Moe-Lobeda challenges the rhythms of our lives in their constant temptation to complacency. If the liturgy is intimately connected to the world then why is it not transformative of the world? If the eucharist suggests an economy in which there is food for all, why does a western world, steeped in eucharistic practice, hoard the wealth of the earth? These haunting questions irrupt and yet point to the same openings of which praise, space and time have made us aware. The rites of baptism and eucharist, our very ritual enactments, have the potential of empowering us to see morally (Moe-Lobeda, page 166). It is as if *koinonia* and *eucharistia* makes us first aware of the deep breath of life within us; a breath which is not our own, not for our own sustenance, but for the world – to be "body of Christ" in the world. The transformative action of the eucharist, and, we may add, the transformative action of liturgy itself, is not a spiritually centered moment aiming at the salvation of the individual. This transformative action is always social. It calls into question all our political, social, economic constructions without ever absolutizing, without ever proposing itself as a definitive program.

The same movement from within to without is witnessed in Herbert Anderson's chapter on rituals of pastoral care and the world in which we live. "What kind of rituals will reweave the social fabric, renew our visions of hope and be the source of joy?" (Anderson, page 188). Anderson calls on worship leaders to rediscover the rituals of lament and, through lament, honesty within our rituals. These rituals unlock secret pain perhaps permitting communities to be honest with themselves. Again, the juxtapositions of worship help us avoid absolutizing (Anderson, page 195 - 196).

Anscar J. Chupungco, OSB concludes this section on Liturgical Orientation with a reflection on the ecumenical movement. Chupungco also wrestles with the question Lathrop poses: what other thing might be juxtaposed to the *ordo* itself? "Unity" in *ordo* "does not negate the fundamental freedom of any church to determine its pattern of worship under the guidance of the Holy Spirit" (Chupungco, page 214). In other words, unity avoids both unification and centralism; it is, perhaps, much more that invitation into the community, into the church – into a "space for preaching the word, celebrating baptism and Eucharist, and welcoming all the members of Christ into our house" (Chupungco, page 213).

This festschrift in honor of our teacher, mentor, pastor, brother, and friend is subtitled "A Liturgy Primer." The label "primer" can be misleading. It can be understood as a book simply providing the reader/student with the basics on a particular subject. This is not how "primer" is understood in this collection. Rather than simply providing the reader/student with the basic insight on a particular subject, this collection embodies the second lexicographical sense of "primer:" *a device for priming, an object "containing percussion powder or compound used to ignite an explosive charge"* (Merriam-Webster Dictionary). You are invited into these juxtapositions. You are invited into this irruption.

# Preface

The idea for this volume came while I was still studying with Gordon Lathrop at the Lutheran Theological Seminary at Philadelphia. The first persons with whom I spoke encouraged me immensely – they know who they are. But realizing that a *Festschrift* is not always of general interest and wishing this volume to reach more people than only those who studied with or have known Gordon Lathrop, the structure of the volume was conceived as an introduction to the field of study that Gordon Lathrop has invigorated and profoundly renewed.

I am deeply grateful to the scholars who contributed to this *Festschrift*. Each one, without a hesitation, accepted the invitation. Each one, with unique gifts in thought and writing, has shared part of their on-going dialogue with the work of Gordon W. Lathrop. The greatest acknowledgement is fruitful, energetic, creative engagement on the proposed subject. Dwight W. Vogel has been incomparable in assisting me through the editorial process. And special thanks to Nancy Bryan Crouch and the late Timothy Crouch for immediately embracing the idea of this "Liturgical Primer."

> Dirk G. Lange
> September 2$^{nd}$, 2005
> Philadelphia, Pennsylvania

It took only a heart-beat for me to accept the invitation to collaborate with Dirk G. Lange in co-editing this volume in honor of Gordon Lathrop. Gordon and I have been long-time colleagues in the Liturgical Theology seminar of the North American Academy of Liturgy. I had the privilege of being a respondent there to his pre-publication presentation of *Holy Things: A Liturgical Theology* more than a decade ago. His perceptive and creative contributions to the discussions in that seminar have taught me much. I have never taken a class from him; yet I count myself not only his colleague and friend, but also one of his grateful students.

The idea of a "festschrift in a different key" was Dirk's. He is the parent of the book; I am the mid-wife. What we have set out to do, with the help of other colleagues whose life and thought have also been greatly influenced by Gordon Lathrop's work, is to "prime" the liturgical conversation across a broad liturgical spectrum. The authors have been invited to address specific topics so that a panorama of liturgical themes may be addressed. It is our hope that teachers and students, pastors and people concerned with the liturgy of the Church may be stimulated to further conversation through the provocative chapters included here. Gordon Lathrop's work has centered on liturgy in the life of the Church for the sake of the world. Perhaps the greatest way to do him honor is to foster further conversations on the liturgy.

Dwight W. Vogel
Feast of Matthew the Evangelist, 2005
Pilgrim Place
Claremont, California

# Tribute

Theologians working in the fields of ritual studies and liturgical practice here pay tribute to the liturgist Gordon Lathrop. One reason why I join in this praise is his care for combining liturgical studies with biblical exegesis. The consequence of this method is that he is always sensitive to hold together, never to separate, the holy rites of sacramental liturgy and the religious dimensions of our human daily life. It is important that we resist any break between anthropology and theology, between daily life and liturgical life. It is precisely Lathrop's combining of biblical reflections with liturgical considerations that vouches for both our human experiences, the positive as well as the negative ones, and our ecclesial symbolic actions, which we discover can and do interrupt our worldviews.

In honor of the liturgical work of Professor Lathrop, I decided to subtitle my contribution "Ritualizing Religious Elements in Human Daily Life," for I heartily agree with Gordon Lathrop's recent statement:

> The Christian experience of the broken symbols makes a proposal to all worldviews, scientific, religious, philosophical: let them be held critically, with room for lament, room for the others, and room for mercy. Our worldviews, especially our religious worldviews, are not themselves God. Only One is holy.*

— Edward Schillebeeckx

*Worship* 77 [2003] 13

# ONE

# Towards a Rediscovery of the Christian Sacraments: Ritualizing Religious Elements in Daily Life

*Edward Schillebeeckx*

## INTRODUCTION

Since Vatican II, sacramental liturgical practice has assumed widely divergent forms. In some countries (including the Netherlands) the verbal aspect of the liturgy, denoted by the traditional patristic term *legomenon* (rooted in the Hellenistic mysteries – I would render it with 'ministry of the word:' verbal expressions) is much accentuated. At the same time, the aspect indicated by the equally ancient word *drómenon* – festive, even dramatic enactments forming an expressive whole of gestures, postures, rhythmic movements, 'doing something' with substances like water, oil or incense in an ambience of music, hymns and moments of silence, light and space – is kept subdued, sometimes eclipsed by treating these things as inessential extras. Elsewhere, for instance in Africa and Latin America, liturgy is embedded in the indigenous culture and is expressed realistically in a recognizable, enthusiastic ritual performance that acts as an identity-forming force throughout the celebrating community. In the first case, what one might call a "protestantization" results in a verbal, sometimes cerebral liturgy, evoking unorthodox connotations. In the second case, the central curial authority in Rome greets these enthusiastic celebrations with a certain hesitancy and transparent forms of constraint. This at a time when these Catholic peoples often interweave their animated, serio-playful festive celebrations with archaic religious images that were once familiar – although, one might ask, for how long?

A truly harmonious blend of *legomenon* and *drómenon*, or word and gesture, is not easily achieved. To my mind that is understandable after so many centuries of stagnation of liturgical creativity, which has been curbed in Catholic churches ever since the Council of Trent. Only recently Vatican

II liberated liturgy from its fixation on rigid adherence to formulas and gestures, and brought some flexibility. The scope this opened up unleashed a fervour that led, in some instances, to an impetuous approach that was hardly justifiable, either liturgically or theologically – counter to the still modest intentions of Vatican II. But no one can be blamed for the fact that a harmonious balance in current sacramental, liturgical practice cannot be taken for granted at this stage. Accusations in this regard, particularly if directed to the proponents of liturgical innovation, I consider plain unfair.

While Christianity may be a school of wisdom, it is not a philosophical institution. Besides the dogmatic tradition, which transmits the substance of the Christian faith through catechesis, and in addition to an authoritative tradition, an academic theological, a popularizing theological and a popular theological religious tradition, there are other ways in which the Christian gospel fans out in all sorts of traditions. The first that comes to mind are the biblical stories depicted in mosaics, sculptures and paintings in old churches, basilicas and cathedrals, thus familiarizing the faithful with the principal stories of the first and second testaments – for many of them their sole access to biblical history, with its message, inspiration and orientation. Nor should one forget the mystagogy from the time of the church fathers, firmly focused on knowledge, instruction in the practice and mystically charged experience of the initiation sacraments: baptism, anointment or confirmation, and the eucharist. Thirdly, there are the vitally important experiential and religious practices that come on the tides of the church's liturgical seasons.

These ritual, liturgical expressions of religious belief are what the Christian sacraments are about, expressing and passing on a shared religious identity. But to many believers these expressions are now in crisis, a crisis so acute that many have turned their backs on sacramental practice.

Archaic Religious Images Deter Believers from Joining in Liturgical Celebrations

In my experience, many peripheral Catholics cite all sorts of outdated religious images as their main reason for distancing themselves from the institutional church and its sacramental practices. These images are dictated ever more categorically by ecclesiastic decree the more scepticism about them grows among believers; yet, as images, they stem from another age and are hard to affirm rationally today. I think this motive is closer to the truth than the oft-repeated charge of secularization, even though the latter, on account of its own acquired truths, has an indirect bearing on the issue. Archaic religious images cause many people to experience sacraments as things that have become irrelevant.

One of the axioms of traditional sacramental theology is that the sacraments are intrinsically effective, at any rate for those who put no impediment or obstacle (*obex*) in the way of these gifts from

# Ordo: Bath, Word, Prayer, Table

God. But in our time a major obstacle to church attendance and active participation in what happens there in liturgical celebration is that many people no longer have any meaningful conception of what they would actually be celebrating. To many people in our late modern era, some of the images and concepts that have been used over the ages to articulate the Christian content of the gospel have become inapplicable, incomprehensible, even absurd. So what does one celebrate?

Nowadays religious concepts and images of God conflict fiercely. To clarify the point I need merely summarize some of the questions with which believers confront me. How can you seriously claim that the whole world was saved by the historically fortuitous death of one individual? To which some feminists would add: "and a man to boot!" How can one talk of God's kingdom of peace when, at the end of twenty centuries of Christianity, we have lived through two world wars, seen holocausts on an unprecedented scale, as well as any number of massive ethnic purges in various parts of the world, in which Christian were and are involved? In addition, the innumerable images that people have of, or ascribe to, heaven and hell have meant that to many these have become mere fables, in comparison with which the Santa Claus festival, intended for children, seems more comprehensible and rather more plausible. What Christianity calls, to my mind correctly, the "divinity" of the man Jesus is represented in the minds of many believers by images like: "Look! Here God in person walks at the lake of Tiberias or Gennesareth, and over there he steps into the boat." All such metaphoric terms referring to religious realities have lost their spontaneity; many people no longer perceive anything meaningful in them. Yet what is expressed by such terms as *God, Jesus the Messiah, Son of God, kingdom of God, salvation, redemption, reconciliation,* and so on, is real to every Christian. This is the reality that all Christian sacraments are essentially about, unless one experiences them as a popular potpourri, something like a carnival that one can perhaps still value as a human "safety valve."

The *obex* or obstacle to fruitful, salvific sacramental celebration is present in late modern churchgoers themselves even before they enter the church. The *legomenon*, the verbalized message, has long ago lost its comprehensible meaning. And the uncomprehended *legomenon* presages the death of the accompanying *drómenon*, the whole liturgy, for that literally means the dramatic performance or enactment of a liturgical scenario, which I shall spell out in more detail in a postscript to this article. If a sacrament no longer 'says' or 'does' anything to believers, it becomes pointless, even if every step is meticulously followed. 'What's the use?' I heard a twelve-year-old girl say in the United States after a Sunday mass, which struck me, too, as pretty well meaningless, with its accompanying banal talk on video tape. Even though it was all conducted precisely and punctiliously according to the official precepts, there was no bond with the communicants, no inspiration, just a vacuous routine.

This situation shows that a misconception of the faith – whether because of poor preaching, misunderstanding of the proclamation, intra-church polarization, a pervasive criticism of church policy, or for whatever reason – can become an insuperable hurdle to joining in liturgical "performances" where hardly any of the script that is being performed still makes sense, in which people experience nothing that orients or inspires them or keeps them going. Let's be honest: that is the situation of many Western Christians today. And I want to add: the situation (at least in itself) has nothing to do with a decline in religious feeling among Christian believers, as some (counter to realistic studies) persist in maintaining with naively candid ingenuousness. The very people (lay people and pastors, whatever you choose to call them) who still try to do something about the problem are singled out as scapegoats. They are said to be the cause of the flagging of Christian religious feeling (and if they do not get the blame, then their theologians do).

I want to state explicitly that I advocate a lifestyle nourished by the sacraments as a distinctive form of religious experience, but at the same time I object to publications that, in justifiable reaction against intellectualistic explanations of the sacraments, do not allow for the distinction (not rigidly enforceable but nonetheless real) between 'faith', including its knowable *content*, and religious *images*. Thus visualizing (bodily) resurrection as the raising of *the deceased body* in no way reflects the Christian meaning of the raising of the dead or human eschatological salvation, for that includes spiritualized corporeality as *human* salvation. The face or the eyes of an animal, however touching and endearing, is not the same as a human facial expression, in which matter is spiritualized. What, then, would be the spiritual facial expression of a dead person who has been taken up and sanctified by God? Any images we may form of it are inappropriate, but their religious implications become intelligible if they point to the Mystery that will befall people as fully *human* beings! That is why our religious tradition emphasizes that people's Christian salvation necessarily includes the body. Tertullian already harped on it: 'The body is the pivot of salvation' (*Caro, salutis est cardo*);[1] or, in modern terms, people, in all their sensory corporeality, are the vital link, the hub, the pivot of everything when it comes to true salvation and bliss. In this regard, commenting on the resurrection texts in 1 Corinthians 15, Thomas Aquinas dared say: "My soul is not 'I,' my ego cannot be reduced to 'my soul.'"[2] From a Christian perspective human salvation is not salvation of souls, as some spiritual gurus keep insisting; it is bliss that befalls us in our full spiritual corporeality or embodied spirit. People are certainly not angels with material bodies, they are not incarnated angelic spirits, but their spirits are corporeal and their bodies are spiritual. This is not dualism but two dimensions of the one human being. In order to understand the resurrection and sacramental celebrations, this sensitive, expressive corporeality is of cardinal importance: it is the *cardo* or pivot of salvation.

In this regard it should be noted that religious content, the soul and dynamo of every form of Christian rituality, is never found in isolation, on its own (hence "culture-less" or transcending all cultural roots). Believers' relation to the changeable cultural present always enters into the substance of their faith. That is why every form of dogmatism, even when it assumes the hermeneutic form of neo-orthodoxy, is an *obex* or obstacle to sacramental praxis. That is also why the Christian faith can survive in troubled times, not merely through superficial, homogeneously evolving continuity but also by way of ruptures, for humans are by nature (hence also as believers) cultural, historically conditioned beings. This applies to both religious individuals and religious institutions. In their faith in God or religion Christians are never outside or above the culture in which they live. Temporality is part and parcel of our humanity. That is why religious *images* may be experienced as outdated from time to time.[3] Christian faith is not possible outside or beyond culture. What is commonly known as "orthodoxy" is in fact *Christian faith,* nevertheless *articulated* in highly specific, culturally conditioned conceptions and images of humankind and the world: a world from a bygone cultural era. In the process, a particular cultural era from the past is wrongfully declared the norm or the 'golden age,' which effectively makes the notions prevalent in those times heterodox in our day, counter to all sorts of (I trust) sincere intentions.

The Christian faith is situated *in* history and is embedded, moreover, in diverse cultures; even within the same cultural tradition there may be variations in periods and interpretation. Hence Christian religion can refer to the Absolute only in a historically relative way: it refers to absolute truth in the sense of pointing to that which transcends every concretely historical articulation.

## Reactions to the Breach between Anthropology and Theology in Traditional and Modern Sacramental Doctrine

### *Theological and empirical scientific reactions (including the ritual studies school)*

As far back as the 1950s hylomorphism (i.e. the interpretation of the sacraments in terms of the Aristotelian distinction between matter and form) came in for serious criticism from Karl Rahner and myself. We did not reject the familiar, traditional terminology out of hand but criticized it, especially the way canon law narrowed it down by linking isolated formulas with impoverishing, punctual use of elements such as water or oil. At that time Rahner, on the basis of his "transcendental" philosophical/

theological project, stressed that an adequate interpretation called for more extensive use of philosophical anthropology. For my part, inspired by the then current phenomenology of, *inter alia*, G. Gusdorf and Maurice Merleau-Ponty, I adopted a phenomenological-anthropological approach to symbolic activity or metaphoric acts. Since then the positive sciences have presented new analyses and theories of rituals from various ethno-anthropological and folklore angles, some scholars also incorporating the already familiar linguistic insights of what is known as semiotics.

Louis-Marie Chauvet followed the course marked out by Rahner and myself, modifying and refining the theory of symbolic acts.[4] Since then many others have taken this route, so that by now this trend is fairly widely accepted; in the Netherlands, developments in the (mainly Catholic) theology of sacraments between 1950 and 1991 were thoroughly surveyed by a Protestant scholar, M.E. Brinkman, in a study of creation and sacraments.[5] Unfortunately, his study was confined to the problem as defined at that time and the corrections already contributed by Rahner, myself and Chauvet.

A more fundamental reaction came from the empirical sciences, *inter alia* from what is known as the ritual studies school. In the 19th and the first half of the 20th century ethnographic studies of ritual concentrated mainly on traditional rites, which were consistently limited to, and identified with, religious rituals. In addition, empirical researchers at that time, insofar as they were Christians, worked on the assumption that rites were phenomena pertaining to nature religions and fertility cults – 'pagan' religions – whereas Christian rites had a distinctive, unique character and were given the exclusive name of 'sacraments.' Christians who studied foreign religious rituals usually judged these from a Christian perception of sacraments; studies by non-Christians of the same ethnographic material often arrived at very different conclusions. By the same token, Christian sacraments were studied on the basis of certain biases against the Christian understanding of what inspired sacramental rituals.

Both approaches assumed, moreover, that rites had originated in an irretrievably distant past, and that modern ritualizing or "rites in the making" could not exist, hence, were inconceivable. Thus ritual creativity appeared to be a contradiction in terms: rituals, it was thought, were inviolable, sacred, and that was an immutable fact for all time. Various elements from early studies by scholars like Mircea Eliade, James George Frazer, Carl Gustav Jung and Paul Tillich strengthened researchers' conviction that rites and symbols, as they were known, could 'not be generated': they were ancient, unalterable certainties, leaving no room for new rituals.

A new generation of researchers in ethnology and cultural anthropology, assisted by what semiotics, folklore studies and linguistics have produced in the meantime and by the expertise of modern electronic information science, approaches the material from a very different angle. These scientists have discovered that contemporary TV commercials, for example, are crammed with ritualizations, that is, "rites in the making," which are part and parcel of our late or 'post'-modern age. This new generation deliberately uses the terms "ritual" and "rituality" to indicate a new approach to what used to be known simply as rites; thus they speak of the "study of ritual" and look for "ritual as such," being a theoretical model or construction shared by all forms of profane and religious rituals as a specific form of behaviour or action. The term is meant to accentuate a distinctive, new interest in rituals, for they are asking different questions from their predecessors. Within this new scholarly trend, there is a small group of researchers who regularly collaborate and to some extent set themselves apart from their colleagues by using a new technical term: 'ritual studies' (more specific than the general term 'study of ritual,' although it is not easy to demarcate the field). I find these researchers to be on the whole quite cautious and modest, in the sense that they are less inclined to pronounce categorically on new insights. Actually they are not bound by any normative consensus, neither in their theorizing nor in their assessment of empirical data. The only idea they consider to be beyond all doubt is that ritual is one of the ways in which people structure and interpret their worldly environment. But in this new approach, many ideas from earlier generations, especially from the 19th and early 20th century, continue to feature in one way or another, albeit in a new framework, along with insights from phenomenology, functionalism, semiotics and structuralism. One early study in particular, dating back to 1966, of ritual in human and animal behaviour was an eye-opener to many of them.[6]

Some years ago these researchers – sometimes called ritualists, even rituologists – concluded that there is a highly suggestive and fruitful distinction between rites in the sense of existing traditional rituals or ritual systems (which were previously conceived of almost exclusively as religious rites) and ritualization, implying processes of rites in the making.[7]

For the past decade, then, empirical scientists have been researching and analysing rituals, irrespective of whether these were magical or religious or, for example, ritual eating customs. Thus their work is indisputably a new contribution to the understanding of 'ritual as such,' a construct which, while abstract in itself, helps to explain a number of phenomena. Christian liturgiologists and theologians, too, can make use (with due regard to the requirements of interdisciplinary scholarship)[8] of their clear methods and criteria to trace the origin or birth of postmodern rites. This in fact clarifies the structure and origin of traditional rites, which previously were thought to have vanished behind the hazy horizon of a distant past. Nowadays we are no longer looking for the prehistoric origin(s) of ancient rituals. The focus has shifted to the immediate 'roots' or living matrix of rituals. And these origins are not in some distant past and are no longer sought in 'primitive cultures' (the very term is no longer accepted by these rituologists), but in the here and now of what is known as live performance. Current scientific interest in rites can be ascribed to the recognition that 'ritualizing,' the origin of rituals, entails trying to discover how the preconscious, latent process that gives rise to ritual behaviour is triggered and develops.

Until quite recently myths and rites tended to have a bad or unfavourable connotation among some scientists. Rituals were identified almost exclusively with religious rituals. And in a world where, to many, God has disappeared from the scene, it was thought that the end of rituals, too, was looming on the horizon. But ritual studies show that the distaste for concepts (and realities) like myths and rites has proved to be a judgment based on a relative perception from the perspective of a particular worldview. It has also become clear that religious rites are only one segment in a far broader ritual spectrum. All rituals, both profane and religious, have their 'matrix' in our biophysical corporeality. Let us first look into this more closely.

In the 19th century and until the 1960s philosophers of religion debated endlessly about what came first in religious practice: myths (religious contents and their images) or rites. At the time my own position was that the two formed a complex whole: religious content (with its variable interpretations) and sacramental or ritual praxis, in its ritual form, are inseparable. I still stand by that, with a slight yet significant shift in emphasis: biologically, after all, ritual appears to precede myth. From documentaries on animal behaviour, TV viewers know that in the animal world rituals already play an important role in the search for contact, in the area of their many forms of communication with one another. This occurs in animal communication in situations of love and procreation, of hunting and killing their prey, no less than in those of birth, sickness and death. Ritual has to do with the need to communicate. In the great cosmic evolutionary scheme, the phenomenon of ritual among animals had long been an innate and acquired behavioural pattern, even before this same pattern arose in the part of the animal world that eventually evolved into human beings. From their "spiritual bodies" or "corporeal spirits," human beings inspire the equally human corporeal, "spontaneous" rituals through myths or other forms of religious or profane beliefs that become the carriers of human ritual behaviour.

Empirical scientific studies show that already at the animal level, rites start with a process of ritualizing everyday occurrences, in which at certain times recurrent behavioural patterns become stylized and fixed in symbolic movements, accompanied by communicative sounds. In the animal world ritual behaviour ultimately serves biological, bio-psychological and socio-biological needs, but through stylization and repetition, certain actions become "symbolic" even among animals, in codes that are intelligible to members of that species. If one looks only for immediate efficacy, then symbolic, ritually stylized actions in themselves are irrelevant, dysfunctional. The meaning of a gesture or the entire ritualization process is "indirect," since if viewed directly it seems to be a play of meaningless, pointless gestures or aimless actions, albeit often so aesthetic that dancing couples can learn something from them. In the play behaviour of young animals, too, one often discerns forms of ritualization, more particularly of socialization, which playfully initiate the young and familiarize them with the harsh world of hunting and killing in which they will have to survive. It is a kind of theatre, a game of searching for communication, for certain contacts or a safe way of evoking longings through play-acting and apparently aimless, superfluous gestures. It entails all kinds of postures, often accompanied by "cries:" noises, even artistic songs, in call and response, challenge, playfulness, feigned rejection and canny acceptance. Thus ritual behaviour seems to be a ritualization of certain everyday actions; it consists in periodic performances, arising from agreeable and disagreeable experiences in non-stylized daily life, which afterwards restore the performers to the complexities of everyday life, but enriched by experience and brightening.

Even though humans are more than just members of the animal species, nonetheless, generically or by virtue of their biogenetic corporeality, they belong to the animal species that performs rituals. It implies, *inter alia*, that corporeality, the human body, plays a key role in *human* rituals as well. This is evident, almost paradoxically, in most religious rites, which, at an anthropological level, have to do with eating and drinking, sprinkling and anointing, reproduction or procreation, sickness and healing, love, awareness of failure and guilt and a need to make up for it, the stages of reaching adulthood and of aging and dying. Forms of ritualization have to do with living and surviving. Rituals are about everyday things that are reduced to their ultimate meaning: a matter of life and death, of living again, of birth and rebirth.

Researchers of the study of ritual have not yet reached agreement on whether or not the need for ritualization is an intrinsic, universal category of our common humanity and hence *in fact* an anthropological constant, of which I am convinced. As both an animal and a human need, or even a human imperative, ritual is rooted in biogenetic, psychosomatic and ecological elements, the latter being both natural and cultural. Our bodies are not only full of biorhythms with a biological calendar of which we are hardly conscious, but as human beings belonging to the ritualizing animal species, we are also programmed and embedded in a society with a distinctive, unique culture, with an immediate worldly context and its own notions about people and reality, whether bound up with transcendental powers and forces or not. To us, human rituals are a key to the way people see, structuré and interpret their world. Within that framework there is freedom of choice, but people are also pre-programmed for ritualization. For we cannot stealthily bypass our bodies; corporeality entails biological, biosocial and biophysical needs. Human life is only possible within rhythms and structures and in socio-cultural contexts. Rites are never purely decorative or some sort of etiquette, even though a ritual system may be given a decorative setting. Thus table manners as decorum form part of ritual: they ease the gathering, make it agreeable and ensure conviviality around the table. Not all moments of everyday life are a matter of "to be or not to be," hence many behaviours are not incorporated into rites. Indeed, ritual becomes more understandable when viewed against the backdrop of day-to-day behaviours that are not ritualized, or if ritual behaviour is compared with related actions, for instance, in the theatre.[9] Ethno-anthropologists have noted that in some cultures there is no distinction between rites and drama (consider the ancient *drómenon*) and many of them see a kinship between liturgy and theatre, notwithstanding profound differences and the fact that they represent different forms of speech and action. Thus liturgical ritual is not theatre! Yet one must remember, also in the case of liturgical rites, that because of people's bio-sociological and bio-psychological corporeality, their behaviour and attitudes always display a pre-conscious or latently conscious behavioural pattern. Hence ritual is rooted in a network of interrelationships between people, who, through their corporeality, are embedded in a natural and socio-cultural ecosystem. In rites, these multifaceted dependencies surface. Unintended connections betray the existence of latent ritual gestures and behaviours.

In the context of what I have just said, especially the phenomenon that natural or biological rhythms acquire a cultural dimension in human ritual, certain features of the rituals of what are known as historical religions become more comprehensible. What Thomas Aquinas called "nature sacraments," that is, seasonal feasts, are often incorporated into new rites that commemorate and re-enact historical events, such as the exodus from Egypt and, in the New Testament, the resurrection of Jesus Christ. Thus the Christian liturgical seasons reflect a merging of typical data from the Christian tradition with Jewish feasts, themselves a historical *re-actualization* of agrarian nature festivals. Regardless of how such a custom is legitimized theologically and apologetically, the various layers of, for example, a particular Christian liturgical feast (think of Easter) can be traced to the even deeper dimension of ritual; a consequence of the real matrix of all ritual, namely the human body with its natural and cultural-historical ecosystem.

When it comes to religious rites, ritual studies show that religions have an essential social and socializing dimension: religion is more than individual 'faith.' This compelled theorists of science (in this particular field) to look for common structures that lurk behind the manifest differences between religious beliefs. In the process they learned that ritual systems have a logic of their own; hence, one should look for their meaning rather than the way they function. Catherine Bell rightly criticizes European and American scholars for their inclination to interpret rituals simply as performances of prescribed or canonical texts; they forget that within human beings, deeper than religion, there is a hidden, fundamental (bio-psychological) ritualizing dimension, namely the insistence on *doing* something in such a way that the 'doing' itself gives the action a special, privileged status – that of ritual.[10] It follows that rituals cannot be reduced to texts, scripts and scores, scenarios, even detailed directions, no matter how important these may be. These aids are secondary to the actual ritual event, for they form part of a whole ritual *system*. The ritualist Roy Rappaport mentions this with reference to the distinction he makes between the 'canonical elements' (ganglions or codes) of a ritual and its 'index elements,' that is those that primarily provide information on immediate situations: shared psychological or physical states of participants in the ritual (real-life connotations of the celebrating community here and now).[11] A liturgical text, for instance, is no more than a sediment. A ritual performance is not the present performance of ancient texts or prescribed gestures. To my knowledge Richard Schechner, Victor Turner's co-worker, was the first scholar to refer to rites not only as performance but also as 'transformance.'[12] With this term he wanted to emphasize that the performance of a music score by, say, Mozart is not identical with the available score and may not even correspond with Mozart's own intentions. In other words, the proposition that rituals are fundamentally static and immutably, even mandatorily traditional, has been empirically falsified. If one tries to keep a ritual system unchanging, it eventually puts pressure on the celebrating community, with the danger that it may disintegrate as a result. Ritual and creativity are in no way mutually exclusive. The cultural context, of which rites are a component, plays a decisive role in these rites – at any rate, if one does not want to incarcerate the participating believers in an archive, a historically accurate replica of ritual celebrations in bygone ages.

Ritual analyses also show that rites are mutable and offer scope for new rituals (or sacraments). This mutability has to do with the interrelationship between a ritual and its context, the ritual field. Rituals also appear to be a particularly appropriate means of striking a proper balance between people's appropriation of change and their sense of cultural continuity.[13] Thus ritual *per se* does not reinforce the status quo – as some ritualists think or even would like it to do – but can also express and articulate protest. The carnival ritual, for instance, is manifestly a temporary interruption of everyday life; it is an 'anti-structure' and as such playfully ridicules the everyday order, hierarchies and fashionable notions or happenings.[14] In Latin America, eucharistic and prayer services are sometimes held which are explicitly socio-politically charged and thus display a similar "anti-structure."[15]

A common weakness of liturgiologists and theologians is that they are not interested in what rituality is 'in general,' whereas such structural knowledge could further their search for the distinctive meaning of their *particular* ritual traditions.[16] The fact that no decisive victor has emerged as yet in the battle for consensus on a conclusive theory of rituality does not detract from the reality that ritual studies have already produced sufficient scientific gains which Christian liturgiology cannot ignore. Universal acceptance of the findings of these empirical theoretical analyses alone would obviate the danger of an exclusively intellectual approach. Ritual "potential" is part of our humanity, and we share it with the animal world. But in human ritual, that which, among animals, primarily serves biological needs becomes the vehicle and expression of meaning and sense, and leads to emotional communication of profane or religious convictions, orienting and inspiring people's lives: a process, whether profane or religious, that has been 'distilled to ritual.'

If Christian sacraments are included under the common denominator of ritual, the crux is that they enact and express the Christian faith in a performance based on a scenario or *score*. As ritual, this performance already has its own rules and logic in a general sense; at the same time it is controlled and directed by religious belief which, in and via the performance, deepens and intensifies to actual religious transfer. After all, faith does not live primarily by cognitive reflection on religious subject matter, even though such reflection is equally necessary and up to a point precedes faith; but only once it is practised in responsible brotherly and sisterly love does faith become the soul of Christian life. This faith is lived and actualized in profane everyday life and is also ritually celebrated and 'embodied' in sacramental praxis. These two forms of religious expression nourish Christian life. In symbolic actions faith acquires meaning and power; the celebration calls to mind what actually happens in the religiously inspired lives of people in everyday profane situations, the condition in which their lives are enacted.

## Questions that are Inadequately Answered, and Pointless Questions that Need No Answers

This section is not so much about unsolved problems in the field of sacramental doctrine or liturgiology as about all kinds of issues that have been debated traditionally (in some cases since the Middle Ages), often resulting in very elaborate or diplomatic, sometimes insincere answers. Some of these questions, moreover, turn out to be pointless.

It should be clear that it makes no sense for Christian liturgiologists and theologians to scrounge blithely from ritual studies or other scientific ritualists. Empirical theoretical analyses of ritual in general, with its own logic, rules and codes, obviously cannot pronounce judgment on Christians'

# Ordo: Bath, Word, Prayer, Table

sacramental self-understanding and certainly not on the religious substance which underlies the Christian sacraments with their religious mysticism and ethical awareness. Theologians who want to learn from scientific findings must necessarily apply searching hermeneutic criticism and be critically alert to actual theological notions assimilated into ethno-anthropological discussions of the specifically Christian sacramental heritage. After all, historically that heritage owes its existence to the message and praxis of Jesus, who is confessed as Christ, the Son of God, our Lord.

Reliable findings of scientific approaches to ritual (and Christian sacraments fall in this category) could also include criticism of certain interpretations by Christians and even of Christian rituals. Thus one finds that Christian theologians have disqualified the rites of other religions, including Jewish or Old Testament rituals. While acknowledging them as meaningful symbols of grace (salvific for those who perform them as *opus operantis*), they deny their sacramental salvific power (which even Thomas still affirmed); indirectly this perception of non-Christian rituals or sacraments is already a form of discrimination. Whereas Christian sacraments have a distinctive Christian core and manner of performance, as religious rituals their structure and performative efficacy are no different from those of rituals informed by other religions. On the other hand, my study of ritualists gives me the impression that they, for their part, often put Christian sacraments in categories that are wholly inapplicable to a properly interpreted Christian ritual. For the rest I would say that, by and large, it is little more than a matter of different terminologies. Some ritualists insist on calling all rituals that actively accomplish or 'do' something magic. In this context magic does not have a negative but, on the contrary, a positive connotation (this applies, e.g., to the work of Roland Grimes). But in terms of the ancient controversies of Catholics and Protestants such use of terminology can be misleading and confusing.

1. *The institution of the sacraments, and how many there are?* Research in the field of ritual studies has demonstrated that the Christian sacraments as human rituals cannot be inferred directly from religious faith. As noted already, the soil in which ritual as such (and that includes the Christian sacraments) is rooted is human corporeality. Rituality grows from a matrix with biogenetic (natural and cultural), ecological and psychosomatic components. This implies that where religious faith exists, it will express itself spontaneously, anthropologically, in ritual, so that searching for the actual 'founder' of these rituals (from a Christian point of view, sacraments) is not an issue of primary importance. The religious pioneers who founded a particular religious tradition, in which rituals have spontaneously developed over the ages, together with their message and way of life that are embraced by their followers, are the factor determining the origin of rites, even though they may never have thought of instituting

any rituals whatever. That applies to the Christian tradition as well. Whether Jesus himself wanted to institute the sacraments, maybe some of them, or all of them (and how many are there?), or none of them, is a purely historical question that can only be answered historically, either affirmatively or negatively.

In this perspective the number of sacraments, too, is a moot point. The history of the 'sacred septet' (*sacrum septenarium*), that is of seven sacraments, no more and no less (as the Council of Trent declared), is not a dogma, despite the *anathema sit* that concludes each canon. In the late 11th, early 12th century a dispute arose among theologians about whether there were four (Lanfranc), five (Abélard), ten (Bernard) or twelve sacraments (Damian), which continued until the 14th century. In the days of the church fathers and the early Middle Ages scores of *mysteria* or *sacramenta* were in use. The two terms were in fact extremely fluid. The debate on whether *mysterium* or *signum* was most characteristic of what was known as *sacramentum* hardly abated; but meanwhile the term *sacramentu* became dominant, while the meaning of *mysterium* as a cultic act disappeared. At that stage the question of how a sacrament should be defined was still undecided. Until the controversy about the "septet," the only distinction was between the major sacraments (*sacramenta maiora*, the initiation sacraments of baptism, confirmation and the eucharist, which the Reformation preserved) and all other rites (*sacramenta minora*).[17]

When it came to creating some order in this medley, the medieval theologians, after much controversy, settled for the *septenarium*. Seven was already a sacred number in both Jewish and Christian tradition, but the theological decision on only seven sacraments was clinched, I learned to my surprise, by the mystical, indeed awe-full reverence (repeatedly eulogized in lyric poetry) of the seven planets that arose in the 12th century. In the first three documents I discovered in which medieval theologians opted for seven sacraments, the decision, on their own admission, was prompted by their reverence for the seven planets. By the time the council met at Trent the "septet" was an accomplished theological fact, which, however recent (at that time), was approved by the council. The *anathema sit* that was appended to this decree referred (according to the council's own interpretation) solely to the fact that the church leadership reserved the right to determine which and how many sacraments (in the technical sense of the word) it would recognize officially; anyone who did not accept that policy was canonically disowned.[18] The canon of Trent did not explicitly exclude the possibility that the church could introduce new sacraments, if serious pastoral needs in the religious community were to require it. For the rest the canon was directed solely against the Reformation, in effect against the rejection of certain sacraments by the Reformers.

# Ordo: Bath, Word, Prayer, Table

2. *Not isolated* materia et forma, *but a broadening of the liturgical field, both materially and spiritually*. The new Christian view of the sacraments faces a twofold task: firstly, to avoid a purely intellectualistic approach to the category of *signum*, that is, an exclusively cognitive analysis of the phenomenon of sign and symbolic activity; and secondly, to prevent a ritualistic approach which, in a roundabout way, would once again objectify the flexible ritual feast to the extent that it would again contain covert magical aspects, as is evident in some publications. We have to avoid both the Charybdis of a purely hieratic and, at the same time, 'objectifying' liturgy, and the Scylla of an exclusively 'subjectivistic' approach to sacramental liturgy, which might even lead to banalization.

We should also get rid of the obsession with just one given formula or one particular gesture as the be-all and end-all of sacramental liturgy. Older people will still remember how many priests were reduced to trembling by anxious scruples when pronouncing the eucharistic institution formula. What is relevant, however, is the overall liturgical field with all its dimensions, which in a sense constitutes a single ecosystem where each element refers to all the others, where light, space, silence and song are just as important as what is often regarded as an isolated peak element. Naturally, and quite rightly, there are dominant symbols, but they should be viewed in proportion, an interactive relationship in which no single component can be elevated to an all-determining position. Everything has its place in the broad ritual field of the performance. Anyone who does not preserve that complex whole and over-accentuates isolated elements (even the institution formula of the eucharist), thus separating them from the celebration as a whole, turns the ritual into magical ritualism simply by concentrating frenetically on a formula. This form of ritualism whipped up into psychological frenzy should be regarded as a residue of the physicalist, 'pseudo-Catholic' interpretation of the real presence in the eucharist and the death of anthropological ritual activity, which in its turn provides the basis and concrete form of sacramental *grace*. The intertwined 'dual element' of anthropological dimension *and* level of grace is in fact just *a single Christian religious event*, in which the one is not infrastructure and the other superstructure!

In my view a crucial point in this inquiry is to realize that the real subject of any liturgical sacramental celebration is both the collective religious community and the individual members of the liturgical community.[19] In God's assembled congregation various liturgical roles, including that of the officiant, are assigned – each with its own place and capacity, without mystification of any particular role.

3. *Opus operatum* and *opus operantis*. My main aim in this subsection is to find a new way of closing the traditional gap between the *opus operatum*, the objective side of the sacrament, and the *opus operantis*, its subjective side, even more fundamentally than I tried to do in 1952 in my book, *De sacramentele heilseconomie (The Sacramental Economy of Salvation)*.[20] The *opus operantis* is intrinsically part of the *opus operatum*, for the two aspects combined are the actual performance that mediates God's gratuitous condescension and are not tagged on to it afterwards. The *opus operantis* is the *opus operatum*, though I would not put it the other way round, as if the *opus operatum* were the work of whoever performs it. In the first place, I want to avoid the casuistry of the distinction between a 'valid' and a 'fruitful' sacrament that can lead to disastrously over-generalized conclusions. Secondly, I want to uphold the insight that in the *opus operatum* (of which the *opus operantis* is an essential part) God's free, gratuitous gift is decisive: through devoutly experienced human ritual performances – independent of human merit – it allows participants in the liturgy to share in the abundance of God's goodwill.

The traditional division between the objective and subjective sides of a sacrament actually derives from Augustine of Hippo, who made a sharp distinction between a valid (*validum*) and a fruitful (*fructuosum*) sacrament. That happened at a time when his reaction to the doctrinal aberrations of the Donatists (who maintained that the personal integrity of the officiant affected the quality of the sacrament) put him in a dilemma and he could find no solution other than this distinction. At the time, in view of its theological potential, it was an extremely opportune solution and served its purpose. Historically, however, it led to a gradual, almost magical attenuation of the sacraments, especially in eucharistic liturgy. In the 10th and 11th centuries, for instance, farmers used to take a consecrated host with them from church to bury in their fields, expecting it to ensure a bounteous harvest. The theology current at that time, based on a crudely realistic physicalism, offered only vague, if far-fetched, legitimation for this practice; at any rate the local church leadership, often with minimal theological training, tacitly permitted it.

4. *Linking "sign" with causation: a categorical error*. Some empirical anthropological studies of ritual rightly criticize the physicalist approach of traditional Catholic sacramental theology, at any rate since the Middle Ages. The fact that Thomas Aquinas in particular made his own contribution in this regard is often overlooked. To be sure, one must concede that he, too, used categories derived from physics. One need merely recall his use of hylomorphic theory, with its distinction between *materia* and *forma*, as a framework to make Augustine's famous proposition, *"Accedit verbum ad elementum*

# Ordo: Bath, Word, Prayer, Table

*et fit sacramentum"* (by adding the word to the element – e.g. water or oil – a sacrament comes about), intelligible in Aristotelian terms. In this hylomorphic philosophical framework, a human ritual action, with or without the use of an object (laying on of hands, sprinkling with water), linked with a ritual formula (e.g. 'I baptize you in the name of…') becomes, through the objective operation of the rite (*ex opere operato*), the instrumental 'cause' of grace, in the same way that a physical cause has a physical effect. If one faults Thomas for this, one is forgetting the traditional premise of his entire sacramental theology, namely that sacraments belong in the category of signs (*sacramentum est in genere signi*), that is of symbolic reference and representation – though one must concede that, particularly in his eucharistic theology, Thomas did not consistently adhere to this premise because of his choice, all but unavoidable in his day, of the physicalist model of matter and form, especially in regard to the conjunction of cause and sign. At the very least, locating sacraments in the category of signs implies that their salvific action has nothing to do with physics or physical change. Even what Thomas calls eucharistic transubstantiation – indeed philosophically non-Aristotelian, in the sense that 'substance' is divorced from its 'accidents' – he considers proper to the category of symbolic signs, hence not referring to any *physical* changes in the bread and the wine. It shows that, whereas he does use the hylomorphic model, he prefers to interpret the instrumental causation of the sacraments non-physically, that is, analogously. In the Middle Ages there was simply no alternative to such an identification of the operation of the sacraments with physical instrumental causation. To complicate matters further, in our late modern era the use of both these concepts – causation and sign – have become philosophically suspect, especially among analysts of language.

This critical suspicion and semiotic difficulty are compounded by the fact that theology – as was almost unavoidable in the Middle Ages, given the lack of phenomenological and semiotic insights – conjoined the two problematic concepts in a formulation, brilliant for its day: *"significando causant;"* that is to say, through the dynamism of their signification the sacraments *causally* mediate God's readiness to extend grace and the resultant forgiving, healing and sanctifying blessedness. In a different philosophical framework, however, the performative signification of a religious ritual as a whole is sufficient; anthropologically the sacraments have no need whatever of a supplementary instrumental cause transcending the efficacious ritual of the Christian faith. The meaningful ritual in its entirety, being the human expression and vehicle of (ecclesial *and* individual) religious inspiration of all participants, *is* the actual gift of grace.

In post-Thomistic times, thomistic epigones, and subsequent modern theological textbooks even more so, have by no means interpreted the application of hylomorphism to the sacraments analogously. Some textbooks went so far as to look for some mysterious transformation of the atoms and molecules in the eucharistic bread and wine. In the process the distinctive character of metaphoric action and symbolic speech was totally disregarded. In short, the peculiar meaning, structure and "aim" or intention of symbolic activity and ritual were overlooked, particularly the fact that one has to invoke symbolic language and metaphoric actions to articulate and actualize the reality of grace;[21] after all, we can never express that dynamic reality in terms of our meagre terminology or our conceptual, controlling and "objectifying" knowledge. The ritual event as a significatory expression surpasses pure reason downwards from above and upwards from below: rituality has its own logical rationality, but that rationality cannot be located or pinned down with a measuring rod. Hence, rather than speak of "healthy irrationality," as has been proposed, one could call it trans-rationality.[22] The "operation" coming from God and the "operation" upwards from below (coming from the faithful believers) is one and the same *opus operatum*, for the ecclesiastic and personal faith of the Christian participant in the sacramental liturgy is still embedded in the 'ritual performance' itself.

OUTLINE OF A NEW VIEW OF SACRAMENTAL LITURGY, THEOLOGY AND PASTORAL PRACTICE

*Religion in everyday life, stylized and flexibly distilled to symbolic rites*

The word 're-discovery' in the title of this essay is not a random or opportunistic insertion. I derive the term from a theological-methodological approach which, thanks to the new findings of empirical ethnology and cultural anthropology (of roughly the past decade), has truly given me fresh theological insight. To me the wealth of empirical material and explanatory analyses unearthed by these anthropological sciences that study the phenomenon of rites in terms of the model of 'rituality' (which assumes that this phenomenon is recognizable in both profane and religious rituals) became a veritable theological treasure trove, despite some critical reservations and circumspection in handling the material. Hence it was indeed a theological discovery.

Inspired partly by the scientific insights of this new approach to human ritual activity, I strolled once more through my old theological garden, *De sacramentele heilseconomie* (1952) and *Christus, sacrament van de Godsontmoeting* (*Christ, Sacrament of the Encounter with God*) (1958, 1959), weeding and planting a little here and there to give it a look more appropriate to the 21st century. To conclude this article I want to lift the veil over this new pathway just a little through my old garden – an image I owe to my colleague Hermann Häring.[23]

# Ordo: Bath, Word, Prayer, Table

The eventual title of my new book on the sacraments will probably be *Sacramenten — Jezus' visioen en zijn weg van het rijk Gods* (*Sacramental Liturgy – Jesus' Vision and His Way of God's Kingdom*), with the succinct subtitle, *Zin- en contrastervaringen tot ritueel gelouterd* (*Experiences of Meaning and Contrast Distilled to Ritual*). I added the second part of the subtitle ('distilled to ritual') in July 1999, following a new book that its author, Huub Oosterhuis, presented to me as a gift: *The living One who sees me.*[24] In it I found a stanza that I want to insert immediately after the title page of my book, partly in grateful acknowledgment of what he has meant for liturgical practice in my country and beyond its borders. Freely translated it reads

> Be present here so what we do
> may be well done: sharing his words
> of grace as bread and wine until he comes,
> vision distilled to ritual.

This image, a "vision distilled to ritual," appealed to me strongly. Distillation implies undergoing some sort of process of catharsis: one lets it happen, the way a substance is purified by fire. It implies surrender, although it requires training: letting God be, for sacraments are special moments of grace when we celebrate what tends to be hidden in profane daily life, a reality present fragmentarily, in flashes. Surrender is one of the key words expressing the mystical process of the human search both for the Ineffable Mystery, "the Sacred," and for expressive ritualization of religious surrender to the Divine Mystery. That word (*legomenon*) and the actual practice (*drómenon*) belong to the experiential tradition of the major world religions, often in rebellion against "established," somnolent religiosity. Distillation or purification, likewise, essentially belongs in the mystical tradition.

1. How did Jesus arrive at his vision of God's kingdom, the source of his preaching and life work, and of his road towards that kingdom, proclaiming God's rule which, for individuals and nations, spells divine salvation: happiness, justice and rightness, love and peace among people in their life and world in God's creation?

Put in a nutshell: Jesus' personal vision took shape in the experiential tradition of Jewish religion, in which the coming of the kingdom of God, God's reign or rule, was a known concept, albeit somewhat obscured in Jesus' day. Such a dream or vision presupposes powerful negative experiences, described as negative because they are contrast-experiences: they derive from a shocking experience of a contrast sensed between the way things are and how they can and must become different and better. This contrast generates the dream, the project, and also the commitment to it. That is the essence of negative experience on whatever scale: it can destroy people, but it can also build them, for as *contrast-experience* it implicitly includes a positive, albeit sometimes vague, vision, which suddenly or gradually clarifies. It is not for nothing that in the Gospels Jesus' decision to have himself baptized by John is followed by a forty-day spell in the silence, but also aggressively menacing desolation, of the wilderness to contemplate and even wrestle with his dream or his life task.

Jesus' own contrast experience was between the human history of suffering, upheaval, wars and injustice that he observed around him in his occupied country one the one hand, and on the other his personal experience of God, whom he called "Abba" or "dear Father," an experience of a God who cares for creation and people, the whole of humankind, destined for goodness, not for evil. Jesus experienced this God as a beloved Parent (combining male and female concern) intent on humankind; a God he experienced as caring, opposed to all evil, and as a Presence who refused to recognize the power of evil in the world and to let it have the last word. For Jesus, God is a *Deus humanissimus*: "God's glory is the living human being" (as the patristic theologian Irenaeus later proclaimed).

The *Abba* experience, not isolated but located in the real-life context of its contrast with what he experienced in the world, sheds light on the man from Nazareth. Mystical experience of God, *in contrast* to what he observed and experienced in the world around him, became the source of his life's work, of his message and way of life, and of the revelation of who he actually was: a human being, fully indwelt by God, and the mediator of God's liberation and salvation. Before his death, maybe since the murder of John the Baptist, he found himself confronted with a new contrast experience. His disarming, loving attitude, in solidarity with God and people, provoked opposition in "this world," posed a threat to what power always means in the world; it made love in this world vulnerable. Jesus' dream was thwarted by human beings, who duly got rid of him. But his faithfulness to a silent but everlastingly present God and his love of human beings remained intact: uncomprehending yet trusting surrender to the living God.

Hence Christian believers should be alert to problems in the world around them and should respond in keeping with their faith, for that is how we draw closest to God's active presence. At such times, when the two forms of presence coincide, when we are both involved with people and revealing the face of the Lord in a worldly situation, something of God's kingdom is realized. Mystics call it the *pati divina*, receptiveness to experiences of God: *letting God be God* and *letting God happen to us*. Jesus did not proclaim a kingdom for a distant future hereafter. Nor did he proclaim a kingdom that is realized invisibly within us. In innumerable, decipherable, historical moments, in ordinary daily life among people in the *here and now,* we can discern sparks of the grace of God's kingdom which continually 'irrupts' into human history in and through our faithful commitment to the resolution of the world's problems. We can share, experience and interpret those sparks of divine grace *in* our human behaviour. As people, as believers, we also 'ritualize' it at appointed times, celebrating what happens and praising God.

2. Hence the sacraments have two dimensions: one anthropological, the other – merging with it – focussed on God. In the *sacramenta fidei ecclesiae*, the vision of God's active kingdom – our letting God's work be done in our daily living – is ritualized. There God's world and the human world are at one. Our spacio-temporal human world is God's world. But to us God's cause is a human cause. What is close to people's hearts is also close to God: it is God's concern. Thus there is the so-called profane level of everyday life where people and the world converge, in which we perceive flashes and facets of the active God – what we call our day-to-day Christian life with its worldly tasks. And there are the sacraments and the liturgy as a whole, in which we ritualize what transpires, both everyday and not everyday, both joyous and tragic. Ordinary actions are 'interrupted,' in the sense that, at given times, such everyday behavioural complexes are stylized and, up to a point, fixed in symbolic movements. The ritual material is intrinsic to our very humanity; Christian faith is its soul and dynamic inspiration.

Scientific studies of ritual have shown me that rituals are an existential, emotional and festive interpretation of existentially relevant actions, whether religious or profane – postures, gestures, behaviours, protocols, eating customs, marriage customs – expressed in a culturally specific manner and embedded in specific cultural, social and even political structures. To my mind these scholars – because of understandable irritation with presumptuous intellectualism – lose sight of the fact that in its own way the dynamics of a ritual performance also refers to knowledge. After all, the logic of metaphoric, symbolic actions is not the same logic that forms the premise of modern, "scientific" manipulation of matter, and hence of relations of cause and effect.

As mentioned already, ritual has two components: the *legomenon* or words in many forms – messages, promises, admonition and exhortation, stories of the living Jesus, and such – and the *drómenon,* comprising gestures, music, chanting, silence, objects like bread, wine, incense, candles, light as well as spatial arrangement and the liturgical order or *taxis* which, as Paul tells us in 1 Corinthians 14:40, should prevail in any authentic, decent liturgy. These two components jointly constitute ritual or, in a Christian sense, sacrament. Hence the latter is a single, indivisible, performative, dynamic, and meaningful happening executed in word and actions, in silence and song, in light and incense – in short, in playful earnest. To Christians this ritual totality itself *is* God's means of grace, actualized at a cognitive, emotional and aesthetic level, in and via the inherent performative power of liturgical celebration inspired by the Christian faith. Just as the performance of, say, a musical score can, *via the performance,* evoke and genuinely bring to life something in the performers, so in sacramental liturgy the salvific action accomplishes efficaciously (*efficax*) what it intends! Only then is the ambiguous and abstract classical axiom that a sacrament is an efficacious sign of grace (*signum efficax gratiae*) truly justified. This interpretation is indeed far removed from so-called physical, instrumental causation, however analogously it is understood. Both anthropologically and religiously, causation in this sense falls wholly outside the richly textured signification that is peculiar to (sacramental or other) ritual. This active signification with its performative efficacy is operative at the anthropological level of a genuine liturgical performance.

Hence the gift of grace is not a vertical addendum to the liturgical celebration, in the sense of a sort of superstructure. Human symbolic celebration of the church's faith by a celebrating community and being transported by it *are* God's gift of grace, not something that is added to it. The Christian faith of all participants in ritual liturgy (as the local representation here and now of what, fundamentally, the universal church confesses worldwide) is nonetheless the essence of all this, and is, at the same time, the conduit of God's act in Jesus Christ; he, after all, is the "pioneer and perfecter of our faith" (Heb. 12:2) – the faith of God's church in the sense of the assembled religious community, the *ecclesia*, aptly expressed by the term "congregation:" God's congregation gathered in the church for liturgical celebration.

A perception of the sacraments based on the ideas of semiotics, the linguistic sciences and ethno-cultural anthropology has far-reaching implications, particularly for pastoral theology. It also explains why, by and large, traditional sacramental practice no longer works, and why the Christian faith is increasingly questioned by Christian believers themselves – the result not so much of declining religious feeling or religious needs as of outdated religious images, because neither religion nor the sacraments are embedded in a socio-cultural environment that is authentically rooted in the here and now (even though critical detachment from, and even protest against, that real-life environment may sometimes be warranted). Sacramental phenomena cannot be reduced to physical events. Sacramental grace is not designed for physical consumption. Sacraments belong in the category of symbols or signs, but in the full compass of height and depth, length and breadth of the wealth of meaning – cognitive, emotional and aesthetic – that the cultural human sciences have deciphered in what is known as ritual or symbolic activity: a playful yet serious activity that approximates the density of reality more accurately than dogmatic formulas and doctrinal pronouncements (which does not mean that the latter are not also needed as always *provisional* – being culturally and historically restricted – definitions of certain *uninfringeable horizons,* especially when the church's religious life is in crisis).

Only when the contributions of the various cultural anthropological sciences have been interpreted theologically does it become clear – unlike in the past – that sacraments are an existentially emotive encounter with God in Christ Jesus. Such an approach is primarily a way of deepening symbolic praxis as a special way to 'knowledge of God' that is more accurate than purely theoretical, thematic knowledge of God (even though the church cannot do without such knowledge either). Over the centuries the gospel message has, on the whole, been communicated to believers more emotionally, more sensitively and especially more vividly by sacramental liturgy and depictions in the liturgical space of churches and cathedrals than by theoretical doctrines. The sacraments involve both the expression *and* the construction and growth of a fundamental identity of Christians and Christian communities or churches, and of the universal Church.

In sacramental liturgy we celebrate the Christian dream of God's kingdom proleptically, in anticipation. That kingdom, the basis of the celebrations in the Christian community, is also actualized fragmentarily in an openness to eschatological liberation and salvation, which entails more than individual or socio-political liberation. In fact, ritual celebrations show how God's footprints in Christians' profane engagement are the *presupposition* of their sacramental celebrations, and how these celebrations – the occasions when Christians are *nourished by God* in and through Jesus in the power of Christ's Spirit – in their turn give courage, orientation and inspiration for their earthly endeavours, to which the liturgy returns them. Thus the eschatological vision of God's kingdom transcends both actual Christian praxis in the world and Christian ritual or sacramental celebration. Yet the anticipatory or proleptic realization of the eschatological kingdom through both profane endeavour and liturgical celebration falls under the proviso of God's startling judgment, which in this respect, too, is always new to us.

The Christian sacraments effect an encounter with God in a special way. To Christians that makes Jesus Christ truly the "sacrament of the encounter with God," thus endorsing Tertullian's dictum, *caro salutis est cardo*: corporeality is the pivot of salvation. This applies particularly to sacramental ritual, as a protest against the evil, absurdity and sinfulness in our worldly lives, and at the same time a festive celebration of the encounter with God already realized in that 'profane' life, *especially* in encounters with fellow human beings. That, at bottom, is the meaning of Tertullian's dictum.

++++

POSTSCRIPT TO THE TERM 'PERFORMANCE'

1. Throughout this article I have used the term 'performance' without defining or explaining it. Nowadays the word is commonly used with reference to films, television, the theatre, shows and the like. According to the 1989 edition of the *Concise Oxford Dictionary* the word means "execution (of command, etc.); carrying out; doing; notable feat; performing of play, piece of music, or public exhibition...; achievement under test." The main overall meaning does appear to be a public show, with the added connotation of a successful show, and play-acting. It also suggests achievement.

Since about 1965 a performance has indicated an artistic performance in many genres and forms. Initially there was no audience participation: the audience watched or listened. But the concept soon broadened. A performance was no longer or not entirely self-contained: as entertainment it had to be infectious. Performances evoke a certain emotional involvement, including criticism.[25] Performers tend to fight shy of the traditional stage, or to extend it to the auditorium or the street, in order to involve the audience actively in the show. They want to offer a kind of alternative entertainment. Hence a performance entails more than just bodily expression and/or artistic verbal and musical proficiency, showmanship and accomplishment.[26] In many kinds of performance – a music recital, pop festival, ballet and the like – the term refers mainly to the dimension of artistic forms of communication. Over the years these have increasingly turned into artistic communication in which aesthetics merged with ethical criticism.[27] A few years ago this was evident in Dario Fo's 'Mystero Buffo', and recently in 'The Emperor's Dream' (about Charles V), performed in Nijmegen by the Flemish Royal Ballet Company. In the same way aesthetics may merge into, and be subordinated to, religiosity.

Most recently, however, 'performance' explicitly acquired the down-to-earth meaning simply of 'efficiency' (which was one of its original meanings), more particularly the capacity to excel of, for instance, industries, investors and entrepreneurs.[28]

In addition 'performance' and 'performativeness' are key terms in linguistics (and this usage, too, has a bearing on liturgical ritual). Especially since J. L. Austin, the pragmatics of speech-act theory refers to 'the performative character' of certain speech acts.[29] This means that the intended action is performed in the actual act of speaking (e.g. 'I promise that...', 'I swear that...', 'I baptize you...', 'I forgive you...'): The *legomenon* itself accomplishes or effects something. Performative speech acts are part of what is known as illocutionary speech. In Noam Chomsky's generative grammar, performance as 'speech behaviour' contrasts with 'competence,' being the human language faculty or system of linguistic rules. Hence speech behaviour or performance is equivalent to what structural linguists call *parole*, whereas competence corresponds with *langue*.

2. In this essay (and in my forthcoming book) I use the term 'performance,' with many of the aforementioned connotations, to indicate ritual or liturgical (religious ritual) performances. *Leiturgia* (liturgy) derives from the Greek words *'leitos'* (from *laos* or 'people,' in this case the Christian faithful) and *'ergein'*, meaning 'to act, to perform, to do.' The primary meaning of the word is profane; a public office or service is called *leiturgeia:* a service or function 'relating to the people.' In Christian liturgy it is not a matter of just one performer (the officiant) but of the assembled religious community, which collectively constitutes the active subject of the entire performance (even though the roles are divided among various individual participants). As both *legomenon* and *drómenon* a liturgical celebration has performative dynamic signification: words and gestures, each with their own context, together determine what is said or done symbolically or metaphorically. As performances, religious rituals, hence the sacraments as well, have something of an artistic, consistent *mise en scène*, which is both a summons to and an expression of action: adoration, thanksgiving, praise, *'theologal'* brotherly and sisterly love, and contemporary ethos or ethical behaviour. Sacramental liturgy is not theatre, is not a concert, ballet or show; but as a performance it has a family likeness to all these that reveals reciprocal affinity.

The word 'performance,' which the ritual studies school uses as a matter of course, is also appropriate to designate Christian sacraments, in contrast to an exclusively intellectualized approach to them. Nonetheless it calls for consciously circumspect usage, which is my explicit intention.

ENDNOTES

[1] Tertullian, *De resurrectione mortuorum*, VIII, 6-7: PL 2, col. 806.

[2] 'Anima autem, cum sit pars corporis hominis, non est totus homo, et anima mea non est ego': Thomas, *Super 1 ad Cor.*, c. 15, lect. II (*Super epistolas S. Pauli Apostoli lectura*, ed. R. Cai, 1, Turin/Rome 1953, no. 924).

[3] See E. Schillebeeckx, "Breuken in christelijke dogma's" in *Breuklijnen: Grenservaringen en zoektochten*, (Baarn: H. Nelissen, 1994), 15-49; L. Boeve, *Onderbroken traditie: Heeft het christelijk verhaal nog toekomst?*, (Kapellen: Pelckmans, 1999); L. Oosterveen, "Tussen band en breuk: De theologische verhouding tot de christelijke traditie" in *Tijdschrift voor Theologie* 39 (1999) 3, 217-227; Daniel Speed Thompson, *The Language of Dissent. Edward Schillebeeckx on the Crisis of Authority in the Catholic Church*, Notre Dame, Indiana, 2003.

[4] L.-M. Chauvet, *Symbole et sacrament: Une relecture sacramentelle de l'existence chrétienne*, (Paris: Cerf, 1987); *Du symbolique au symbole: Essai sur les sacraments*, Paris 1979; "La structuration de la foi dans les célébrations sacramentelles" in *La Maison-Dieu* 174 (1988) 75-96; "L'avenir du sacramentel" in *Rech. Sc. Relig.* 75 (1987) 241-266; "Le sacrifice de la messe: représentation et expiation" in *Lum. et vie* 29 (1980) 69-106; "La ritualité chrétienne dans le cercle infernal du symbole" in *La Maison-Dieu* 133 (1978) 31-77; "Sacrements" in *Catholicisme: Hier, Aujourd'hui, Demain*, 13, Paris 1993, col. 326-361; "L'Eglise fait l'Eucharistie, l'Eucharistie fait l'Eglise" in *Catéchèse* 71 (1978) 178-180; "Le sacramentologue aux prises avec l'eucharistie" in *La Maison-Dieu* 137 (1979) 65-70; *Liturgie et prière: Eléments de réflexion anthropologique, théologique et pratique*, ib. 195 (1993), no. 3, 49-90.

[5] M.E. Brinkman, *Schepping en sacrament: Een oecumenische studie naar de reikwijdte van het sacrament als heilzaam symbool in een weerbarstige werkelijkheid*, (Zoetermeer: Boekencentrum, 1991).

[6] "A Discussion on Ritualization of Behavior in Animals and Man," ed. J. Huxley in *Philosophical Transactions of the Royal Society of London* (Series B, New York/Cambridge) 251 (1966) 247-525.

[7] The use of the term 'ritualizing process' stems from J. Huxley (see note 6). Theoretically this has had a beneficial impact on the work of two theorists, both of whom also did empirical research: Ronald L. Grimes, professor at the University of Waterloo, Canada and founder of the Journal of Ritual Studies, and the more circumspect Catherine Bell, associate professor at St Clare University, California. R.L. Grimes's main studies were *Beginnings in Ritual Studies,* rev. ed., (Columbia: University of South Carolina Press, 1995); "Reinventing Rituals" in *Soundings* 75 (1992), no. 2, 21-41; "Emerging Ritual" in *Proceedings of the North American Academy of Liturgy* 1990, 15-31. C. Bell's principal works are *Ritual Theory, Ritual Practice*, (New York/Oxford: Oxford University Press, 1992), and *Ritual: Perspectives and Di-*

*mensions*, ib. 1997. I also mention the long famous inspirer of many other scholars, V.W. Turner, whose numerous publications drew my attention to the new trend in the study of ritual: *The Forest of Symbols: Aspects of Ndembu Ritual*, (Ithaca, NY: Cornell University Press, 1970); *The Ritual Process: Structure and Anti-Structure*, (Ithaca NY: Cornell University Press, 1977); *From Ritual to Theatre: The Human Seriousness of Play*, (New York: PAJ Publications, 1982); *Celebrations: Studies in Festivity and Ritual*, (New York: PAJ Publications, 1982); *The Drums of Affliction: A Study of Religious Processes among the Ndembu of Zambia*, (Ithaca NY: Cornell University Press, 1981); *Process, Performance, and Pilgrimage: A Study in Comparative Symbology*, (New Delhi: Concept, 1979); "Symbolic Studies" in *Ann. Rev. of Anthropology* 4 (1975) 145-161; "Process, System and Symbol: A New Anthropological Synthesis" in *Daedalus* 106 (1977) no. 3, 61-80; *The Ritual Process*, (Chicago: Aldine, 1969); "Forms of Symbolic Action," in *Proceedings of the 1969 Annual Spring Meeting of the American Ethnological Society*, ed. R. F. Spencer, 3-25,( Seattle: Univeristy of Washington Press, 1971); *Dramas, Fields, and Metaphors: Symbolic Action in Human Society*, (Ithaca NY: Cornell University Press, 1974); *Revelation and Divinisation in Ndembu Ritual*, (Ithaca NY: Cornell University Press,1957); "Worship and Ritual in Christianity and other Religions" in *Studia Missionalia* (Rome) 23 (1974) 11-21; *The Anthropology of Performance*, second edition, ( New York 1986) (copy text from the 1st ed.); *The Anthropology of Experience*, ed. V. Turner/E.M. Bruner, (Urbana 1986). I also refer to the main authors who introduced modifications and corrections to Turner's work: Roy A. Rappaport, E. Erikson, Stanley Jeyaraja Tambiah and R. Schechner. A book considered important by some scholars, J.M. Greer, *Circles of Power: Ritual Magic in the Western Tradition*, (St. Paul MN: Llewellyn Publications, 1997), is extremely interesting but somewhat esoteric.

[8] Cf. A.K. Giri, "De grenzen van disciplines: Het heroverwegen van theorieën en methoden" in *Conc.* 35 (1999) no. 2, 64-71; S. Bauman, *Hermeneutics and Social Science: Approaches to understanding*, (London: Hutchinson & Co, 1978); Cl. Boff, *Theology and Praxis: Epistemological Foundations*, (Maryknoll NY: Orbis Books, 1987) (originally in French, a doctoral thesis, mainly on interdisciplinary study, at the Faculty of Theology, Louvain). Compare these studies with: J. A. van der Ven, "Op weg naar een empirische theologie" in *Meedenken met Edward Schillebeeckx*, ed. H. Häring e.a., , (Baarn: H. Nelissen, 1983), 93-114 (and his many subsequent publications on this subject), and *De theologie uitgedaagd: Spreken over God binnen het wetenschapsbedrijf*, ed. R. van den Brandt/R. Plum, (Zoetermeer: Beokenscentrum, 1999) (especially the article by E. Borgman, 129-165).

[9] See A.N. Terrin, "Rito e teatro: Riflessioni a partire dall'antropologia culturale e dalla storia comparata delle religioni" in *Studia Patavina* 38 (1991) 565-594.

[10] Bell, *Ritual*, l.c. (n. 7), 166.

[11] See R. Rappaport, *Ecology, Meaning and Religion*, (Richmond CA: North Atlantic Books, 1979), 179.

[12] R. Schechner, *Essays on Performance Theory, 1970-1976*, (New York: Routledge, 1977), 71.

[13] In her latest book Bell gives an impressive analysis of the dialectics in ritual between tradition and change: *Ritual*, l.c. (nt. 7), ch. 7, 'Ritual change', 210-252.

[14] See Turner, *The Ritual Process*, l.c. (nt. 7).

[15] See the book by the Brazilian F. Taborda, *Sakramentos: praxis e festa*, (Petropolis: Vozes, 1987). It remains a classic, influenced not by the trends of ritual studies but by empirical scholars of playful celebration, which the author locates in a situation of 'resistance and surrender.' This sacramental theology was written from the angle of a resistance and liberation movement in the Latin American context.

[16] By particular traditions I mean the various rituals of Christians, Jews and Muslims and rites from Asia, Oceania, Africa, Australia and South America.

[17] Yves Congar, "De idee van hoofd-sacramenten of voornaamste sacramenten" in *Conc.* 4 (1968) no. 1, 23-34. Also see L.M. Chauvet, "Sacrements" in *Catholicisme*, l.c. (n. 4), 13 (1993), 333ff.

[18] For the meaning of the expression *anathema sit* at Trent (which certainly does not imply 'condemnation to hell', as some people think), see the analyses of P. Fransen, in the collected volume of his articles: *Hermeneutics of the Councils and Other Studies*, ed. H.E. Mertens/F. De Graeve, (Louvain: Leuven University Press: Peeters, 1985), esp. 69-94, 95-125 and 198-213.

[19] Yves Congar in particular fought for this as far back as the 1960s: "L'Ecclesia ou communauté chrétienne, sujet intégral de l'action liturgique" in *La Liturgie après Vatican II*, ed. J.P. Jossua/Y. Congar, (Paris: Cerf, 1967), 241-243.

[20] See *De sacramentele heilseconomie: Theologische bezinning op S. Thomas' sacramentenleer in het licht van de traditie en van de hedendaagse sacramentsproblematiek*, I, (Antwerpen: 't Groeit; Bilthoven: Nelissen, 1952), part II, section I, 561-619.

[21] Some scholars hold the view that metaphors do not deal in truth, but to my mind metaphors are very much concerned with the relation between meaning, thought (in concepts and images) and reality. In religious (especially Christian or sacramental) ritual, too, the cognitive relationship remains a vital ingredient which should not be papered over, under pressure from the new notion of performative efficacy, with 'anti-intellectualist' emotion. Concern about the 'cognitive relationship' of propositions, metaphoric or otherwise, has nothing to do with intellectualism; that would be the case only if it entailed suppressing all other relations and not giving them their due.

[22] This debate can also turn into a battle of words. What many scholars now call trans-rationality is worked out by Thomas as *intellectus*, the antithesis and implicit basis of conceptualizing and analytical *ratio*. In Thomas's thinking *intellectus* (hence intellectualism) means something very different from rationalism and even comprehends more than 'intentional knowing'. It also embraces all inner life, which in the medieval classification of human faculties was not included under *ratio*, even though Thomas was sufficiently familiar with the interrelationship or *circuminsessio* of human faculties. One would have to circumscribe the current usage of 'intellectualism' somewhat more accurately.

[23] "Twice he passed through the garden of theology – certainly not a garden of Eden" (our translation): H. Häring, "Met mensen op weg, voor mensen op weg: Over het theologisch denken van Edward Schillebeeckx" in *Mensen maken de kerk* (Report on the symposium on the 75th birthday of Edward Schillebeeckx), (Baarn: H. Nelissen, 1989), 27-46, cit. 40.

[24] Huus Oosterhuis, *Levende die mij ziet*, (Kampen/Tielt: JH Kok/Lannoo, 1999), 76.

[25] See J. Jaeger, *Stijlgids: stijlen, stromingen en begrippen in de kunst van 1860 tot heden*, (De Bilt: Cantecleer, 1985), 86.

[26] Cf. *Lexicon van literaire termen*, H. van Gorp e.a., Groningen 1991, 80-81 and 299-300.

[27] See Th. Baumeister, *De filosofie en de kunsten: van Plato tot Beuys*, (Amsterdam: Damon, 1999), 479.

[28] M. Schweitzer, *Performance of Institutional Investors* (Thesis, University of Maastricht), Maastricht 2000.

[29] J.L. Austin cf especially his *How to do things with Words?*, (Cambridge: Harvard University Press, 1962); for speech-act theory: J.R. Searle, *Speech-acts: An Essay in the Philosophy of Language*, (Cambridge: Cambridge University Press, 1969).

# TWO

# Liturgy and the Truth about Human Suffering

*Don E. Saliers*

*"...but we also boast in our sufferings, knowing that suffering produces endurance, and endurance produces character, and character produces hope, and hope does not disappoint us, because God's love has been poured into our hearts through the Holy Spirit that has been given to us." Romans 5:3-5*

From the beginning Christian faith and life has acknowledged human suffering. In writing to the church at Rome, Paul expresses extraordinary confidence that God is in the midst of our tribulations. The fledgling Christian community is to boast not only in the hope of sharing the glory of God in Christ, but even to boast in its suffering various trials and persecutions. The letter of James opens by admonishing us to "count it all joy when you meet various trials." Under severe persecution, Christian faith and hope flourished in the face of suffering and death. The very act of assembling, as Justin Martyr[1] reports – to hear the prophets and the memories of the apostles and to share the common meal – was a claim of Christ's victory over death in the midst of martyrdom.

By all human accounts this is a most difficult claim to comprehend. We may try to avoid the fact that Christian liturgy must face death and suffering by saying that this attitude was the special circumstance of early Christianity with its expectation of an imminent *eschaton*. But the question of its truth will not go away, for human suffering has continued to impinge upon the lives of worshiping assemblies in every age. Intersections between suffering and the worship of God go beyond the severe tests of religious persecution and martyrdom. An abstract theodicy does not suffice for discerning and understanding how Christian liturgical life illuminates matters of human suffering.

# Ordo: Bath, Word, Prayer, Table

A voice from the late twentieth century speaks to a deeper complexity:

> History shudders, pierced by events of massive public suffering. Memory is haunted, stalked by the ghosts of history's victims, capriciously served from life in genocide, holocaust, and extermination camps. The cries of the hungry, the shrieks of political prisoners, and the silent voices of the oppressed echo slowly, painfully through daily existence… For most of the world's population in the present and the not-too-distant past, to live is to suffer: to be born is become a victim.[2]

Thus Rebecca Chopp wrote in the introduction to *The Praxis of Suffering* nearly twenty years ago. Perhaps these words are even more pointed for us in very recent times. Our awareness of massive public suffering brings a range of moral pain to those who do not directly experience these things. This awareness also challenges easy assumptions about prayer. One might even argue that attentive and faithful liturgical participation arouses and sustains such awareness.

The sheer enormity of suffering haunts Christian public worship. To speak truthfully of human suffering in all its variety in the brute prose of historical and social/political description is one thing. To speak truthfully out of the resources of the Christian liturgical assembly is another. In all too many cases Christian public worship attempts, in sermons, song and prayer, to avoid honest engagement with such reality. Soon or late, however, assemblies gathered in the name of Christ about the Word, the Table and the Bath must come to terms with the reality and enormity of suffering. This juxtaposition of the good willed by God and the suffering undergone by human beings generates both the necessity and the desire for truthful liturgy.

To be human is to suffer. This is a primordial fact. Yet the range of human suffering is vast, for while so much pain and misery is circumstantial, life is vulnerable and mortal, embodied and finite. Natural disasters continue to occur – earthquake, storm and drought. But war and violence of all kinds continue even more to mark human history. This has led many critics to accuse the practices of prayer and liturgy of being opiates or projections of immaturity. As Nietzsche recognized, prayer and worship can be the refuge of untruth, falsifying and diminishing our sense of humanity. Christian theologians have seen that liturgical prayer can be, as Johannes Metz observed, a "eulogistic evasion of what really matters."[3] "What really matters" – for Metz and for most liberation theologians – is precisely the elimination of social/political conditions that are at the root of so much human misery. So we must ask: can Christian liturgy be truthful about suffering when its very nature is regarded as avoidance of the real? What wisdom is available that will speak to these undeniable features of human existence? What can speak and heal; or at least speak truthfully? To speak in the form of words is crucial, but words alone are not enough. It is the liturgical "transaction" with God – to use Aidan Kavanagh's phrase – that matters: "…the church's worship does not merely reflect or express its repertoire of faith. It transacts the church's faith in God under the condition of God's real presence in both church and world."[4]

This essay explores the resources of Christian liturgical life in light of these questions. The Gospel claims that created life belongs to God who alone is holy, yet who redeems and sanctifies the world in, with, and through Jesus Christ. There is no escaping the contrast between this claim and how we "suffer" the way the world is in its actuality. This is the gap between "holy things," "holy people," and the world as it has come to be. How does Christian liturgy address the gap between the "is" and the "ought to be" of the world? Can liturgical participation illuminate anything about human suffering that we do not already understand by moral reasoning alone?

## Biblical Sourcing of the Church's Liturgical Life

When Christians gather in worshiping assemblies week upon week, year upon year, human lives are constantly being brought to the glorification of God and the sanctification of humanity. Every assembly is conjoined by baptism to the on-going word, prayer and action of Jesus Christ which is his 'liturgy' in the world. Any thinking about liturgy and suffering must begin by recalling that baptism is "into his suffering and death." While there are many New Testament texts that reflect this primary fact, Paul's letter to the Romans forcefully states a key implication of baptism: "I consider that the sufferings of the present time are not worth comparing with the glory that is to be revealed to us."[5] Our baptismal entrance into participation in the worshiping assembly takes seriously the fact of human suffering, even placing it in a cosmic reference. "The whole creation is groaning in travail" to be liberated from suffering and death.

The world we inhabit is filled with beauty and terror, goodness and violence, joy and pain. Human societies live always amidst such contrasts, and we bring these things with us to our worship of God. Various churches in all their liturgical diversity live in the tensions peculiar to their time and place. Yet to each time and place Christian liturgy brings narratives, prophecies, wisdom, song and the prayers of biblical sources to the *ordo* of Christian worship. In his writing, especially in *Holy Things: A Liturgical Theology*,[6] Gordon Lathrop has convincingly demonstrated how the dynamics of liturgical rites are intrinsically biblical. The ancient biblical texts are used in worship to speak a new and relevant Word. The pattern of the use of scriptures in the liturgy is itself biblical – "the liturgical pattern is drawn from the Bible."[7] This point is crucial to how we may unfold the biblical sourcing of Christian liturgy, while yet recognizing the great diversity of social and cultural contexts in which Christian assemblies exist.

Indelibly etched in the whole range of the biblical witness is the reality of human suffering. So the very stories that constitute the core of the liturgical lectionary (whether canonical or informal) carry the marks of pain and misery. Biblical literature contains sources that face and name the vulnerabilities and collusions of human existence.

For all the realism of sacred Scripture about human life, worshipers are often engaged in strategies of avoidance. Suffering may be avoided, or even (as in some traditions) denied as illusory. But all attempts to avoid or to deny the ubiquity of human suffering finally falter before the honesty of Scripture about the whole range of human vicissitude. The founding narratives, the lament/praise juxtaposition of the psalms, and cries of the prophetic literature all move against such strategies of avoiding the real. The Wisdom literature continues to remind hearers that, in the language of Ecclesiastes, "for everything there is a season." The deep contrasts of human life are figured in the canonical literature, from Genesis to Revelation. Liturgical worship carries within its own ordering of Scripture a prophetic critique of all attempts to deny or avoid the range of human suffering.

I propose that Christian liturgy, insofar as it takes into itself the biblical sources and modes of perception, does not simply name or affirm suffering; it engages it in a surprising way. It tells us something new about suffering. We will return to this point; but first some reminders about the intrinsic ways in which major biblical resources resolutely keep God and human experience, praise and lament, in generative tension.

Written into the founding narratives is this tensive engagement. The Exodus story emerges out of the suffering of Israel under Pharaoh's oppression. The very songs of triumph we find in the canticles in Exodus 15 (Miriam and Moses) encode the contrast between oppression and liberation. The Joseph cycle contains the conspiring jealousy of his brothers and Joseph's being sold into slavery as a crucial feature of the surprise outcome of reunion in Egypt. It is no wonder that African-American preaching features these stories so prominently as woven into its own sense of history.

Narratives of King David contain the suffering he created. While we may rejoice in the surprising choice of the young shepherd boy, David, to be the king of Israel as recorded in I Samuel 16, we also must hear of David's own faults as the story of his rule unfolds – Bathsheba and the death of Uriah, and eventually his own deep grief.

Thus biblical readings do not shy from naming and engaging human suffering, and the role of human agents in creating misery. But imprinted deeply in the poetry and prayer of the Bible is a contrast between praise and lament. It is appropriate that the older traditions spoke of the "psalms of David" since the narrative of his life is mirrored in the full stretch of the psalms as poetry and prayer. While Christian liturgy has tended to use the psalms of praise and thanksgiving in the development of liturgical prayer, it is still the case that the majority of the psalms are laments. Individual and communal lamentations cry out of pain and suffering, as well as in anger and frustration. While most lament psalms turn also to trust and praise, the heart of their witness is to the suffering of life that is spoken directly to God. "Out of the depths I cry to you" (Psalm 130). In the season of Lent (arising from the practice of baptismal preparation) the so-called "penitential Psalms" echo the cry of the broken-hearted. Praying through this season in the Christian assembly must confront a range of suffering – especially the suffering caused by sin. But other psalms, which may only surface in the daily offices, take us more deeply into the cry of the heart. Psalm 88 plunges relentlessly into the depths of despair, with no turning to praise at all.

Here, of course, we recognize that the psalms have not always been used as the Church's song in their entirety. The notable exception for worship on the Lord's Day was the Reformed traditions' insistence on the entire Psalter (in metrical form) over time.

In our own time, the recovery of the whole range of biblical song in the psalms and canticles has enabled some communities to acknowledge that Christian assemblies can and must sing "honest, aching songs"[8] to God as well as praise.

The truth about suffering caused by human neglect is at the heart of so much of the prophetic literature that is the necessary tap root of Jesus' own prophetic teachings. Time and time again the prophets, major and minor, address the suffering resulting from the neglect of the orphan and the widow. No worshiping community can escape the warnings of Amos, of Jeremiah or of Isaiah. There is, for the Christian assembly, a constant drum beat of reminders of the suffering of the poor, the oppressed, and of all subject to human injustice and violence. Thus Amos can utter harsh words against liturgy itself: "…I take no delight in your solemn assemblies. …Take away from me the noise of your songs; to the melody of your harps I will not listen. But let justice roll down like waters…" [Amos 5:21, 23-24]. The critique of Israel's failure to alleviate suffering places the truth of human suffering at human hands squarely before the worshiping community.

A central biblical claim, from Genesis to Revelation, is that God does not turn away from human terror, violence and pain. The Christian community focuses on the incarnation of God in a fully human life. This in turn sets at the heart of worship an immense and mysterious solidarity with all creation and with all the brokenness and travail that human beings undergo. This leads us to the specific christological sourcing of liturgical truth about human suffering, namely what J. Metz and others have called the "dangerous memory" of Jesus Christ.

### HUMAN SUFFERING AND THE DANGEROUS MEMORY (*memoria passionis*)

Johannes Metz, in establishing a style of political theology, proposed that Christian proclamation and worship can only be salvific in our present world if it is grounded in the *memoria passionis* of Christ. Drawing on earlier work by Walter Benjamin and steeped in Adorno and the Frankfurt School, Metz turns to this "dangerous memory" of Jesus Christ as a way of facing the enormity of human suffering in our time. He is interested primarily in how "developed" societies are at present dominated by technological reason and market forces. In his judgment human suffering results from such systems. Those caught in such systems may also be aware of such world-wide suffering. He does not develop the idea of the moral pain resulting from a kind of "radial" awareness of such suffering and our complicity; I think this is an accompanying crucial feature of what many bring to Christian liturgical assemblies as well.

Metz does not offer a systematic account of how the "dangerous memory" of the suffering, death and resurrection of Christ permeates the liturgy. But he does call for the practice of such a memory by the Christian community. In his own work he gradually came to see the origins of this truthful address of human suffering in the Eucharistic *anamnesis*. I propose that it is precisely the practice of the *memoria passionis* that draws together all the biblical resources mentioned above into a Christian liturgical life that addresses the question of truth about human suffering – in all its range.

I propose that an appropriate recovery of the *memoria Jesu Christi* in the whole ecology of Christian worship is crucial to any adequate attempt to answer questions about suffering in our contemporary situation. This requires both a theological re-interpretation of the whole canon of Christian liturgy *and* a living "practical hermeneutic" in the assembly's liturgical formation. That is, we must see the major structures (baptismal rites – including continuing renewals of baptismal covenant – eucharist, daily prayer, rites of passage – all pastoral offices – and the cycles of time [week, day and year]) as continual deepening of the *anamnesis* of Jesus Christ. This requires a renewed reading of the Christian *ordo* as Gordon Lathrop has convincingly argued.

Bruce Morrill claims:

> In the *memoria Jesu Christi* Metz is able to identify the history of suffering as a history of freedom. As the eschatological memory that anticipates the promised future of the oppressed, the hopeless and failed, it is at once dangerous and liberating, compelling…Christians continuously to change their attitudes and actions with this specific future in mind.[9]

I propose that this is more than a theological claim or even an ethical admonition. It is itself what the liturgy effects, even when actions are not available, or are tragically ambiguous in the face of the complexities of our radial awareness. In this sense liturgy is not only an eschatological motivation, it is already the reality given. This allows for a sense of eschatology broader than a particular social/political realization. The eschatological and saving force of this practice of *anamnesis* is relevant to both social realization and action and to the hope for eternal life – both participation now and hope for eternal life in God.

Sourced in biblical realism about human suffering and about the full stretch of life before God, Christian liturgical life has its own profound center in the passion, death and resurrection of Christ. This is at the heart of all eucharistic and baptismal rites. When this connection with truthfulness about the divine engagement of human suffering is lost, liturgy loses its ability to speak to the real world. A liturgy without the "dangerous memory of Christ" at its heart is subject to all the idolatrous and trivial projections of human religiousness.

## THE PARADOXICAL CHARACTER OF LITURGICAL PARTICIPATION

Two initial images will illuminate a central mystery of liturgical participation: Simone Weil's reflections on affliction and the crucifixion that creates "the infinite distance between God and God" juxtaposed with Julian of Norwich's saying from her *Showings*: "Betwixt God and ourselves there is no 'between.'"[10] This opens the paradoxical faces of God in Christ we receive in the liturgy over time which, in turn, opens the deeper mystery of God "hidden and revealed."

The whole canon (or "ecology") of Christian liturgical rites is rarely fully available to a given local church or community, or perhaps even to a whole tradition. Even a partial range available in the Sunday liturgy of Word and Eucharist, surrounded by Scripture reading and devotional prayer is enough to form us in the paradoxical character of a Christian "reading" of the world and ourselves. God is continually self-giving in Word and Eucharist as the Holy One, Holy Three. We are joined to the continuing liturgy in Jesus Christ in such a way as to approach God who is creator of all things visible and invisible, and Spirit both within our hearts and at work beyond our ken in the cosmos.

The way of the liturgy is in and through what Jesus Christ is and does: feeding, healing, liberating, proclaiming, Spirit-conferring, suffering and associating with all sorts and conditions of human beings. Without attention to these features of his crucified and risen life we cannot understand the larger sweep of the God of history, hidden and revealed.

So liturgical action is *anamnetic* in the particulars of the life, teachings, deeds, suffering, death, resurrection and Spirit-conferring of Jesus Christ. But this narrative cannot be fully received until the whole of the divine life becomes its construal. By this I mean that the whole of Scripture must be apprehended in its richness. Thus until Jesus Christ is remembered within the whole ecology and economy of Scripture, the fullness of his person and work is diminished. At the same time, until Jesus Christ is remembered under the impress of lived history –including suffering and joy, terror and beauty, human evil and human good, forces of nature for ill and for plenty – the reality of his redemptive manifestation of God is diminished. Thus a further element of paradox emerges: the world cannot be discerned truthfully without the dangerous memory of Jesus Christ; yet what the incarnation, death and resurrection effects cannot be discerned without a truthful acknowledgement of the suffering of the world.

Perhaps no other theologian has addressed this paradox so poetically as has Hans Urs von Balthasar in his meditation on Holy Saturday, the "middle day," entitled *Heart of the World*.[11] Here in the total emptiness between death and resurrection, we are left without recourse. The intensity of the "passion" and the liturgy of Good Friday take us to the deeps of experienced suffering. Yet to come is the ritual culmination of Easter's shocking reversal. In the time between, however, there seems to be an "infinite distance between God and God." We are left in silence. It is a moment at the heart of Christian worship where we can do nothing, not even lament. Here it is that out of the utter emptiness, out of the very weariness of God who bears the sufferings of the world, a "slow drop" of life begins which we cannot fathom. Thus in the liturgy of Holy Week, culminating in the three days of Maundy Thursday through Resurrection morning (the "Triduum") we live through the paradoxical participation of God in our humanity!

Understanding this, Gordon Lathrop reminds us that the *ordo* is a living pattern of participation in God that requires deep Scriptural memory and engagement in life. "Holy things for holy people; yet [God] alone is holy." If this is so, then we are taken in, even beyond our understanding, into the compassion of God which is paradoxically present in, with, and under the things and people God graces in the midst of the human condition. This, of course, is not simply a Lathropian insight – this insight belongs at the heart of Christian faith, worship, and belief.

## Liturgy as a "School for Compassion"

Two dangers appear in speaking of liturgy as a school for compassion. The first danger is the possible reading of compassion in the direction of sentimentality. It is easy to regard compassion primarily as a form of "tenderness" or "tender care." There is much in Christian worship that has to do with God's tender care for creatures. Here one thinks immediately of the appearance of Psalm 23 in funeral rites as in its appearance in the Sunday lectionaries, as well as its widespread use as devotional prayer. The Canticle of Zechariah sings of the "tender compassion of our God" when "the dawn from on high shall break upon us."[12] Many prayers and collects certainly emphasize this attribute of God, and many teachings of Jesus found in the Gospels show remarkable tenderness. Yet the divine compassion also carries more than "pity" toward humanity. We can easily take a conception of love from our cultural needs and conceptions and project it onto God. The divine compassion contains elements of correction and the call to practice compassion toward others, the most strenuous of which is Jesus' call to love the enemy.

The second danger is to read compassion as human moral sacrifice. Here again, there is much to support the concept of sacrificial love as the paradigm for the Christian response to God. As God's Son was sacrificed for us, so we should sacrifice ourselves for others. However, a severe consequence may result if the practice of compassion lead to forms of self-abnegation, and even a certain pride in this. The difficult side of discipleship, especially the call to leave everything to follow Christ is particularly dangerous when construed as a form of self-hatred. In such instances, the liturgy can seem to turn compassion away from the tenderness of God for the creature as a grace, and move toward a presumptive or heroic self-emptying of the human subject.

But the "school of compassion" that attends eucharistic participation holds together the "tender compassion of our God" and the moral demands of love for the other. The liturgy itself schools us away from sentimentality; but it also schools us away from presumptive and romantic heroism of making self-hatred a moral virtue. Mature and comprehensive intercessions of the community over time make this clear. We pray for "all sorts and conditions" of humanity, including those of the church and of ourselves.

Over all our liturgical participation stands the sign and reality of baptismal grace – we who are finite and sinful are paradoxically made worthy to stand and praise the God of all creation. This was, of course, a constant theme in Luther, but not his only. Rather, precisely because we are incorporated into the living *memoria Jesu Christi* – baptized into his suffering, death and resurrected life – we can face suffering with compassion.

These considerations lead to a renewed sense of liturgical participation as a formation in the "compassion of God." This is far more than empathy or certainly than pity for the suffering. It is a radical solidarity that faces the limits of human love. It is based on the perception that God's compassion is even "greater than our hearts." This distance and intimacy in the face of human suffering is required. This has immense social/ethical and moral implications for liturgy and a new form of the *imitatio Christi* in our present social/political world.

Earlier we proposed that Christian liturgy engages and tells us something new about human suffering. Christians, shaped by the *memoria Jesu Christi* can never say that suffering and death do not matter. Senseless suffering and massive death is an enormous indignity to those created and redeemed by the whole pattern of Christ's incarnate life and death and resurrection. Despite our tendencies to sentimentalize death, Christian funeral rites are, rightly enacted, the antithesis of sentimentality. If we follow the *ordo* of such rites we find the engagement with the mystery of death located in the very compassion of God… but compassion tested by real separation and distance without the Trinitarian life. The cry of abandonment hovers in the background of texts such as Psalm 23. The rites appropriately supplicate God for mercy. For those Christians who find a more intimate connection between Jesus Christ and his mother, it seems appropriate to supplicate Mary – she who witnessed his suffering and who was the *Pieta* in the flesh – "pray for us now and in the hour of our death."[13]

## The Limits of Liturgy in the Face of Suffering

Finally we must come to terms with what liturgy does not do. It cannot spare us from suffering. Neither do the rites of the Church guarantee that God will act in specific events of human pain and travail. Liturgical participation is not a talisman or a shamanist ritual. Rather, the on-going prayer of the Christian assembly in both lament and praise continually re-orients us to the elemental facts of existence before God. This wondrous creation is also finite and fallen (not as depravity, but as turned away in freedom). More to the point, by its own continual rhythms, and the constant juxtapositions of Scripture, prayer and eucharistic meal – all baptismally permeated, Christian liturgical life rehearses and participates in the truth about human suffering. Liturgy enables human beings to anticipate death and future suffering – to practice a liturgical *ars moriendi* (art of dying) without morbidity or denial of life. This is more than the rehearsal of a philosophical idea or a set of resigned Stoic attitudes; it is a bodily practice – an engagement between human community and the God in whose name that community gathers.

At its heart, Christian liturgical participation in adequately celebrated rites holds mystery and suffering together. It holds honesty about what befalls us and the hope beyond all ills as figured in the divine *kenosis*. God and the whole created order are bound together, but do not collapse into one another. The terror and the beauty, the sorrow and the joy, the infinite distance and the "no between" are together in the *memoria Jesu Christi* at the heart of our life. But this life must be practiced.

In some degrees of suffering there is no evident resolution; in other instances pain and suffering are transfigured in the actual experience of the believers. The eschatological hope is neither otherworldly nor collapsed into what we can achieve in this world. In addition to the eternal rest and the glory of the *communio sanctorum* (communion of saints), there is always and also a vision of the "new creation," and the vision of the transformation of the structures of violence. The mystery of grace is that even our very complicities in the sufferings of others are thereby named and challenged. This is the permanent tension of all Christian liturgical participation.

Thus, even though liturgy is permeated by praising, blessing and thanking God, we are driven to live compassionately in this world, and moved to alleviate suffering wherever we can. Despite the fact that so many seem so easily to settle for so little of the mystery, Christian liturgy ought always to place the reality of human suffering into the cosmic promises of God. Hope is not only for what is resolvable or even healed in time and space. Eternity is still a feature of the holiness of God. East of Eden, and in the vagaries of human history, human sufferings will persist, no matter how much justice and peacemaking is brought to life by liturgical participation. This is why the permanent tension between our earthly liturgies and the heavenly liturgy are also sounded and enacted over time in the liturgical year. So in the great feast days of the Church do we from time to time encounter the wedding of heaven and earth. In this way our *Alleluias!* co-mingle and animate our laments, and our *Kyries* anticipate the *Gloria in excelsis* of those living eternally in the presence of God.

# Ordo: Bath, Word, Prayer, Table

ENDNOTES

[1] See Justin Martyr, *First Apology*, 67.1

[2] Rebecca S. Chopp, *The Praxis of Suffering: An Interpretation of Liberation and Political Theologies*, (Maryknoll, N.Y.: Orbis Books, 1986), 1.

[3] Johannes Metz, *Faith in History and Society: Toward a Practical Fundamental Theology*, trans. David Smith (New York: Seabury Press, 1980)

[4] 4 Aidan Kavanagh, *On Liturgical Theology* (New York: Pueblo, 1984), 8

[5] Romans 8:18. Cf. the baptismal instruction from Romans 6:3-4, "Do you not know that all of us who have been baptized into Christ Jesus were baptized into his death? We were buried therefore with him by baptism into death, so that as Christ was raised from the death by the glory of the Father, we too might walk in newness of life."

[6] Gordon W. Lathrop, *Holy Things: A Liturgical Theology* (Minneapolis: Fortress Press, 1993), 15-32 and passim.

[7] Ibid., p.19.

[8] The phrase comes from a recent hymn text by Brian Wren, *God, Give Us Freedom to Lament*: "We'll walk beside you,/come what may,/to you our hopes and hearts belong,/ and when we've nothing else to say,/ we'll sing an honest, aching song." *New Beginnings* (Carol Stream: Hope Publishing, 1993), #26.

[9] Bruce Morrill, S.J., *Anamnesis as Dangerous Memory: Political and Liturgical Theology in Dialogue*. (Collegeville: The Liturgical Press, 2000), 31.

[10] Cited in Wendy Farley, "Natural Suffering, Tragedy, and the Compassion of God" in *Second Opinion* (18, no. 2), p. 28

[11] Hans Urs von Balthasar, *Heart of the World*, trans. Erasmo S. Leiva (San Francisco: Ignatius Press, 1979).

[12] Luke 1:78

[13] The repetitive prayer of the rosary based on Luke 1 – "Rejoice Mary, full of grace, the Lord is with you. Blessed are you among women and blessed is the fruit of your womb, Jesus. Holy Mary, Mother of God, pray for us sinners now and at the hour of our death." – calls upon Mary and the mysteries of Redemption.

# THREE

# Gathering, *Ordo*, and Baptism

*S. Anita Stauffer and Dirk G. Lange*

PART I - S. ANITA STAUFFER

One of Gordon Lathrop's favorite quotes is from a (now-destroyed) church bell in Luck, Wisconsin:
To the bath and the table
To the prayers and the word
I call every seeking soul.[1]

To Baptism and the affirmation or remembrance of baptism, this bell called those in the parish of West Denmark Lutheran Church. To the Eucharist they were called, and to intercessions for the Church and the world, and to the proclamation of the Gospel. The central things. The central actions. All called by the church bell, the "mouth" of God.

"I call every seeking soul" to gather in that place. To assemble to sing, to celebrate, to do penance, to eat the holy meal, to pray. To *do* things. To meet together to do the central things of the Church. Not passively to watch actions, but to join in doing them. These actions are called the liturgy, and we do them still today.

Gordon Lathrop is largely responsible for the popularization of Alexander Schmemann's term *ordo*.[2] Usually this word is used to refer to the Eucharist, to the organizational shape of the eucharistic liturgy. As Lathrop expands and explains,[3] this eucharistic *ordo* has four components:
Gathering
Word
Meal
Sending

# Ordo: Bath, Word, Prayer, Table

So the people gather for the purpose of hearing the Word proclaimed, participating in the Meal celebrated, and finally leaving to bring the Gospel to the world. They prepare for worship at home, and come to the church to participate actively in the liturgy.[4] Indeed, this gathering defines the church: According to the Augsburg Confession, the church "is the assembly of all believers among whom the Gospel is purely preached and the holy sacraments are administered according to the Gospel."[5]

Gordon Lathrop summarizes the eucharistic *ordo* in this way: "This ordo organizes *a participating community together with its ministers gathered in song and prayer around the Scriptures read and preached, around the baptismal washing, enacted or remembered, and around the Holy Supper*. This *ordo* is these things done together, side by side."[6]

The liturgy in which the people participate when they come together has several parts – the components or shape of the *ordo*. Yet it is important to note that the gathering begins at home, and then continues in corporate worship with several variable constituent parts: usually greeting fellow worshipers while entering the narthex, singing an entrance hymn, and being greeted by the presiding minister. The gathering may also include an explicit remembrance of baptism, and/or a rite for confession and forgiveness. One must be careful, however, not to overload the gathering rite to the point that it draws attention away from the central parts of the eucharistic liturgy: Word and Meal.

Baptism also has a shape or *ordo*, though perhaps not so clearly defined as that of the Eucharist. Lathrop refers to it as "the patterns of Baptism: teaching, bathing, and welcoming into the assembly."[7] This hearkens back to the catechumenate of the early church with a period of teaching and spiritual and moral formation of the adult candidates, the water bath, and welcoming into the assembly for the first Communion. Today this pattern is known as the catechumenate, and forms for it are used in a variety of Catholic and Protestant denominations. When the baptism is for infants and children, the instruction is for the parents and sponsors.

Examining these resources, we discover that baptism often follows an augmented pattern, beginning with the parents and sponsors gathering at the font, an address by the presiding minister, and the presentation of the person to be baptized. Then comes the major section of the rite: the consecration of or thanksgiving for and over the water, (commonly known as the Flood Prayer, and commonly derived from Luther's *Sintflutgebet*), the questions and answers of the candidate (or sponsors) and the congregation (the Apostles' Creed), and the washing in water with the Trinitarian formula. The third part of the baptismal rite is a series of ritual actions: commonly consisting of a prayer for the Holy Spirit, the chrismation or anointing with oil on the forehead, the optional presentation of a white garment, and the optional presentation of a candle lit from the Paschal candle. Finally, there is the welcome by the congregation.

After recognizing the baptismal *ordo*, one can give attention to the several hallmarks of the baptismal rite.[8]

First is its **paschal essence**. Baptism is a sacrament of the paschal mystery, that is, it is our participation in the death and resurrection with Christ (Romans 6:3-5). This has been a central understanding of baptism (especially in the West) since the fourth century, evidenced by the mystagogical writings of Ambrose of Milan among others. It was also Martin Luther's central meaning: "The sinner does not so much need to be washed as he [*sic*] needs to die, in order to be wholly renewed and made another creature, and to be conformed by the death and resurrection of Christ, with whom he dies and rises again through Baptism."[9] This paschal understanding of baptism helps correct and transform the common understanding of baptism as a cute little ceremony with babies; this is especially clear when the candidate is immersed or submersed.

Baptism's second hallmark is its **pneumatic nature**. This is apparent in many denominational rites, in which there are two prayers invoking the Spirit. The first is in the prayer of thanksgiving over the water, in which the Father, whose Spirit moved over the waters in creation and anointed Jesus in his baptism, is asked to send the Spirit now, that new life may be given to the neophyte. A second *epiclesis* is during the laying on of hands. Thus the neophyte is given not only new life in Christ, but also the seven gifts of the Spirit. Immediately after the laying-on-of-hands is the sign of the cross, which may be made by anointing with oil. Here again is reference to the Spirit, but here it is in the past tense: "... you have been sealed by the Spirit . . . ." (One can argue that this is confirmation, and that any adolescent rite should not repeat or overshadow what was done in baptism.) And for those who wonder: baptism by water and baptism in the Holy Spirit constitute a single unified action which we do sequentially. It must never be forgotten that we are baptized into Christ by water *and* the Spirit.[10] As one stanza of a new hymn puts it:

> In life, in death, we trust in God's most holy name,
> forever traced by water sign, and sealed by Spirit flame.[11]

Third is the **corporate understanding** of baptism. Baptism is always simultaneously personal and corporate. Most liturgical churches today indicate that baptism is celebrated within corporate worship. Various elements of the rite help avoid a privatistic connotation of this sacrament. Such elements include the participation of the congregation in prayers, the Creed, the welcome, and the Peace. A representative of the congregation may present the baptismal candle and white garment, if they are used. Participation in the Church is a corporate, not a private, matter. That is why baptisms (except for emergencies) are normally conducted at the font during Sunday worship.

Candidates are baptized into the whole communion of saints in heaven and earth. As the old Latin hymn puts it:

> Christ is made the sure foundation,
> Christ our head and cornerstone,
> Chosen of the Lord and precious,
> Binding all the Church in one.... [12]

The fourth hallmark, **eucharistic context**, is closely related to baptism itself. It can be said and even emphasized that "[t]he gift of Communion is the birthright of the baptized."[13] Even when a young child is baptized but may not yet receive at the Lord's Table, the eucharist remains the culmination of baptism. The connections between the two sacraments are several. First, there is an ecclesial connection: baptism creates the church, and the eucharist nourishes and sustains it. Second, there is the soteriological connection: baptism brings and the eucharist renews the gift of forgiveness. Third is the afore-mentioned paschal connection: in baptism we are joined to Christ's burial and resurrection, and in the eucharist we remember *(anamnesis)* those events as *"we remember his death, we proclaim his resurrection, we await his coming in glory."*[14] Because of these connections, most mainline churches today expect baptism to be celebrated within the context of the eucharistic liturgy. Baptism is entrance into the community that feasts at the Lord's Table.

Baptism has a **ritual character**. We have already touched on the fact that in many traditions, the baptismal rite is full of rich actions and signs which distinguish it from earlier rites. Since baptism involves the whole person and the whole church, it cannot be merely an intellectual or verbal exercise. In baptism, actions, words and symbols all relate to provide a rich constellation of touch, sight, smell, and hearing (and taste if communion follows the baptism immediately).

Water is the principal element in baptism. In scripture, water is a powerful image: an element of creation and a symbol of primeval chaos, an enabler of life and an agent of death. Water is both friend and enemy. It sustains cellular life, cleanses and refreshes; it can also destroy and drown. These multivalent meanings of water are all present in Baptism: creation, flood, crossing the Red Sea, drowning/burial, cleansing/bathing, etc.

There are other ritual signs in baptism. Most of them derive from the early Church. Chrismation is baptismal anointing with oil, deriving from a second-century Christian liturgical practice. Since the oil is imposed in the sign of a cross, this is also known as the signation. Another action is the presentation of a white garment as a symbol of the life of the resurrection which is conferred in baptism. (See Galatians 3:27 and Revelation 7:9) Finally, a small white candle lighted from the Paschal candle may be presented to the neophyte or sponsor: this is a visual symbol of the primal relationship between baptism and Easter. It is often encouraged that this candle be lighted at home on baptismal anniversaries. Other ritual actions of the early church are not generally used among churches in western cultures today: exorcisms, exsufflation (the ritual opening of the ears and mouth for baptism), and additional anointings with the cross. While some would find meaning in such actions, the danger is in their potential to overshadow the central action itself: the water bath.

In its multivalence, baptism by water and the Spirit signifies that our sinful nature has been drowned by God's grace. We honor that intent when we seek to let baptism be a true sign of what it signifies – death and resurrection with Christ.[15]


PART II – DIRK G. LANGE

Baptism as paschal essence, in its pneumatic nature, its corporate understanding, its eucharistic context and its ritual character points the believer towards life. In *The Large Catechism*, Luther begins the commentary on baptism by stating that it is the sacrament by which we are received into the Christian community.[16] Baptism orients us towards life, towards life in and as the communion of saints. Traditionally understood as a rite of passage, baptism has become synonymous for us with initiation and, in a strange way, with independence. We've "come into our own." (This can be particularly true for those denominations practicing adult baptism but also for churches practicing infant baptism – confirmation then plays the role of a rite of passage or initiation into adult life.)

S. Anita Stauffer has pointed out the various metaphors and uses of baptism in the ritual practice of denominations. Her exposition pushes us to ask another question of our baptismal practices: have we over-emphasized one of these images and forgotten others? Has 'initiation' taken over? Has 'confirmation' or one's conscious 'choice' of Jesus as Savior led us away from the baptismal emphasis on the infusion of the Holy Spirit – infusion of the Spirit embedding us within a community of the Spirit, the church?[17] Why would Luther insist on this simple and seemingly obvious characteristic of baptism: we are received into the Christian *community*?

What does this reception entail? Is Luther suggesting that baptism is something more than a coming of age, something different (maybe even opposed) to an initiation rite? Isn't baptism the immersion into dependence: dependence on family and the community around us for health, nurture, safety, education, joy, life? Isn't baptism, first of all, immersion into death – a confrontation between life and death?[18]

### BAPTISM: A CONFRONTATION

The confrontation begins with baptism. At the beginning of a Christian life – at least according to one metaphor – is a death. We first die with Christ in order to be raised with Christ. Cyril of Jerusalem in the *Mystagogical Catechesis* (the instruction given to those newly baptized) writes:

> O strange and inconceivable thing! We did not really die, we were not really buried, we were not really crucified and raised again, our patterning was but in a figure, while our salvation is in reality. (…) O surpassing loving-kindness! Christ received the nails in his undefiled hands and feet, and endured anguish; while to me, without suffering and toil, by the fellowship of his pain he vouchsafes salvation.[19]

Baptism into Christ, for Cyril, is specifically a "fellowship of his pain." As an individual the baptized has received salvation, but it is in the "fellowship of his pain." In other words, baptism is both an individual and a communal reality. When I enter the waters – whether as an adult or as a child – I enter into the fellowship of Christ's pain, of Christ's suffering and death.

But how is this unique "fellowship" or communion accomplished? The believer cannot return and re-experience the suffering of Christ even if many pietistic texts and popular spirituality would desire it.[20] Fellowship in Christ's suffering is nothing less than fellowship in the suffering of the world, fellowship in the suffering of the "very least of these" (Matthew 25).[21] Fellowship in Christ's pain is deeply fellowship in the community of the gathered assembly, fellowship in the suffering of the communion of saints, fellowship in the pains, tragedies, joys of the community – in human pathos.[22] It is strangely in this "fellowship" that salvation becomes a reality for the believer. In other words, it is not our choice that saves; through the abandonment of our independence into the life of the community something of salvation is intuited. Isn't this what Isaiah was already prophesying?

> Is not this the fast that I choose: to loose the bonds of injustice, to undo the thongs of the yoke, to let the oppressed go free, and to break every yoke? Is it not to share your bread with the hungry and bring the homeless poor into your house... Then your light shall break forth like the dawn and your healing shall spring up quickly... then your light shall rise in the darkness and your gloom be like the noonday. The Lord will guide you continually, and satisfy your needs in parched places, and make your bones strong; and you shall be like a watered garden, like a spring of water, whose waters never fail. (Isaiah 58:6-11).

We are raised up – our light "shall rise" – we will know the resurrection when we are immersed in the fellowship of Christ's pain, immersed in the suffering of this world. This immersion turns us into a wellspring whose waters never fail. "The water that I will give will become in them a spring of water gushing up to eternal life" (John 4:14).

As if to underline the importance of this "immersion," this "fellowship in his pain," Cyril further emphasizes: baptism is not only for the remission of sins. John's baptism conferred only the remission of sins, but baptism into Christ is, as Paul writes "a baptism into Christ's death." It is a "communion with Christ's true sufferings."[23] And let it be repeated: this "communion with Christ's sufferings" does not mean going to see a movie such as "The Passion of Christ." This "fellowship" means coming to the assembly in order to share the death and the resurrection with and in the assembly, to be a *memoria Jesu Christi*.[24] This fellowship means coming to the assembly but only to be sent out again, renewed in one's baptismal covenant – sent out again to encounter God in the neighbor. "God says, 'I do not choose to come to you in my majesty and in the company of angels but in the guise of a poor beggar asking for bread.' (...) Christ replies, 'I have revealed to you in my Word what forms I would assume and to whom you should give (...) I place flesh and blood before your door with the plea: Give me a drink!'"[25]

We are sent out from the eucharistic table to remember to the world our baptismal identity: clothed with the body of Christ. "Remembering our baptism" then is being present in the world as a people who have been encountered, confronted, immersed, killed and resurrected. We are the memory of the body of Christ, the memory of the cross and the resurrection in the world but also our neighbor, the outsider, in a strange Gospel reversal, is a *memoria Jesu Christi* for us.

# Ordo: Bath, Word, Prayer, Table

### BAPTISM AND FAITH

If baptism is this immersion in the fellowship of Christ's pain, an immersion into a dependence on community, even an immersion into death, then it can only be life through the gift of faith, through the promise. Faith is not an individual possession for the self-satisfaction of the believer but a "being let-go" into death – a *continual* "being let-go." Like the bread of life, we are broken and distributed; like the rivers of living water, we too flow out ("out of the believer's heart") for the world (John 7:38). "Filled with the Holy Spirit, we nourish one another. We are a cup of cold water for one another."[26] We are poured out for the world, for Christ and neighbor.

Faith cannot be a possession. Faith cannot even be a gift for which we could give something in return. It is a gift with no return. It is Abraham and Sarah setting out not knowing where they were going, setting out never to return. The faith received in baptism – the promise believed – is at the heart of the sacrament. "What is the good, then, of writing so much about baptism and yet not teaching this faith in the promise? All the sacraments were instituted to nourish faith."[27] It is immersion in a 'not-knowing.' Perhaps this is what, primarily, distinguishes baptism from rites of initiation or rites of passage. Yes, baptism as initiation comforts the believer. Baptism as initiation comforts the believer with the promise of a way, a new way. Comfort, however, on its own quickly submerges into self-satisfaction: I am on the way, I have been saved. But then, we know only individual grace and the community has been forgotten. Yet, "to be baptized is always to be identified with the one whom himself identifies with the outsiders and the marginalized."[28] The rite of initiation is already punctured.

Comfort offered in baptism is itself in constant need of confrontation – not to create anxiety but to point towards the reliability of the gift of grace. Baptism calls forth this juxtaposition. In Luther's attempt to free baptism from its "captivity," he states that baptism as simple washing away of sins is "too mild and weak to bring out the full significance of baptism."[29] Baptism as "passage," as the "regeneration" of the human person is too weak. As S. Anita Stauffer has reminded us, Luther says even more: "The sinner does not so much need to be washed as he needs to die, in order to be wholly renewed and made another creature, and to be conformed to the death and resurrection of Christ."[30] Baptism confronts the believer with death and, in that confrontation, the believer is without any resource. Only in the recognition of this inability to accomplish salvation is the believer fully conformed to the death and resurrection of Jesus Christ. Only in the recognition of this inability is the believer able to rest in the newly found "comfort" of God's gift of grace.

And this "conformity to the death and resurrection of Christ" is nothing other than the "fellowship in his pain" – it is the deep fellowship with the suffering, joy, life of the community. But it means also more: it is discovering the Paschal Mystery among those who are not part of the Sunday assembly but in whom we see and hear the body of Christ. Through that "conformity to the death," life is given. Faith is born. In that immersion into the 'not-knowing,' God steps in and leads us into life. And isn't that the light of the Resurrection?

# Ordo: Bath, Word, Prayer, Table

## ENDNOTES

[1] See page 89 and footnote 3 of Lathrop' *Holy Things: A Liturgical Theology* (Minneapolis: Fortress Press, 1993).

[2] Schmemann, *Introduction to Liturgical Theology* is an expansive exploration of *ordo*. (New York: St. Vladimir's Seminary Press, 1966).

[3] In his chapter "The Shape of the Liturgy: A Context for Contextualization" in *Christian Worship: Unity in Cultural Diversity,* S. Anita Stauffer, ed. (Geneva, Switzerland: Lutheran World Federation, 1996).

[4] In this chapter, the word *liturgy* is reserved primarily to refer to the Word and Table model in its entireity; other services are referred to as *rites*.

[5] "The Augsburg Confession" (1530), Article 7 in *The Book of Concord: The Confessions of the Evangelical Lutheran Church,*. Robert Kolb and Timothy Wengert, eds. (Minneapolis: Fortress Press, 2000), 42.

[6] Gordon Lathrop, *Holy People: A Liturgical Ecclesiology.* (Minneapolis: Augsburg Fortress, 1999), 106-7.

[7] Lathrop, *Holy People: A Liturgical Ecclesiology.* p. 58. In the recently approved *Renewing Worship* project of the Evangelical Lutheran Church in America, this pattern has been described as follows: "The pattern for the celebration of Christian baptism has a simple yet profound center: washing in water and speaking the word of God. From this center the pattern unfolds to include a gracious presentation of those to be baptized, the public profession of the faith of the church, other visible signs that amplify the meaning of baptism, and a welcome into the community of faith. Baptism is celebrated within the larger pattern of the Christian assembly's gathering around the word of God and the eucharistic meal. The powerful event of baptism in the assembly takes place within a larger pattern of formation in the faith, a lifelong process of discipleship." *Holy Baptism and Related Rites* in *Renewing Worship* series (Minneapolis: Augsburg Fortress Press, 2002), 2.

[8] This construct was prepared initially for the author's article, "Holy Baptism in the Lutheran Book of Worship" in *Currents in Theology and Mission,* December 1986, 13:6.

[9] "The Babylonian Captivity of the Church" in *Luther's Works* (American edition), ed. Abdel Ross Wentz, vol. 36 (Philadelphia: Fortress Press), 68.

[10] See John 3:5

[11] "Remember and rejoice," hymn text by Ruth Duck, © 1992 GIA Publications.

[12] 7th century Latin; translated by John Mason Neale

[13] Notes on the Liturgy, *Lutheran Book of Worship Ministers Edition,* (Minneapolis: Augsburg Publishing House and Philadelphia: Board of Publications, Lutheran Church in America, 1978), 31.

[14] Eucharistic Prayer B of *The Holy Communion, Rite II, The Book of Common Prayer,* (New York, Church Hymnal Corporation, 1979), 368.

[15] See S. Anita Stauffer, *On Baptismal Fonts: Ancient and Modern* (Cambridge, England: Alcuin/GROW Liturgical Study 29-30; 1994) and the video, *Re-Examining Baptismal Fonts: Baptismal Space for the Contemporary Church* (Collegeville: Liturgical Press, 1991).

[16] See also Evangelical Lutheran Church in America, *The Use of the Means of Grace: A Statement on the Practice of Word and Sacrament*, (Minneapolis: Fortress Press, 1997), Application 14B.

[17] For a further and very rich discussion of baptismal imagery, see Gail Ramshaw, *Treasures Old and New: Images in the Lectionary* (Minneapolis: Augsburg Fortress, 2002), 401-409.

[18] "…baptism is not merely a onetime event but involves a daily dying and rising with Christ." *Holy Baptism and Related Rites* in *Renewing Worship* series (Minneapolis: Augsburg Fortress Press, 2002), Introduction.

[19] Cyril of Jerusalem, "Mystagogical Catheses: On the Rites of Baptism" in *The Nicene and Post-Nicene Fathers,* vol. VII. Second Series, (Grand Rapids, MI: Wm.B.Eerdmans Publishing Company, reprinted 1996), Part II, Section 5.

[20] See for example the beautiful tenor aria in Bach's St. Matthew's Passion "Ich will bei meinem Jesu wachen, so schlafen unsre Sünden ein." ("I will be with my Jesus watching, that slumber may our sins enfold.") Today, many turn to the film by Mel Gibson to "experience" this fellowship of his pain.

[21] See further my chapter on the eucharist, page 96 - 97.

[22] See the chapter by Don E. Saliers, page 39.

[23] Cyril of Jerusalem, "Mystagogical Catheses: On the Rites of Baptism", Part II, Section 6.

[24] See above, Saliers, page 44 ff.

[25] Martin Luther, "Commentary on the Gospel of John," *Luther's Works* 22:519-520.

[26] Gail Ramshaw, *Treasures Old and New*, 408-409. "The Greek of John 7:38 is ambiguous: is the source of the living water Jesus, or the believer? The sacramental Christian responds Yes to both. Christ the water, incarnating God's water of creation, flows continuously in the Spirit, who waters the believers, who themselves become the spring of living water in the world."

[27] Martin Luther, "The Babylonian Captivity of the Church" in *Luther's Works* 36:68.

[28] Gordon W. Lathrop, *Holy Ground: A Liturgical Cosmology* (Minneapolis: Augsburg Fortress Press, 2003), 118.

[29] Ibid., 191.

[30] Ibid.

# FOUR

# Proclaiming and Preaching

*Samuel Torvend*

### NOW YOU ARE THE BODY OF CHRIST

One of the most alluring temptations in contemporary Christianity is the willingness to espouse the ancient docetic view that Jesus of Nazareth was not a real human being.[1] Oh, he may have looked human, acted in a human way, and even appeared to suffer as humans do when whipped or nailed to a cross, but in truth, he was a spirit disguised in human form or one who shed his humanity at the moment of resurrection. A kissing cousin of gnosticism (the assertive dualism that favors spirit over flesh), the docetic stream in Christianity looks askance at the natural world, the gifts of the earth, and the pleasures or needs of the body. As a voice alive in Christianity, it steadfastly turns a suspicious eye toward the flesh-and-blood Jesus and dematerializes him into the ether. Indeed, we can hear in some later writings of the New Testament, the whisper of this spiritualizing influence, unable to reconcile itself to the contingency of life. In other writings, we can hear its shout. Thus we find the Christian teacher Origen speaking of the body of Christ as a "school of souls" being illuminated in its "spiritual" and otherworldly destiny by a divine Savior.[2] Thus, we hear Richard Fox arguing in a convincing manner that "most Americans believe Christ to be a transcendent and unchanging divine person."[3]

There is, of course, another viewpoint. It has been said this way: God did not become an idea so that only idealists or philosophers might contemplate the idea of God; nor did God become a spirit so that only spiritual people might experience the presence of God; rather, God became a human being so that all humans – all humans – might be drawn into the merciful and life-giving body of God.[4] One could say it this way as well: "Christian faith is more than an 'idea.' It is the encounter with the grace of God present in Jesus Christ and it involves the encounter with those concrete, flesh-and-blood things which connect us to the flesh of Jesus."[5] Or say it this way: the continuing and deeply shocking claim of

Christian faith is that in the body, in the words and actions of a first-century Palestinian Jew, one encounters "the great fire of the love of God for us, whereby the heart and conscience become happy, secure, and content."[6]

Indeed, we might say, to follow a medieval adage, that God communicates with human beings in a manner through which humans can receive that communication; that is, through another human being, through the words and gestures of that human being; indeed, through all the senses: through speaking, hearing, touching, eating and drinking. Thus, Mark, deeply skeptical of spiritualizing tendencies among the miracle-worker christologies of his time, presents Jesus as one who washes (1:9), speaks (1:15), touches (1:31), listens (2:5-12), eats and drinks (2:15); the one who becomes tired (6:31) and famished (11:12). Thus Paul, after indicating his own visual infirmity in writing to the Christians at Galatia, ends his letter with that poignant and sublime reference to the mystery of the flesh: "I carry the marks of Jesus branded on my body" (6:17). Without the body, it would seem, there is, quite simply, no life.

## THE NEEDS OF THE BODY

What does the body need in order to survive in this world? Clearly, the infant as well as the adult needs *air to breathe*, for without this invisible gift of the creation, this most abundant of earth's elements, all living things would quickly expire. Thus, life out of the womb begins with a slap and sudden intake of breath, just as life ends with the last exhaling of breath. Indeed, humans are, with *adam*, the primal earth creature, 'dead and inactive clods' until animated with the breath of life.[7]

The body also needs *water* if humans are to survive for more than a few days. Or, we could say it this way: we not only thirst for water but we are water beings. Yes, humans may be attracted to many things throughout life, yet we remain in profound need of water and are drawn to its many sources: to lakes and streams and pools, to showers and baths and springs. If one ever doubts this primal attraction, taste the tears that mark the cheek. They are not fresh but salt-water: a natural sign the body holds of our distant origin in the ancient seas where life first emerged so many thousands of years ago. Indeed, a moist membrane – an invisible sea – surrounds the entire globe, air and water, as it were, combining to nourish life, to keep life green and growing. Yes, humans are drawn to and need this natural element because it dwells within, surrounds, and nourishes us.

No doubt humans need *food and drink* if the body is to grow. And so Luther writes, "I believe that God has created me together with all that exists. God has given me and still preserves my body and soul: eyes, ears, and all limbs and senses ... and abundantly provides food and drink ... along with all the nourishment for this body and life."[8] Yes, with all other life forms, humans hunger for food and will do almost anything if living is imperiled because food is lacking or in short supply. Who, then, would be surprised to hear Jesus pose the question, "Is there any among you who, if your child asks for bread, will give a stone? Or if the child asks for a fish, will give a snake?" (Matthew 7:9).

Of course, one of the most obvious needs humans hold is the yearning for each other. Quite simply, human beings need *other human beings,* other bodies from the very beginning of our gestation in the womb until we breathe our last. Ask any psychologist about the fundamental task that confronts every infant and she will tell you that it is the need to know a mother or father will come when the infant cries out. In other words, the fundamental task is learning to trust – to trust – that other humans will care for and nourish this fragile life so that it might grow and mature.

Finally, it would seem that humans need to hear the *human voice*, not only to recognize the other, whether that other is parent or spouse, friend or stranger, but also to hear the tone, the sound, the word that guides and comforts, warns and wails. Word placed next to word not only offers information but also evokes meaning so that humans might discover or make sense of the meaning of their embodied lives. But perhaps we need to hear the human voice – its stories and its songs – because we are forgetful, forgetful of who made us and what our purpose might be in this troubled and beautiful body we call the earth. Or perhaps we even need, in this presumably post-modern age with its presumptive death of any meaningful word set next to word, a shared story so that we might be awakened again and again to the fragile and vulnerable condition of things.

But, of course, this is all to say that the needs of the body, the life and well being of the body, the "life, health, and salvation" for which we yearn in the body, are met in a mediated manner. That is, one encounters and receives the means to live *as* one is gathered and held against the breast, *as* one hears the murmur of the familiar voice, *as* one is refreshed in the bath that cleans the sweat and mess, *as* one is nourished with food and drink. In other words, the great qualities of life, what Christians call the gifts of God – love, mercy, grace, hope – are always, always, *mediated bodily* through word and gesture, word and sign, human voice and earthy sacrament. The docetist may be baffled by the mystery of the body yet a deeper voice whispers, "flesh-and-blood things connect us to the flesh of Jesus."

## The Movement of the Body

Needless to say, the image of the body is a powerful word and profound symbol in the Christian story, elaborated in the Bible and invoked in the church's worship.[9] "By water and the Spirit," says the leader in one baptismal liturgy, "we are made members of *the body* of Christ."[10] Or this: "We receive you as *fellow members of the body* of Christ, children of the same heavenly Father," says the assembly in the same liturgy.[11] To be received into this 'body,' then, is to enter an organic, living communion, a body that does not create itself but rather is vivified – breathed into life – by another: by the breathing of the Spirit. Thus, as the bishops of the Second Vatican Council made abundantly clear in their recovery of an ecclesiology rooted in the metaphor of the body, the fullness of the body is alive in the gathering of individual bodies united in the local assembly.

It is in this assembly, then, that the needs of the body are present in ritual pattern, a series of real, flesh-and-blood things rooted in human experience but reinterpreted, transfigured, by the Spirit's breathe: a *common story*, the *water of life*, and *food and drink*; that is, the proclamation of the gospel and the enactment of that gospel in baptism and the Eucharist.[12]

Or we might say it this way: The Spirit, the breath of life, animates the body with reading from a book, a washing in water, and the sharing of a meal. Indeed, one could argue that throughout their history, Christians have received no more and no less than these simple actions, all other ones serving as elaborations that return to these essential ones. When they are used or enacted, they benefit the body. If they are overlooked or forgotten or taken in small measure, the body suffers. This is to say that these actions possess a dynamic movement through which the body – the local assembly – is continually *awakened to faith in God* and *love for the neighbor in need*, again, not one without the other.

## THE BODY BREATHING OUT

Whether one studies the *Book of Common Prayer*, the *Lutheran Book of Worship*, or the *Roman Sacramentary*, Christians can discern this dynamic movement that leaps from the page into bodily action, one that possesses a beginning and an ending. Between this gathering and sending of the body, there is a center where "two or three meet together." Here, it would seem, the body is gathered, the needs of the body are attended to, and the body then leaves. In Lathrop's words: "To be part of the community of word, baptism, and meal is to be gathered by the power of the Spirit into [Jesus Christ], under the grace of God who sent him."[13] And so, just as the body breathes in and out in order to live, so too the movement of the liturgy possesses this dynamic: a gathering in that moves along a trajectory which leads to a sending. The body – this body of Christ – may gather in the name and presence of the Trinity, but the flow of the liturgy sends that body outward "in peace, to serve." To say it simply: people gather in order to leave. But between that gathering and sending, it would seem that humans need to hear the human voice placing word next to word, sound next to sound, evoking the meaning of both word and sign.

# Ordo: Bath, Word, Prayer, Table

It goes without saying, however, that the body, any body, dwells within space and time and, as a matter of fact, not just any space or time. Since we are not capable of time travel, we cannot journey to the distant past or into an unknown future. Christian communities dwell in particular cultures and at specific times. The trouble for many North Americans is that we live with the artifice of time travel: films can give the impression of being accurate historical documentaries just as theme parks can lead people to think that they are really experiencing Bible Land or Tomorrow Land as it was or will be. Indeed, the temptation has always been alive in Christianity (one not so different from the docetic lure) to focus on words *from* the past as cherished memories *of* the past. Living in the present – in this local place, with these other people, at this particular time – can so easily evaporate into a miasma of wishful words that lead the speaker and listener to "back there then" or "out there tomorrow," to be free of the body's constraints. Such a temptation – the conscious or unconscious move to wrest one from the present moment and the local place – is so easy to accept. Who doesn't cherish lovely memories of the past, even biblical memories? After all, "what they recall is presumed to be settled and closed."[14]

Yet we live in the present moment, in this place. And it is here and now that we can be awakened to faith and to love. It is here and now that the "murmur of the familiar voice" needs to be heard, not leading the listener to an imagined past but asking how ancient words and old dreams shape the present; not leading the listener to a dematerialized future but asking if the ancient words and even older dreams shed any light on the troubling question of this age, a question thought unimaginable by every generation of the past, "Will there actually *be* a future for the generations if humans continue to despoil earth's body and create weapons of death?" How safe, how easy it is to ignore the pressing needs of the present while one constructs with words a world of imagined safety and comfort. Poet and novelist Annie Dillard hints at the difference between these two worlds when she asks:

> Does anyone have the foggiest idea of what sort of power we [Christians] so blithely invoke? Or, as I suspect, does no one believe a word of it? The churches are children playing on the floor with their chemistry sets, mixing up a batch of TNT to kill a Sunday morning. It is madness to wear ladies' straw hats and velvet hats to church; we should all be wearing crash helmets. Ushers should issue life preservers and signal flares; they should lash us to our pews. For the sleeping god may awake someday and take offense, or the waking god may draw us out to wherever we can never return.[15]

Perhaps there is a fatal truth in what Dillard suggests: maybe no on really does believe a word of it, at least for us, for now. That is, maybe far too many voices, many with the most sincere intentions, actually deaden Christian assemblies to their own contingency as well as their capacity to "awaken someday" and be drawn out into this tragic, beautiful, and contingent world. Maybe Dillard is right when she diagnoses the middle-class captivity of so many North American assemblies, gatherings unable to discern the volatile mixture of chemicals alive in its body. Maybe there is some shred of truth in Fox's assessment that most North Americans yearn for a "transcendent and unchanging divine person," a person *unmoved* by nothing but the prayer for personal security or individual healing. Indeed, is not the expectation alive in so many Christian assemblies that the Jesus proclaimed and preached during the liturgy will simply conform to our culturally formed expectations? One is reminded of the telling words written by Dietrich Bonhoeffer in 1937:

> We gave away the word and sacraments wholesale, we baptized, confirmed, and absolved a whole nation unasked and without condition. Our humanitarian sentiment made us give that which was holy to the scornful and the unbelieving. We poured forth unending streams of grace. But the call to follow Jesus in the narrow way was hardly ever heard … [Yet] happy are they who, knowing the [costly] grace [of Christ], can live in the world without being of it, who, by following Jesus Christ, are so assured of their heavenly citizenship that *they are truly free to live their lives in this world*.[16]

## THE MOVEMENT OF THE BODY

Between Bonhoeffer, the German Lutheran theologian and Dillard, the American Catholic poet, is there not a truth that corresponds with the dynamic outward movement of the liturgy: that it is possible to be "drawn out" with others who are "truly free to live their lives in this world" even though one may go to a place from which one might never return?

Thus we come to the pattern of word set next to word, one leading forward to the next, as it were, through public proclamation, interpretation, prayer, baptismal washing, thanksgiving meal, and sending into the world. While textbooks and worship books can readily give the impression that the ecumenical pattern of the Christian liturgy is a list of texts to be read or sung, a string of bullet points to be performed, a more ancient yet contemporary perspective suggests that the pattern is an organic whole, an ensemble of actions placed next to each other, an ordered cacophony of diverse voices and actions that both proclaim and critique, that invite the body of the assembly to enter the world without being of it. As Gordon Lathrop observes, "In the history of the Christian liturgy, the essential matters are always juxtaposed to each other and are always made up of at least two juxtaposed elements: readings *and* preaching, teaching *and* bathing, thanksgiving *and* receiving food." [17]

One reading, usually from the Jewish Scriptures, is set next to another one, usually from the letters of the Christian Scriptures: one Jewish voice set next to an early Christian voice. And yet the pattern pulls one forward to another voice: the voice of Jesus as interpreted through a gospel written for a Christian assembly. The simplicity of the pattern, of diverse voices set next to one another, should not be underestimated; it begs the profoundly simple question: How might these ancient words and even older dreams shape the present for this assembly gathered in the presence of God? The reading or proclamation of the texts alone is not enough, as if they were simply historical documents about a vanished tribe. They beg for a voice to interpret their meanings in the present moment. Indeed, the texts themselves are understandings and interpretations of the encounter with the living God in this world: in the soil of this earth and among diverse peoples. The one who stands to speak from these words engages in the anamnetic task of awakening the gathered assembly to that which it may have forgotten: that it is been breathed into life by an Other so that the body might "truly live in the world." It is not surprising, then, that we find this pattern already in the Christian Scriptures where Luke notes "that beginning with Moses and all the prophets, [the risen Lord] *interpreted to them* the things about himself in all the scriptures" (24:27). Thus, the one who speaks from these words, these diverse voices, is called to speak the truth about Jesus Christ. But in this speaking the truth about Jesus Christ, one is reminded of the outcome of such interpretation in Luke's story: "they got up and returned to Jerusalem" (24:33). They did not return quietly to their homes or escape to the hills. Rather, they went forth and *entered the city*, that place of seeming failure and grief, that metaphor of the larger world, with good news for a group of people experiencing nothing less than collective paralysis.

Such a movement in the Scriptures and in the pattern of the liturgy stands as a cogent reminder that the one who speaks – the homilist, the preacher, the minister of the word – does so within the context of a larger trajectory: reading is set next to preaching but preaching itself is set next to prayer.[18] Indeed, if one can speak of this liturgical pattern as a "remedial norm," it is here that we recognize its value since the prayers bring to awareness, even when preaching fails to do so, the truth of this world, of its injustice, fear, and sorrow. Within the centripetal movement of the liturgy – its gathering in of the body and the ever-present temptation to imagine that this body *alone* is the object of God's presence or grace or love – the prayers of the people are an opening outward to the "city," to the truth of national or local failure, to the truth of personal and communal grief.

It is, after all, not that difficult to film or produce a passion play, a sustained and dramatic focus on the suffering of Jesus. It is not that difficult to preach about the death of a first-century Jew, especially knowing that the preacher will enjoy a satisfying meal after the liturgy. It is much more difficult, however, to ask how *that suffering then trains this assembly now* to recognize the suffering of real bodies in the world. Is this not, in part, what Bonhoeffer means when he writes that "the call to follow Jesus in the narrow way was hardly ever heard" – that thousands of German Christians could flock each year to the Passion Play at Oberammergau or sing "Herzliebster Jesu" every Good Friday yet utterly fail to recognize those who suffered unjustly in their midst and this, no less, in one of the most highly educated and scientifically sophisticated nations on the face of the earth?

## Nourishing the Body

Yet the trajectory of the liturgy does not end with communal *Amen* to the prayers of the people. While humans may long to hear the "murmuring of the familiar voice," they also need to eat and drink. Christians place thanksgiving to God next to sharing the fragment of an ancient meal. Standing with the assembly and giving thanks, "in all times and in all places," a leader – the presider, the pastor, the priest – places word next to thankful word for the gifts of this earth, for the life, death, and resurrection of Jesus Christ, for the Spirit alive in the assembly. Thus, the assembly hears and participates in two proclamations, that of the 'great reading' (the gospel) and that of the 'great thanksgiving' (the eucharistic prayer), one a mirror of the other: a feeding in the ear, a hearing in the mouth.

Thanksgiving yields to eating and drinking at table. After all, who would offer thanks over food and drink only to walk away or reserve the meal for a few people? The juxtaposition of these two actions – thanksgiving and eating – allows the words spoken or sung in thanksgiving to frame the eating of bread and drinking from cup as gift of God and the earth's abundance, the life of Jesus broken and poured out for the many, the Spirit binding the body together through this shared loaf and cup. But this eating and drinking takes place within the trajectory that moves from gathering to sending. It is not a separate or private act cut off from the earlier proclamation of word and its interpretation in preaching.[19]

This is to claim that the task of proclamation and preaching does not end with completion of the homily or sermon or prayers. Indeed, *the preacher is called to ask how these biblical texts interpret the action of the thanksgiving meal.*[20] Thus, when this particular act of proclamation is placed within the larger trajectory, the act of preaching rightfully leads or guides the assembly toward the thanksgiving meal at table. The preaching, in effect, is intended to open and deepen the diverse meanings possessed in the eating and drinking as viewed from the perspective of the diverse voices and images present in the biblical texts.

At the same time, such preaching through the trajectory of actions allows the preacher or homilist to ask the question, to what end do this assembly eat and drink in the presence of God? If the preaching does not follow this trajectory, if the fundamental pattern of word-set-next-to-sacrament is forgotten in the preaching, then – even though the Eucharist may be celebrated every Sunday – it can nonetheless remain a significant yet *un-interpreted event* or become only a dramatic appendage, an exercise in forgiveness only, or a strategy for community-building only. As a deeply symbolic action, one that is filled with a surplus rather than a paucity of meaning, the meal of Christian community cannot be reduced to one meaning, otherwise the action is deprived of its richly varied biblical meanings: it is transformed from multi-vocal symbol into a univocal sign. Yes, there is the promise of forgiveness, the promise of union between Christ and communicant, the promise of community. Yet the many biblical meals themselves – present in that list of readings Christians call the lectionary – always expand the circle of meaning and thus allow other voices to be heard in the assembly, voices that may move the body in the narrow way, toward the city.

## The Body Given Away

It should come as no surprise that the earliest Christian communities made collections for the needy and gave their bread away freely to the hungry and the poor *at the end of the communal meal*. It should come as no surprise that the New Testament offers tantalizing hints of Christian communities caring for the bodies of their neighbors who were in need. For some, however, it may be surprising to note that the New Testament also reveals the failure of early Christians to serve people in need both inside and outside their gatherings (e.g., Matthew 25:37-40; 1 Corinthians 11:17-34; James 2:1-13; Jude 12). It would seem, on the one hand, that early Christians intuited in the ministry of Jesus among the marginalized and the poor their own mandate for service in "the city" arising from the words proclaimed and the meal given freely to all in the assembly. And yet these same texts, alas, demonstrate the ever-present temptation to forget this movement from being served by God in the liturgy to serving the neighbor in need.

In the culture where Christians gather, proclaim, preach and pray, give thanks, and eat together, so many people tend to see religion solely as a source of comfort or entertainment. The expectation among so many Christians in North America is that the God proclaimed by the liturgy will simply conform to expectations derived from a consumerist culture. Or say it this way: one might agree that with the theological claim that "God's grace is poured out in Jesus Christ, encountered in the spoken word and enacted sacrament." Yet one asks, for whom? How far is the "pouring?" Poured out only for the little me? Poured out only for this assembly? Or, poured out for the world, even a world that may not care to know the words and actions of the Christian assembly? As Marianne Sawicki observes:

> The epistles and the gospels were written to convey memories about Jesus from those who had know him before [his death] to those who wanted to know him afterward. But in addition to memories, these texts were written to convey instructions for recognizing the Lord in real time, that is, *for finding Jesus incognito in our present circumstances*. [Of course] memories are easier to accept than instructions, because memories refer back to a past time; what they recall is presumed to be settled and closed. Thus it is relatively easy for us ... to take up bread and cup in remembrance of the fact that Jesus lived here once upon a time. It is much less [easy] to seek Jesus in the present, even though we know where he is dwelling. It is difficult to worship in expectation of ... responding to the invitations he gives us right now in the needs of the hungry, the thirsty, and the homeless (Matthew 25:31-40). Their pleas for help are coming from Jesus ... incognito.[21]

What might this mean, then, for those who proclaim, preach, pray, give thanks, and eat together at table? Between a gathering and a sending forth in the liturgy, do Christians not receive broken bread – a "broken body" – in order to learn to recognize that Body present in the broken and hungry bodies of this land? In American culture, where healthy, productive, and seemingly "useful" people are rewarded for creating economic growth and where hungry, malnourished, and seemingly "unproductive" people are hidden or ignored, the temptation will always be present to let the needs of the former – the healthy and the productive – interpret the meaning of the gospel and its enactment in the liturgy of Christians. But what if ministerial leaders let their imaginations and work be shaped by the One who spoke and shared bread with those who were deemed useless, impure, and hungry?

Of course, the temptation will always be present to ignore the pleas of the hungry and little ones who dwell on the margins. The temptation will always be present to imagine that the purpose of the proclamation we call "liturgy" is to reassure the comfortable and distract the anxious with entertainments. Yet – Kavanagh tells us: "The Sunday liturgy is not the Church assembled to address itself. The liturgy does not cater to the assembly. [Rather], it summons the assembly to enact itself for the life of the world."[22]

# Ordo: Bath, Word, Prayer, Table

And so, we come to the final juxtaposed pairing of the liturgy: sending set next to service in a world yearning for, yet seemingly incapable of, creating a justice and peace that passes its cloudy understanding. If there is any truth in the claim that the liturgy summons the assembly to give itself to this real world, in humble service to real bodies, then one might expect that homilists and preachers and musicians and intercessors will help bring to the assembly's awareness those instructions as to where the body of Christ will be found in "the city" that surrounds the assembly. Indeed, one may expect and even long for a clear word that points the assembly along the trajectory that leads to the narrow way, "so assured of their heavenly citizenship that they are truly free to live their lives in this world."

All this is to say that the assembly – the body – is, in the end, *not* the center. The center is God graciously sending Christ among us in word and sign so that the Christian assembly might go forth to offer its life in prophetic service to this complex, enchanting, and troubled world. But is this too much for which to hope, that homilists and preachers might point to such prophetic service? After all, the last and the first one, the central figure in the Christian story, embodied such service only to find himself uttering words of dereliction from an ancient psalm outside the city gates.

And yet, and yet, a young man proclaimed to the disciples, "He is going ahead of you . . . there you will see him just as he told you."[23] And so we ask, having heard the proclamation of this good news, will the assembly leave seized with terror or with amazement?

## Endnotes

[1] Docetic, from the Greek, "it seems" [but is not really so].

[2] Origen, *De Principiis*, II. 11, 6.

[3] Richard Fox, "America's National Obsession," in *The Chronicle of Higher Education* (02/20/2004): B9.

[4] Notes taken on a sermon preached by Gordon Lathrop in Spring, 1973, at Pacific Lutheran University (Tacoma, Washington).

[5] Gordon Lathrop, "What are the essentials of Christian worship?" in *Open Questions in Worship* 1 (Minneapolis: Augsburg Fortress, 1994), 6.

[6] Martin Luther, "A Brief Instruction on What to Look for and Expect in the Gospels," in *Luther's Works* 35 (Philadelphia: Muhlenberg Press, 1960), 119.

[7] Martin Luther, "Lectures on Genesis, Chapters 1-5," in *Luther's Works*. Jaroslav Pelikan, ed. (St. Louis: Concordia, 1958) I: 84.

[8] "The Small Catechism," in *The Book of Concord: The Confessions of the Evangelical Lutheran Church*. Robert Kolb and Timothy Wengert, eds. (Minneapolis: Fortress, 2000) 354.

[9] Cf., Romans 12; 1 Corinthians 12; and John 19.

[10] "Holy Baptism," in *Lutheran Book of Worship*, 121.

[11] Ibid., 125.

[12] Consider the ecumenical consensus on the common pattern of Christian worship: "The eucharistic liturgy is essentially a single whole, consisting historically of the following elements in varying sequence and of diverse importance: [gathering with] hymns of praise ... [the] proclamation of the Word of God, in various forms ... intercession for the whole Church and for the world; preparation of the bread and wine; thanksgiving to the Father for the marvels of creation, redemption and sanctification ... the Amen of the whole community; the Lord's prayer; sign of reconciliation and peace; the breaking of the bread; eating and drinking in communion with Christ and with each member of the Church ... blessing and sending. *Baptism, Eucharist, and Ministry. Faith and Order* Paper No. 111 (Geneva: World Council of Churches, 1982), E27.

[13] Lathrop, "What are the essentials of Christian worship?," 9.

[14] Marianne Sawicki, "How can Christian worship be contemporary?" in *What is contemporary worship?* Vol. 2 in *Open Questions in Worship*. Ed. Gordon Lathrop (Minneapolis: Augsburg Fortress, 1995), 29.

[15] Dillard, Annie, *Teaching a Stone to Talk: Expeditions and Encounters* (New York: Harper & Row, 1982), 40-41.

[16] *The Cost of Discipleship*. R. H. Fuller, trans. (New York: Macmillan, 1963), 58, 60. Emphasis mine.

# Ordo: Bath, Word, Prayer, Table

[17] Lathrop, "What are the essentials of Christian worship?" 11.

[18] The designation "prayer" refers to the "general intercessions" or "the prayers of the people" as noted in various liturgical books.

[19] The separation of preaching (by one person) from liturgical or sacramental leadership (by another person), while widely practiced in some Christian communions, effectively breaks the organic unity of the liturgy's trajectory and presents these two actions as dissimilar ones. Perhaps pastoral leaders need to be reminded that they are ordained to "the ministry of word and sacrament," not the ministry of the word some days and the ministry of sacraments on other days.

[20] The same principle would apply to any ritual action following the homily or sermon: baptismal washing, marriage, reconciliation, ordination, or funeral rite.

[21] Marianne Sawicki, "How can Christian worship be contemporary?," 29. See also her *Seeing the Lord: Resurrection and Early Christian Practices* (Minneapolis: Fortress, 1994). Emphasis mine.

[22] Aidan Kavanagh. *Elements of Rite: A Handbook of Liturgical Style* (New York: Pueblo, 1985), 45.

[23] Mark 16:7.

# FIVE

# Teach Us to Pray

*Gail Ramshaw*

## WESTERN LITURGICAL PRAYER

Most manifestations of religion assert that although humans discover themselves to be vulnerable, prey to weakness, hunger, disease, shame, evil and death, they believe that there are beings or principles that exist beyond these dangers. Some force or being is invulnerable, or at least far less vulnerable than humans to the recurring and unending difficulties in life. A religious practice is the system proposed by which its practitioners have access to that invulnerability. Somewhere, we hope, there is more strength than we have, and our religion dictates to us the methods by which we hope to get it. Perhaps we are to make pilgrimage to an *axis mundi*[1], or offer pieces of our flesh to the sun, or sit in attention during the priest's sacred mantra, or cultivate a technique of meditation, or obey the dictates of the authoritative males, or seek from nature its stores of energy. Humans have offered a myriad of suggestions on how to access the power beyond themselves.

One of the primary ways that Christians connect with transcendent power is to pray. Christians believe that there is a God who is the locus of everlasting and almighty power and that because God is beneficent, God hears and heeds our requests. As with other monotheistic religions, Christians claim that God's creative powers did not conclude eons ago, but continues in the form of perpetual care for that creation. God can give to humans – perhaps also to vegetation, to animals, to the forces of nature – more life than they currently have. To access this divine power, the church has fostered various techniques of prayer, from the rigors of pilgrimage to the altered consciousness of the rosary's mantra, from the ecstasy of *glossalalia* to the discipline of contemplation, from perpetual adoration of the sacrament to conversational talk with God over coffee.

# Ordo: Bath, Word, Prayer, Table

The method of prayer used by Christians perhaps more than any other is liturgical prayer. Liturgical prayer is the formalized style of praise and petition practiced by the assembled community. For ritual to function on its deepest possible levels, the community needs to agree on a pattern; with continual repetition that pattern can become the very marrow of our skeleton, the underground river nourishing even our deepest unconscious selves. Because the church has found its liturgical worship to be more effectual than not, the Christian pattern of the assembly's prayer has varied little across congregations and changes slowly over the centuries. Yet even with liturgical prayer, the sacramentaries of the world's churches show different rhetorical styles, the East relying on metaphor and relaxing into repetition, the West preferring objective prose and deleting unnecessary verbiage, while throughout the world are communities that advocate *extempore* prayer rather than an approved printed text. Of all these methods of prayer, this essay focuses on the liturgical prayer of the Sunday assembly in the West by examining the prayer Jesus taught, the eucharistic prayer, the collect and the intercessions.[2] With each of these four occasions of Christian liturgical prayer, we can identify from where the church borrowed the form; how the form was emended by the believers' encounter with Christ in the Spirit; how each prayer functions within the totality of the Sunday's praise and petition; and what reforms of these prayers may be called for in our time.

The great prayer of Ezra recorded in Nehemiah 9 is a primary biblical model for Christian liturgical prayer. God is praised as the creator of the world and the savior of the Israelite people. The prayer reviews the narrative history of salvation, and while acknowledging the people's sin, praises God for continuous forgiveness. The first half of the prayer might well double as a creed, with all the saving deeds of God recalled and divine mercy lauded. After the section of praise comes the section of petition, the "Now therefore." God is asked to continue the same salvific work toward the people by helping them in their current hour of need.

Christian prayer adopts this same outline: first praise, on the basis of which follows the petition. In Christian prayer, the narrative of praise usually culminates in a rehearsal of the death and resurrection of Christ, and the petition is understood as being received by God only because of the saving work of Christ. The characteristic conclusion to Christian prayer, "through Jesus Christ our Lord," means not only to suggest that like a prime minister, Jesus will lobby for our request at the throne of the sovereign, but rather that in the death and resurrection of Christ is finally the very salvation we seek. Not only the benefits of our praying, but our entire salvation comes through Christ. It is because of this fundamental christological understanding that some Christians regard any interfaith prayer that eliminates all mention of Christ as no more effectual for the Christian in addressing the divine than would be

Shinto devotional rites. Christ receives the primary praise, and Christ effects the gifts we receive. Christ constitutes the connection between divine power and human need.

Although the deist beliefs of the eighteenth century remain persuasive in our culture, at least the church maintains that God is not on permanent retirement. Rather, God is alive and well with both the power and the will to improve the human situation. The church asserts that there is genuine literal meaning behind a petition that asks God to feed the poor: God is able to feed the poor, sacred scripture has promised that God will feed the poor, and we are holding God to that promise. Thus Christian prayer is not merely a group consciousness-raising exercise, rather it boldly addresses God, asking God to bring about new life for those who suffer.

Yet in this exercise of coming together to plead for divine action, we discover that the church's prayer is not only christological, it is also trinitarian. As trinitarian doctrine asserts, the Spirit of God is co-equal with the Father and the Son. The Spirit of the risen Christ is operative in the church and through it in the world. So it is that Christians are sometimes surprised to discover that it is through them and their actions that God offers the world new life. The communal exercise of liturgical prayer has helped to transform individual petitioners into an inspired community of service to the earth and its peoples. As is stated in the full doxological conclusion of many prayers, the Spirit of God also lives and reigns; it is also the Holy Spirit whom we worship and praise.

## The Prayer Jesus Taught

Called by different communities the Lord's Prayer, the Our Father, or the Prayer of Jesus, the prayer Jesus taught follows the general Christian liturgical pattern – the new reorienting the old – in which a previous pattern of prayer has been reshaped by the person of Christ.[3] First century Jews would routinely have prayed for the coming of the reign of God. Whether envisioning either a spiritual or a political kingdom, the prayer would have been understood eschatologically. That is, the dominion of God was to arrive sometime in the future, and the praying community hoped for its arrival sooner rather than later. The life of Jewish prayer also included petitions that, granting the widespread expectation of horrific suffering before the end, God would grant the petitioners strength for endurance in the final ordeal.

Onto this Jewish pattern of prayer come several Christian alterations. Christian eschatology is always two-fold: in speaking its truth, the church must always say two things.[4] Because Christ has risen from the dead, the reign of God has already begun. The eschatological age is upon us: this is already the eighth day, the future time brought into the present. Yet the present does not contain all that there is of the dominion of God. More of Christ's resurrection will be manifest sometime in the future. Thus for the Christian, the prayer for the coming of God's kingdom includes not only a petition for God to end this world's evil, but also a faith statement that in the resurrection evil has already been conquered.

Although the *Didache* prescribes that the Lord's Prayer should be prayed by each believer three times daily, by the fourth century the Lord's Prayer had found the place it still retains in many Christian assemblies: the entire people are to pray this prayer together aloud before receiving communion. The forgiveness that the Jewish believer expected would come at the end of time is already shared in the Christian community, while it waits for the final forgiveness of all. The bread for which the community prays is not only today's fare, not only the eschatological feast on the mountain at the end of time, but also this very meal of bread and wine, this bread that *today* is the eschatological bread of *tomorrow*.

The prayer Jesus taught calls us away from the personalized religious quest common in the contemporary West toward the biblical journey of the whole people. Many people, perhaps having imbibed the patterns of their childhood bedtime prayers, think of praying as asking God for the safety, perhaps also happiness, of oneself and one's immediate family and friends. Yet biblical religion calls us to move our individual selves into the community. It is "our," not my, Father, who is addressed, and together we pray for the entire human community. Even if my personal situation is privileged, that of the vast majority of the world's people is not. As we come to the eucharist to commune together, we first place in our mouths petitions for the worldwide community.[5] When Cyril of Jerusalem instructed his catechumens on the meaning of the Lord's Prayer, he said of the phrase "in heaven," "They also are *a heaven* who bear the image of the heavenly, in whom God is dwelling."[6] It is commonplace for religions to imagine God as residing above the sky. Yet this fourth-century bishop reminds the community that where God resides is within the community.

The Lord's Prayer exemplifies the manner in which religion speaks in metaphor. The imagery found in this prayer is the dominant image of the Bible: God is a monarch, the people live under God's rule, and when that rule is challenged, the people beg that God once again show sovereign power and mercy.[7] Onto this ancient Near Eastern religious imagery, Christians add their interpretative layer: Christ is the monarch who, as the son of the god, administers divine authority on the earth. The christology developing in the first century relied heavily on the royal psalms for its understanding of the person and meaning of Christ.[8] The earthly sovereign had been granted his power from the deity, and in that authority rested human salvation. To what degree this biblical use of royal imagery can continue to infuse our Christian prayer remains to be seen. At least we can agree that in a postmodern democracy, considerable catechesis about the royal metaphor is required.

The most obvious Christianizing of the Jewish prayer, and the most controversial in the present time, is that Jesus is remembered as having addressed God with the Aramaic *Abba*, rendered in Matthew's and Luke's citations of the prayer with the Greek noun for father. Scholars of religion are not at all surprised to hear devout petitioners address the divine as their father. Indeed, on those first-century streets of Jerusalem were not only Jewish believers (who probably did not approach God as their *Abba*) but also Greco-Roman polytheists, for whom address to Zeus-Jupiter as father was standard procedure. It might be that addressing God as father came into Judaism as cultural adaptation, more than anything else. Certainly the church fathers, in explaining the language of Father-Son-Spirit, rely for their thinking on their cultural androcentrism, philosophy and biology. Yet Christians have built on this imagery an immense cathedral of speculative language and pious devotion. Free church prayer copies this prayer in its practice of addressing all extempore prayer to 'Father,' and some mid-twentieth century liturgists argued that even though 'father' is not an accurate translation of the term *Abba*, 'father' retains its privileged status in liturgical prayer.

We cannot know what the future of Christian liturgical prayer will decide about this address, its meaning and its frequency.[9] It is evident that Christians will not easily come to agreement about this issue. One small technique that may assist communal prayer for a contemporary assembly in which father imagery is controversial is to introduce the prayer with the bid, "Let us pray to God, our X and our Y, in the prayer Jesus taught." Each week, the X and the Y would be nouns suggested by the liturgy's propers, its biblical readings, the psalm, the hymnody, or the sermon. The images of God may be rather traditional, such as "our Shepherd," "our Light," or more innovative, such as "our Nurse," "our City." It may be that the added imagery can provide a wider context within which the classic prayer that Jesus taught can be prayed.

## THE EUCHARISTIC PRAYER

The contemporary church inherited from primitive Christianity a lengthy table prayer that had as its foundation the blessing at Jewish meals in the home. Jews understood this prayer as blessing God and so as blessing also the food. That is, God is blessed, that is, praised, and in the praising, the created world – here exemplified in the food of the meal – is blessed, that is, transformed. It is as if the Hebrew term *berakah* in one word describes the covenant relationship, the circle in which God connects with the community and the community connects with God. A full Jewish table blessing included praise for

# Ordo: Bath, Word, Prayer, Table

creation, for God's care of the people throughout history and for the food on the table, as well as a petition for a future where good was plentiful for all. We see a parallel idea in the closing call of the seder: "Next year in Jerusalem!" That is, next year, may all eat freely in an abundant promised land.

Jewish table prayer, while serving as the first draft for Christian eucharistic praying,[10] was edited by the community's encounter with Christ: Christ is the ultimate gift of life, and the food that incorporates his life and death is ultimately more life-giving than storehouses filled with the fruits of the earth. Trusting God's promise of plentiful food for all, the prayer invokes the Spirit of God on the meal, on the believing community, perhaps also on society, and in some contemporary prayers on the earth itself. West and East can lay down the quarrel about which part of the prayer effects the mystery of the eucharist, for neither the narrative of the Last Supper nor the invocation of the Spirit ought be imagined as a magical moment. Rather, the Jewish pattern of praising God for all God's salvation comes to Christian fruition in the passion and resurrection of Christ, and the Spirit of the risen Christ is acknowledged as the continuously transformative power in the church and throughout the earth. In much Western eucharistic practice, this prayer is trinitarian in structure: God is praised for creation and a history of salvation; the assembly joins the angels in singing the *Sanctus*; Christ's meal, death and resurrection are bought into the present assembly, by means of narrative and acclamation; the Holy Spirit is invoked upon a narrow or a wide circle of need; and in a concluding doxology the assembly affirms the prayer with its *Amen*.

The eucharistic prayer is the primary liturgical locus of the church's thanksgiving. It can be argued that over the centuries Christian worship has come more and more to be understood as helpful for the assembly: the worshippers get their needs met, either through fervent prayers to God or the enthusiastic interaction with other worshippers. The Christian tradition calls us to balance this humanist dimension of religious ritual with the conviction of faith that the primary reason that we worship is because God is due our praise. Scripture depicts the angels as beings dedicated nearly wholly to the praise of God, and classically in the eucharistic prayer we join with the angels in pure praise. While some forms of Christian worship allot considerable time to singing God's praise, others do not, and all contemporary Christians can learn from the psalms a praise that is not related to one's personal situation or dependent on one's emotion. God is praised, not because my life is going well or because I enjoy that kind of hymn-singing, but because God created the earth, gave life to millennia of the faithful, and once again this Sunday offered this assembly bread beyond our bread. God is praised because God is God.

Perhaps because of its recital of the acts of salvation and its focus on the elements of the eucharistic meal, the eucharistic prayer gained pride of place as the preeminent prayer of the Sunday liturgy. In some church bodies, only an authorized prayer was seen as efficacious, and even the presider's bodily gestures were precisely stipulated. However in the last decades, countless eucharistic prayers have been crafted and prayed, some with ecclesiastical approval, some not. Yet extraordinary care is still called for in the crafting and proclaiming of this prayer, so that the prayer can continue to epitomize Christian worship: the assembly, gathered together over the bread and wine, praises God for all creation, affirms the centrality of the death and resurrection of Christ, invokes the Spirit on the church and the world, and so finds even itself transformed. The fundamental nature of this prayer has led to its characteristic conservatism, and only recently are liturgists beginning to experiment with an alternate outline or a unique rhetorical style.

As with all liturgical prayer that is spoken in the solo voice of the presider, efforts must be made to help the assembly see itself as offering the prayer. Many contemporary eucharistic prayers include responses for the assembly. As well, the eucharistic prayer is a most appropriate time for all the people to stand in *orans* position,[11] demonstrating that they are joining with the presider in this prayer of all the people.

### THE PRAYER OF THE DAY

The contemporary church has inherited from the early medieval sacramentaries a short opening prayer, which by collecting the assembly into one group and collecting their many intercessions into a single petition came to be termed "the collect."[12] Called "the prayer of the day" within the Lutheran tradition, this short prayer can be seen as a model for Christian petition. Rather than being derived from Jewish prayer, the prayer of the day copied formal petition to the Roman emperor. The petitioner addressed the emperor, praised him for some previous action, and asked for a furtherance of the action. In the Christian adaptation of the court pattern, it is God who is praised as the one who has saved us in the past, God who is approached as the one who will continue to save. Although many of the Latin collects are somewhat general and reflect the fear in the early middle ages of the encroaching northern tribes ("O God, without whom we are helpless, protect us from all danger now!"), at least at festivals the content of this variable prayer reflected the readings of the day.

As the church uses historic rituals, it must continuously inquire whether the inherited pattern is so good that the higher value lies in continuing the tradition, or whether the pattern is flawed enough that the higher value lies in trying something new. One instance of this issue concerns the syntax of

# Ordo: Bath, Word, Prayer, Table

classic collects. The Latin language is grammatically concise, and the Roman court aware of time, and so the prayer of the day became characterized by brevity and cohesion. Most current adaptations of the classic collect lengthen the prayer, judging that too brief a prayer is over before the assembly can attend to it. Clearly, if the medieval collect was spoken in Latin, accessibility by the assembly was not judged a high priority, as it is with us.

Indeed, accessibility is so much our concern that in some assemblies this prayer is being put into the mouths of the entire assembly, rather than spoken in a solo voice by the presider. Perhaps this practice resulted from the problematic habit of churches printing out the full text of their liturgy. This innovation suggests that the presider's speech is not effective in gathering up the entire assembly into one voice. If people come to think that the assembly must speak all its words aloud together, liturgical worship as it has developed in the West would require radical alteration. However, if some assemblies wish to adopt this new pattern, the published prayers of the day will need revision, since these prayers were drafted with the intention of being proclaimed by a single practiced voice, rather than read without rehearsal in communal recitation.

A second instance of the inquiry into the continuing life of the tradition lies with the masterpieces of the classic Western collects. As the churches provide many new compositions so as to link a specific prayer of the day with each of the Sundays and feasts of the three-year lectionary, we might keep alive among us some of the treasures of the tradition. Phrases such as "Stir up your power and come," "you wonderfully created the dignity of human nature and yet more wonderfully restored it," "make us love what you command and desire what you promise"[13] are too noble to be set aside. Like the memory of the saints themselves, these words of theirs still resonate with a faith worthy of our attention.

## The Intercessions

Justin Martyr's second-century description of the Sunday liturgy states that after the preaching and before the meal, "We all stand together and offer prayers." Perhaps best referred to as "the intercessions," since indeed all of the prayers in the liturgy are "the prayers of the people," "the prayers of the faithful," or "the prayers of the church," this lengthy prayer comes in many forms: a single text spoken by the presider; a series of collects, with communal responses; bids, followed by silence and a communal response; a litany; in some small assemblies, wholly extemporized spontaneous petitions.[14] Many assemblies craft their own intercessions each week, perhaps assisted by the models provided in their service books or in purchased worship resources. That the intercessions are locally generated can prove to be either a blessing or curse. That the prayer has been crafted by a member of the assembly may insure that the intercessions are fully owned by the people and reflect a welcome immediacy. Yet in many assemblies, guidance for this central task is minimal or nonexistent, and the leader of prayer may be demonstrating an immature notion of prayer, marked by the concerns or the emotional state of only the self. Even prayers that move to the "we" may display only a child's small circle of awareness and interest.

The fullest classic order of intercessions in the West was a top-down list found extant in the Solemn Prayers on Good Friday. Immediately enlarging the circle of our concern, the Good Friday intercessions began with a prayer, not for this assembly, but for the entire church on earth. Subsequent petitions prayed for the clergy, the catechumens, all the baptized, the Jews, people who do not believe in Christ, people who do not believe in God, public officials and all those in need. The outline recommended in many service orders for Sunday morning condenses or omits several of these concerns, adds others and concludes with a petition somehow related to the dead, some Christians praying for the dead, others commemorating the dead in a prayer for the final resurrection. To open our prayer to an always wider field of concern, some assemblies are adding a petition for the earth, its seas, its forests, its animals. We might think of the intercessions primarily as petition for everyone who is not at worship that day, as distinct from the prayer of the day and the eucharistic prayer, which do pray for the assembly itself: the intercessions take as their model Mary at the wedding of Cana, pleading, "They have no wine." One standard Sunday outline includes petitions for the whole church, the earth, the political and social orders of the world, the local community, those in special need, silence for private prayer, and a commemoration of the dead. Were an assembly to decide to alter this pattern, perhaps by reversing the order to give priority to non-church issues, ritual practice would urge that the newly adopted pattern become standard. For the people to join in this prayer, it is helpful to anticipate what is coming next.

The intercessions are a welcome location to experiment with inculturation of the liturgy. Different Christian communities may find their own tone or style appropriate. The intercessions may be formal or improvised, one voice or many voices, relatively short or as lengthy as an assembly freed from time constraints might desire. The assembly standing, in *orans* position, kneeling, bowing, swaying, moving in procession; the words spoken, declaimed, chanted, sung: a single language, several languages: the individual assembly should shape especially this prayer to its liking. Yet there are many caveats that call for our attention, lest this prayer lose its potential as the prayer of the whole people for the whole world.

# Ordo: Bath, Word, Prayer, Table

The intercessions are to be finely crafted in an aurally accessible vernacular. Occasionally one encounters intercessions that are too rhetorically idiosyncratic. Too poetic a text dishonors the assembly by leaving it behind somewhere in the metaphors. Liturgical prose is not quicksand, but a clear-cut pathway into the heart of God.

The intercessions need to be connected to the readings, but they may be too attached, the effect being to repeat or compete with the preaching, a danger particularly threatening in those assemblies where the preacher crafts the intercessions or where the intercessors wish that they were the preacher. According to medieval tradition, the deacons crafted this prayer, perhaps because they were more fully aware than were the priests of the needs of the people and less likely to deliver a second sermon.

The intercessions are not to be deist, assigning to ourselves the solution to our problems, yet neither are the intercessions to be smug, telling God exactly how the world's needs are to be met. Sometimes simply stating the problem, laying the sorrows of the earth before God, is enough. "For the nations of the world" is more humble than "that the nations of the world will . . . ." Along with creative hymnody, the intercessions may be an appropriate place for liturgical assemblies to experiment with diverse images of God. In a petition concerning the political order, the prayer might address God as Sovereign or Judge; in a petition for the earth, as Tree of Life or Rainbow; and in a petition for the sick, as Healer or Everlasting Arms.

The intercessions are to include local concerns, but they may be too narrowly local. The prayers may be only about the assembled community, its family members and friends. The intercessions cannot be finalized until after reading the morning's newspaper. The assembly needs to find the most appropriate time before the intercessions for announcements, without expecting the intercessions to effect these announcements. Some parish decision ought to make clear in which circumstances an individual's name is to be included in the petitions. As to whether a person's last name is to be included, one can argue either way: historically, only the first, that is, the baptismal name, was used; however, historically, people did not have last names. It is useful, after the last petition and before the commemoration of the dead, to allow time for silent prayer or petitions called out from the assembly. This technique adds to the manner in which the intercessions can attend to all the needs of all the world.

The intercessions need to be grounded in the present, but they may be too trapped in the moment. The effect of the concluding petition that recalls the week's faithful departed is that the praying community remembers its past and anticipates its future. The needs of the present are held between the life of the departed and the life of the world to come, and this puts our week's concerns into a continuum of faith that supports our prayer and comforts our anxiety.

Too many assemblies pray too short a prayer. When in the second century Polycarp was arrested, he asked the soldiers to grant him first time to pray, and the record of his martyrdom says that he then prayed for a full two hours, "having made mention of all who had at any time come in contact with him, both small and great, illustrious and obscure, as well as the whole Catholic Church through the world."[15] While we smile at his clever stalling tactics, we might also emulate his practice of full and expansive prayer. Yet what is not mentioned this week can be prayed for the following Sunday.

If the intercessions take their place in a full order of eucharist in which a complete and resonant eucharistic prayer carries the assembly's praise to God, the *Sanctus* is sung, and the joy of sharing the bread and wine celebrated, then the intercessions can focus entirely on petition. However many Protestant Sunday assemblies meet without the eucharist, or they omit the classic praise at the table. In such situations, the classic form of intercession must be adapted so that it includes perhaps half praise. Thus, as in the model of Nehemiah 9, and similar to the prayer of the day, only with our praise comes our petition.

In conclusion, we can admit that believers have high expectations for Sunday's prayers. Having found a worthy precedent for communal prayer in some human phenomenon, and having reshaped this pattern in the light of Christ, the assembly discovers that in its praying, the community itself has been changed, from individual to communal, with the power of the Spirit. Such liturgical prayer sees as its double emphasis the praise of God and intercession for a never-ending list of the needs of the earth and its peoples. It might be said that these prayers are in the business of holiness: the human addressing the divine, the community imagining a reshaping of the petitioners in light of faith, the praise of God, the endless pleading for God's intervention in the things of this earth. In some religions, such a religious task requires words that are themselves somehow holy. This usually means that the prayers employ archaic speech or only authorized phrases, as if only the past or only the priests can endow mere words with the endeavor of holiness. We sense this phenomenon in those assemblies that continue to pray the prayer Jesus taught using the dated vocabulary of the King James Bible, which retained an old pronoun style that, even when the translation was published in the early seventeenth century, was passing out of popular use.[16]

Yet in most of the Western church, archaic speech is not the usual language of prayer. Most of Sunday's liturgical prayers are framed in quite ordinary speech, what we might call a deep vernacular, the wording of the prayers accessible enough to express the hearts of the baptized. For in the mystery

# Ordo: Bath, Word, Prayer, Table

of the incarnation, in God's idea to save the world by the divine becoming human, the church's ordinary speech affects holiness. Just as the baptismal bath uses tap water, and the Bible was written by human beings, and the food of the eucharist can be store-bought bread and wine, so too we find the words for our liturgical prayer in our recent dictionaries, the tone of our prayer in the vernacular of our age. The holiness is not in the words themselves. Rather, the Bible proclaims that God is accessible to humankind first as Word, speaking into the void of creation, declaiming the covenant commandments, inspiring the pen of the prophets and psalmists, evangelists and apostles. All these speakers used ordinary words, and, in amazing mercy, God was made manifest.

Have we succeeded in praying? Yes, no. As the body of Christ, the church carries on through the centuries the blessings and beseeching of Christ himself. As the temple of the Triune God, the church embodies divine mercy for all people according to their needs. It is good that there is always next Sunday, to try once more to pray.

## ENDNOTES

[1] A specific place or plant believed to be the center or pivot-point of the earth or cosmos, the connecting-point or "thin place" between heaven and earth (e.g. the Black Hills for the Lakota, the Temple Mount for Judaism, the Bodhi tree for Buddhists). *Ed.*

[2] For a history of these four occasions of liturgical prayer, see Joseph A. Jungmann, *The Mass of the Roman Rite: Its Origins and Development*, tr. Francis A. Brunner (NY: Benziger Brothers, 1950), II 277-293, II 101-274, I 372-390, I 480-490.

[3] Joachim Jeremias *The Prayers of Jesus* (London: SCM Press, 1967), 82-107.

[4] This central theme of Gordon Lathrop is discussed in *Holy Things: A Liturgical Theology* (Minneapolis: Fortress, 1993), 46-53.

[5] See, for example, Leonardo Boff, *The Lord's Prayer: The Prayer of Integral Liberation* (Maryknoll, New York: Orbis, 1983).

[6] Cyril of Jerusalem, *Lectures on the Christian Sacraments* (Crestwood, New York: St. Vladimir's Seminary Press, 1977), 75.

[7] See Norman Perrin, *Jesus and the Language of the Kingdom: Symbol and Metaphor in New Testament Interpretation* (Philadelphia: Fortress, 1976).

[8] Gail Ramshaw, *Treasures Old and New: Images in the Lectionary* (Minneapolis: Fortress, 2002), 247-255.

[9] For a concise discussion of the language of father, see Gail Ramshaw, *God beyond Gender: Feminist Christian God-Language* (Minneapolis: Fortress, 1995), 107-109.

[10] For an ecumenical discussion of the contemporary eucharistic prayer, see *New Eucharistic Prayers: An Ecumenical Study of their Development and Structure*, ed. Frank C. Senn (NY: Paulist, 1987).

[11] In the Roman catacombs, we find the representation of a woman praying with extended arms. This is known as the *orans* posture—the posture of one who prays. *Ed.*

[12] For a study of the prayer of the day, see Louis Weil, *Gathered to Pray: Understanding Liturgical Prayer* (Cambridge, MA: Crowley, 1986).

[13] *Les Oraisons* II 545, II 385, II 342.

[14] For a full discussion of the intercessions, see Walter C. Huffman, *Prayer of the Faithful*, rev. ed. (Minneapolis: AugsburgFortress, 1992).

[15] *The Martyrdom of Polycarp,* Roberts-Donaldson tr., ch. VIII.

[16] Alister E. McGrath, *In the Beginning: The Story of the King James Bible and How It Changed a Nation, a Language and a Culture* (New York: Doubleday, 2001), 266-271.

# SIX

# Eating, Drinking, Sending:
# Reflections on the Juxtaposition of Law and Event in the Eucharist

*Dirk G. Lange*

## Eucharist and Law

If we ask the "what" question – "What is the eucharist[1]?" – we will be tempted to return to its origin. We will want to know what really happened and, if possible, we will want to "see," re-enact, re-live the scene as in a movie. But through which lens are we going to view the scene? Through the passion? Through the resurrection? Through a notion of sacramentality? Through Aristotelian metaphysics? Through sacrifice or perhaps through testament? Through memorial or *anamnesis*? Perhaps through the Word? No matter how forcefully we state our argument, every approach applies a hermeneutic to the eucharist.

Listen to Luther. Is he not making a different proposal?

> Christ, in order to prepare for himself an acceptable and beloved people, which should be bound together in unity through love, abolished the whole law of Moses. And that he might not give further occasion for divisions and sects, he appointed in return but one law or order for his entire people, and that was the holy mass… Henceforth, therefore, there is to be no other external order for the service of God except the mass.[2]

When Luther writes these words in the "Treatise on the New Testament," is he not proposing that a hermeneutic arises *out* of the event called the eucharist? Isn't Luther proposing that believers relate to life – their lives, the lives of their "neighbor" (in the meaning given that term by the parable of the

Good Samaritan), their cosmology – through the "event" called the eucharist rather than the other way around?

The strange and unexpected irruption of the word "one law" (or order) in this passage will guide our reflection towards an ecumenical hermeneutic – towards a "unity through love." Why would Luther employ a word, or play with a word that he normally sets in juxtaposition to Gospel? We associate the notion of law with the ordering of society and the maintenance of balance between the rights of individuals and the collective interest. We understand law as a system, even a symbol, which represents, protects, and when invoked, re-enacts the rights of people. Why would Luther equate the heart of the Gospel with law? How are we to understand the grammatical peculiarity of this phrase: "one law or order for his entire people, and that was the holy mass"? Could Luther actually intend the eucharist to be the "one" absolute law?

In light of Luther's reticence towards legalism in any form and particularly within the context of worship, we need to answer with a resounding: No! It would be better to reformulate our question: isn't it the "law," when set side by side with the eucharist, that is disrupted? The intrusiveness of the word "law" in this passage yields, I believe, an initial hermeneutical insight: yes, "law" itself is profoundly destabilized or displaced by a liturgical act. The "law" is not imposed upon the event – the eucharist is not compared to a law - rather, the event – the eucharistic event – interprets the notion of "law."

Prosper of Aquitaine's coupling of "law" and liturgical practice in the well-known aphorism *lex orandi, lex credendi*[3] is an appeal not to a universally imposed practice or law but to a law of begging,[4] a law of supplication, an appeal to unceasing prayer. The need of all humanity before God is itself a continual prayer and, for Prosper, this prayer – this need both silent and spoken – is expressed through liturgical practice.[5] The appeal to unceasing prayer, to the condition of needy humanity as the "law" of liturgical practice implicitly acknowledges a foundation that does not rest in any institutional church, in any Magisterium, even in any liturgical tradition. The "law's" foundation is not the solid, unambiguous certainty of a mystical origin that proclaims eternal truths, that insists on absolute values, appeals to universal principles, that unfailingly distinguishes between right and wrong but, in the words of Psalm 42, the foundation is "deep calling to deep" – strangely, oddly, deeply abyss, need, hole. The "law's" foundation is in humanity's need.

When Luther interprets the "law" through the eucharistic event, he is disrupting our uncritically held notion of "law." As it is classically understood, the law is the imposition of a universal to maintain order and justified by an appeal to a foundation – a mythic, idolized, even mystic foundation. In other words, the law's foundation is non-negotiable, beyond criticism and questioning.[6] However, when the foundation is not a mystic origin or a transcendental source but humanity's need of grace expressed through liturgical practice, then both law and its foundation are shaken. By displacing the law and its foundation through liturgical practice – specifically the act we call the eucharist – the law itself is awakened to its characteristic not as absolute but as invention. Through its displacement by the eucharistic event, the "one law" questions its own "origin" – it is called to recognize the deep, the abyss, the hole; it is called to *respond* to that need; it is called to responsibility.

Luther's intention is now clear: by placing "law" and "eucharist" together in one phrase, he places intense pressure on the term "law." Luther contrasts the "one law" that is the eucharist with the old Law of Moses. In other words, the "one law" is contrasted with that older law that has constituted for itself a mystical foundation. The "one law" that is the eucharist displaces the "law" which posits its origins in an absolute authority, in a mystical (or divine) source. The eucharist is the "*one* law," the only law – it is not "a" law but rather the one law that effectively ends the mystical character of all law. Luther is questioning, displacing, deconstructing the violent imposition of a "law" in order to reach the profound "unity through love" for the entire people. The "one law" that is the eucharist challenges all our conceptions of law by interrupting, irrupting, awakening the participant – by awakening us – from the realm of mystical foundations, absolute origins, eternal testaments, perfect memorial. It thereby challenges the very framework of current ecumenical and intra-denominational debate on the "meaning" or theological significance of the eucharist.

In stating that the holy mass or eucharist is the "one law" for the entire people, Luther disrupts the notion of law by displacing its "origin." A liturgical act – the eucharistic event – breaks open the mystical origins of the law. Or, put another way, when we say that Jesus Christ is Gospel – new law – the mystical foundation of all law and religion is challenged. Of course, for Luther, Jesus is God but not the God of mystical origins and absolute heights. Jesus is God in the manger and on the cross. In other words, when we run to God we do not run to the law (or ascend to its mystical origins) but we run to the manger and the cross. We run – dare I interpret it in this way – we run to the singularity of an event.

Eucharist as Event

This chapter began with the question "what is the eucharist?" only to discover that it is unanswerable. Instead, we were led along a path of displacement of meanings. In light of those displacements, we can now reformulate the question and begin again by asking: How do we remember an event?

This question in itself already presupposes a historical perspective for, in order to ask the question, something necessarily occurred. But why do we look back as if the event – call it the Last Supper for example – could be localized historically? This looking back defines the event as an ending rather than as a beginning, as something resolved, as something that we keep as a memorial, rather than something calling us, something ever irrupting, even haunting us. The return of a singular event, the continual irruption of that event in our lives is here opposed to simple imitation and memorial. Something in the event – its singularity – cannot be captured by our memories, by any act of *mimesis*, imitation or remembrance. This singularity continually returns or irrupts into the ordered patterns of our lives disseminating principles, rules, laws, foundations, even reference points of faith. The dynamics of liturgical repetition focus on this singularity. The singularity is repeated, continually repeated, precisely because it cannot be captured or truly remembered. The repetition itself points to an incompleteness in the event. Returning to the opening question of this section, we are called to look for something incomplete, perhaps disseminated and which cannot therefore be totally remembered.

We are confronted then by a second question: what constitutes, in the event, the singularity that resists capture or remembering? Michel de Certeau writes, "An event is not what can be seen or known about its happening, but what it becomes (and, above all, for us)."[7] He is writing about an event (the revolution of May 1968 in France) that had been witnessed and that had, as its own testimony, the chronicles of innumerable newspapers. Yet, a sensory and intellectual/emotive conceptualization does not constitute the event. The event is in its becoming, in its coming to be, and, parenthetically, in a continual and non-exhaustive "coming to be" through the limitless us. In other words, the singularity of the event opposes the facile historical perspective as it opposes the facile theological positing of an origin or mystical foundation as if these could be explanatory. The singularity of the event cannot be remembered by a memorial act or idealistically construed liturgies or correctly defined sacraments or even broad ecumenical consensus – for all of these are only attempts to capture the event.

This singularity as *resistance to remembering* eludes capture by sight or knowledge but it offers also more than just a cognitive resistance: it engages body and soul. The resistance to facile remembering is first of all a dis-membering of our own identity, of our own life and knowledge, of our own body and blood and that of our neighbor. The event irrupts through continual displacements.

The radical singularity of the event has been relegated to a corner by traditional eucharistic theology and practice. Yes, an event is placed at center stage – the Last Supper (for example, Luke 22) – however, traditional eucharistic theology establishes this event as origin. By placing a theological emphasis on origin, the eucharistic celebration receives a new mystical foundation. The eucharistic celebration itself becomes "law" rather than that which interprets and displaces law. In this worst-case scenario, the eucharist becomes a law dictating our ritual remembering and repetition as if through ritual remembering we had ever-renewed access to the mystical or divine foundation – to some special communication of grace. In this scenario, only the (usually male) presider regulates access to the event and the meaning of the event is controlled through faithful observance and imitation of the law. This is not what Luther proposed when he wrote that the "one law" inspires unity through love.

Again, in traditional eucharistic theology, the basic components of liturgical practice are not hotly contested. An event happened – traditionally called the Last Supper. "High" liturgical traditions (those emphasizing shape or pattern) have approached this event through the sacraments: *anamnesis* is an enacted remembering of the event. So-called lower liturgical traditions (those suggesting that the liturgy is much more amorphous) will memorialize the event and consider their "remembering" as an act of public allegiance, a token of their faith. In either case, a previous occurrence (or event) in salvation history (the Last Supper, proclamation of the Good News, gift of the Spirit) is remembered or appropriated by a current/present act. The repetitive ritual act is, in itself, a "communication" of the event.[8] Either of these traditional liturgical approaches to the event enact the ritual as if the event to be remembered and enacted or communicated were already known, as if the outcome were always the same.

A first-century church document illustrates Luther's point. The *Didache*[9] questions this definition of liturgical or ritual repetition. It offers an example of displacement, of a profound resistance to the efforts of memory to capture the event and define speech. In Chapters 9 and 10, there is the description of a eucharistic celebration.[10] These chapters are now dated around 50 CE which would mean they predate the written Gospel accounts and are probably coterminous with the oral tradition of Matthew's Gospel and Paul's preaching.[11] Two things are absent from this account of the celebration of the eucharist: the Words of Institution[12] and any explicit reference to the cross – to the death and resurrection of Jesus Christ. These two missing references unsettle our assumptions: is the "what" of our memorial, the "what" of our ritual action, the "what" of our "event" no longer so clearly definable? Here is an early Christian community, in fact probably one of the earliest of which we have a record, celebrating the central liturgical rite of the eucharist but not remembering Jesus' presence either by means of the Last Supper or of the cross. What and how does this community remember Christ?

The *Didache* disrupts our remembering and it does so at that critical moment in the liturgy when we think we are the closest to remembering. For when we celebrate eucharist, we use the words that

Jesus used – the Words of Institution – the words that have become like a watchword for the eucharist. In the past, when the Words of Institution were absent, scholars even dismissed the liturgical witness as non-eucharistic (which was the fate of the *Didache* for several decades).[13] Repeating the Words of Institution provides the illusion that we are repeating something that Jesus did, something Jesus instituted, something Jesus founded. We cannot repeat the cross every Sunday but we can repeat this meal and thereby "remember" the Passion. But the *Didache* pulls the rug out from under us. It questions our historical, institutional, ritual remembering of an event by questioning our understanding of that event. What then is actually "remembered" in the eucharist? Is it only one meal, only the Last Supper?

When remembering becomes too narrowly focused, the prophet Isaiah's cry is heard again: "Do not remember the former things or consider the things of old. I am about to do a new thing; now it springs forth, do you not perceive it?" (Isaiah 43:16-21). In this prophecy, God first reminds the people of their flight from Egypt, their redemption through the dry passage of the Red Sea. But then God immediately tells the people *not to remember,* in other words, to dis-remember. If the people try blindly to remember in their ritual and their meal-sharing the passage through the Red Sea, they cannot recognize the passage God prepares today, now. If our own ritual remembering in the eucharist concentrates too heavily on one event, we too risk not seeing what new thing springs forth today. We too risk falling asleep through our ritual remembering rather than being reoriented to God's activity and call in the world now.

By its silence on the Last Supper and even on cross and resurrection symbolism, the *Didache* disseminates liturgical "remembering." The *Didache* points toward not one account of the meal, but to the meal-sharing tradition that Jesus practiced. Jesus proclaimed the Kingdom of God through his table fellowship, through the ancient ritual action of a meal. This act of "open commensality"[14] radically disoriented and reoriented the participants in relation to their accepted cosmology.[15] When we look at the meal event in the gospels, we notice something peculiar: Jesus was breaking every ritual norm when he celebrated a meal. He would eat with those deemed unworthy (or ritually unclean) and when he ate with "religious folk" he always introduced an element to unsettle the ritual purity of the event (Matthew 9:9-13; Luke 7:36-50; Luke 19:1-10). Whatever Jesus' intent in the unexpected pattern of these meal events, one thing is clear: the meal sharing became, already in the Gospels, a liturgical act that pointed away from itself as liturgical act and towards a responsibility. The meal event as celebrated by Jesus was so radically new and different (displacing), so radically life-giving in its displacement, that the sharing of bread and wine became the central act by which early Christians repeated that displacement, repeated that reversal, repeated that which could not be captured.

# Ordo: Bath, Word, Prayer, Table

Liturgical repetition, then, is not the remembering of one event but the displacement – the disruption – of all forms of remembering; it is the disorientation and reorientation of this radical commensality. The *Didache*, and of course the Gospels, stand as our witnesses. Disorientation and reorientation are irruptions of the singularity of the event into our daily lives. Remembering is not 'looking back' or 'calling to mind,' but the displacement of our lives so that the event can "become for us" (de Certeau).

We do not know how the eucharist "became" for the community of the *Didache*. We do have, however, a witness in the structure of this text: the meal sharing practice finds expression in a particular relation to the world, to the community, to strangers, and to the poor. The concluding chapters of the Didache reorient the notion of hierarchy in the community and propose a radical generosity, a strong welcome and an equally strong discernment.

The literary form of the *Didache* further underlines this displacement and resistance to memory. For example, Jesus is not the grammatical center of this liturgical text. In fact, the name of Jesus itself is disseminated in the text. The cup and the bread (the promise) do not refer directly to Jesus but come to us through (*dia*) Jesus. The emphasis is not as much on the person of Jesus and what Jesus did as it is on the promise of God – the promise of life, knowledge, Spirit, reconciliation – that comes to us *through* Jesus. This is in sharp contrast to later canonical literature (particularly in the Words of Institution) in which Jesus is the primary referent. In the Johannine writings, Jesus becomes the vine and the community the branches. The name of Jesus is imposed through direct reference and speech: "I am the vine, you are the branches." (John 15:5). The need for a direct, clear reference, the need to capture the event in the "I am" or the "This is my body..." overpowers the call to disorientation, displacement, and reorientation. The eucharistic witness of the *Didache* orients the reader (the participant), not to a single referent, not to a single name, not to an imposition, not to a "law" (and its mystical foundation), but to a radical inter-relationality (see again the call to live as community in and through the sharing of all things, material and spiritual in the concluding chapters of the *Didache*). The dissemination of the referent and the subsequent displacement of the participant is perhaps the irruption of a singularity, the event, or the irruption of a series of related events (a meal gathering by Jesus).

The witness of the *Didache* to the meal event that Jesus practiced is a witness to something that cannot be remembered. Sacramental remembering is displaced. Remembering and repetition are not supplying us with the source or origin or foundation, perhaps not even with the event. The eucharist is therefore not the imitation or mere repetition or simple memorial or even *anamnesis* of the final meal of Jesus but a testament to the continual displacement initiated by Jesus. Liturgical repetition is then the opposite of imitation, for imitation would repeat a closed, self-containing event, a direct referent. Liturgical repetition, however, enacts the dissemination that always breaks itself open, that always displaces itself. In this sense, liturgical repetition is always already an anti-liturgy. The eucharist is the reminder that Jesus died (was broken, fragmented, displaced, disseminated) "for our sins" but it is also a radical reminder that all our liturgical and perhaps especially our sacramental practices point away from any easy meaning we would attribute to them. Meaning itself is in fact disseminated, sent out through the door as many broken pieces of bread.

The eucharistic meal in the *Didache* suggests that performative ritual embodies the irruption of an event – or the awakening to the impossibility of capturing the event *per se*. This awakening is an awakening to the continual call of the event to displace those who participate in it. The irruption does not reduce the eucharistic event to a historical fact or moment, nor does it send us off into the unfathomable grounds of a mystical foundation. The irruption through liturgical repetition expresses the disseminated nature of the event: not only is the bread broken, disseminated, but the "utterer" (the presider) is also disseminated, scattered in plural, grammatical forms. This dissemination is an unsettling experience, an experience the participant (presider included) would prefer controlling. The eucharistic event, however, resists capture, resists falling asleep – it constantly calls us to life.[16]

The eucharistic prayer in the *Didache* concludes with beseeching: "So may your church be gathered . . . ." Even in the rite, the gathering, the "unifying" is not completed. A prayer for completion is added. Another disorientation has occurred, this time from thanksgiving to pleading. The repetition of the meal has brought back the dissemination, not as a negative incapacity but as hope. The remembering has pointed not towards a completed event but something absent, a hole, an abyss, something still becoming "for us" and continually questioning us.

## HERMENEUTICS OF EVENT

Let us return to the two main points before moving on to the third. By equating the "one law" and eucharist, Luther has displaced the origin and foundation of the law. The law – no law – gives us access to the singularity of an event. Rather, the law is itself displaced and re-interpreted through reference to an event. Denying us access to immutable, transcendental, mystical truth and origin, Luther directs us to the singularity of an event – the Christ event. That event disrupts our remembering. We are confronted by an event that cannot be remembered. The liturgical practice of the *Didache* embodies this confrontation by focusing on the radical disorientation and reorientation of the meal-keeping practice of Jesus. Liturgical repetition is the repetition not of a memorial but of a continual displacement.

Leader, people, things and world are displaced in liturgical celebration by the impossibility of capturing, imitating and remembering an event and the recognition of the inadequacy of any form, whether old or new, to express that singularity. This impossibility and this displacement – this time and space – witness to a profound dissemination of meaning. Dissemination (the impossibility of capture) is threatening for high liturgical proponents (because it denies any universal validity to a set *ordo*) as well as low liturgical advocates or free church advocates or mega-church advocates (because it denies universal validity to any method created or contrived for conversion and sanctification). In order to approach this dissemination, we will again turn to Luther. Here, Luther provides an insight into his theological method, a method deeply rooted in a biblical pattern:

> But what could the devil not do? ... He had some of his followers in the Christians' schools, and through them he stealthily sneaked and crept into the holy Scriptures. Once he had wormed his way in and had things under control, he burst out on all sides, creating a real brawl over Scripture and producing many sects, heresies, and factions among Christians. Since every faction claimed Scripture for itself and interpreted it according to its own understanding, the result was that Scripture began to lose its worth, and eventually even acquired the reputation of being a heretics' book?? and the source of all heresy, since all heretics seek the aid of Scripture. Thus the devil was able to wrest from the Christians their weapons, armor, and fortress (i.e. Scripture), so that it not only became feeble and ineffective against him, but even had to fight against the Christians themselves. He got Christians to become suspicious of it, as if it were plain poison against which they had to defend themselves. Tell me, wasn't that a clever scheme of the devil? ... This is the way the plot worked out for the fathers: Since they contrived to have the Scriptures without quarreling and dissension, they thereby became the cause of men's turning wholly and completely away from the Scriptures to mere human drivel. Then, of course, dissension and contention over the Scriptures necessarily ceased, which is a divine quarrel wherein God contends with the devil, as St. Paul says in Ephesians 6[:12], "We have to contend not against flesh and blood, but against spiritual wickedness in the air." But in place of this, there has broken out human dissension over temporal honor and goods on earth, yet there remain a united blindness and ignorance of the Scriptures and a loss of the true Christian faith .... Isn't this also a piece of devilish craftiness? No matter what play we make, the devil is a master and an expert at the game.[17]

Luther's synopsis of the history of the interpretation of Scripture and the devil's role in it reveals a fundamental hermeneutical insight. If we were to rephrase Luther, we might hear him say, "The devil creeps into the Scriptures through the different schools and gets each school to argue for one – its own – interpretation of Scripture. What results are heresies: everyone begins to interpret the Scripture in their own way. And even worse, the Scriptures themselves, become the Christians own worst enemy. Then the church fathers and bishops come along and decide to put an end to all the bickering. They impose one authoritative interpretation, sanctioned by Rome, through the church councils and imposed by the laws of the lands. This is exactly what the devil wanted because this then blinds Christians to the incredible tension, the juxtapositions which are the pattern of the Scriptures."

This passage is revelatory not only of Luther's struggle to free Scripture from the constraints of a monopolistic interpretation but it is also suggestive of his eucharistic hermeneutic. When this passage is placed next to our opening citation (God "appointed in return but one law or order for his entire people, and that was the holy mass"), we will better understand the displacement of the notion of law and its reorientation in the eucharist. In the opening citation, the eucharist is named the "one law" which responds to the many occasions of "divisions and sects." In the second passage, one authoritative interpretation opposes (suppresses) the many divisive, sectarian interpretations of Scripture. Luther interprets the force of opposition in the second citation as a negative move. The one authoritative interpretation is an imposition, a violence. The suppression of voices in the second passage destroys the biblical pattern. On the other hand, the potentially negative "one law" in the first passage is broken open through association with the eucharistic celebration. In other words, the eucharist, rather than imposing itself like one law or order, patterns for the participants (for us), a continual dissemination, a continual displacement and reorientation.

Is it then possible, when the eucharist is considered as an event always breaking open our rituals, always pointing towards an abyss, an absence, always displacing and disseminating, is it possible to discern a hermeneutics? Or is this just another antinomy? Can a hermeneutics of displacement be a true hermeneutic? In a strange way, I will say, yes. This dissemination, this continual displacement and reorientation, is the pattern of the liturgy itself. It is the pattern that Justin invokes when he invites us into the pattern of those good things.[18] This dissemination – the "one law"! – is not a negative move (that of simply scattering, dying) but a pattern yielding an approach to meaning.

We have another term for this pattern that the eucharist embodies for the entire people: the means of grace. The means of grace clearly focuses this pattern – yes, on the sacramental gifts of bread and wine and water, but even more importantly on the promise these hold. "Jesus Christ is the living

# Ordo: Bath, Word, Prayer, Table

and abiding Word of God. By the powers of the Spirit, this very Word of God, which is Jesus Christ, is read in the Scriptures, proclaimed in preaching, announced in the forgiveness of sins, eaten and drunk in the Holy Communion and encountered in the bodily presence of the Christian community."[19] The "one law," the pattern that is the eucharist, invites believers into the simple acts of reading, proclaiming, announcing, eating and drinking, encountering… the Gospel. The "one law" invites into – it gathers the people in – just as the "one law" disseminates at the same time all referents, all foundations, all laws.

The "one law" invites into a pattern and a hermeneutic emerges – a hermeneutic of event. The sharing of bread and wine, the sharing in the body and blood of Christ is all this: reading, proclaiming, announcing, eating and drinking, encountering and we could add bathing and teaching as well. The "one law," the juxtaposition embedded in the eucharistic event itself does not defer to a mystical foundation but takes us to the crux of a sacramental and even more generally a liturgical theology. The sacramental act is not the bridging of the gap between the sacred and the secular – it is not our peephole into God's reality or our high-speed internet connection to God or any form of privileged communication – it is the encounter of God's grace through and in creation's need. In that encounter, human need is reoriented. The "one law" witnesses to the displacement of the mystical foundation – to the displacement of God in vulnerability, need, suffering. The hermeneutic of event – of the "one law" – disseminates and juxtaposes rather than systematizing and concluding. The hermeneutic of the "one law" points to the hole, the abyss in which the "promise" can be truly promise, truly testament. The "one law" that is the eucharist is then a profound "unity through love."[20]

The one law or order awakens from the slumber of mystical origins to reveal itself as the juxtaposition, the crux, the confrontation, the dynamic embedded within the eucharist. This law or order takes us to the cross. The means of grace[21] then is nothing less than the way to the cross – through the water and the word, we are brought back to the death and resurrection of Jesus Christ, to a communion in the paschal mystery; through the bread and the wine and the word, we are brought back to the body and blood of Jesus Christ, to his life offered to each one of us.[22]

But is this not in contradiction to the earlier statement that the means of grace confounds our very method of thinking and remembering? What does it mean to go to the cross? Are we again idealistically remembering that past event as if we were all gifted with liturgical *hypermnesia*?[23] Are we somehow miraculously taken back to the crucifixion as in a film? Does the means of grace accomplish this sort of magical time-machine?

We want to believe that we are able to remember the cross; for example, there are moments in life when we are imbued with a strong emotional response to the cross and are overwhelmed that Jesus died "for me." Our emotions, our memories take us back... Or we fall back in on ourselves, as happens in many parishes today that do not keep up the incessant and necessary dialogue and critique of culture: "This is the way we've always done it!" In uncertainty and insecurity we return to what is known to us, what we remember as being the most vital: "This is how we enact our faith!" – "This is how we remember Jesus!" – "This is how we worship!" Or, on another level, we get excited about a film like the "The Passion of the Christ" that shows it all "as it really was"! Worship would then have to compete with this film. In any of these scenarios, worship patterns are simply attempts to remember and our liturgies become trapped by the different forms of remembering that we have constructed.

In response to these attempts at remembering, the one law speaks a resounding No! The one law confronts us with the impossibility of remembering, with the impossibility of imitating. The one law that is the eucharist refuses our attempts at capturing or containing or hemming in the Christ event. As deep resistance, the means of grace – the juxtaposition of Word, bath and table – redefines our very notion of remembering. Through the perspective of the means of grace, remembering is now not looking back and idealizing a moment in history. It is a continual disruption of our thinking, our remembering, our pieties, our spiritualities. The means of grace confront an all too human way of remembering and say, "This event cannot be repeated or imitated. It is a singular event. And as such, you cannot capture or control it. Rather, it irrupts anew in every situation, in every time, in every culture. It is that moment which is not held by time."

When the event, the singular event, takes the assembly to that moment not held by time, it places the assembly in a singular time, in the eighth day[24] – in the day not of the week. When the means of grace takes the people to the cross – it takes them to the cross present in the world today. The means of grace take us to the cross in human lives, to the cross in the life of family, community, society, nation, world. But it never just takes us to the cross as if Good Friday were the last day – it will always point to the eighth day. When the means of grace take us to the cross, it takes us to the promise: the promise of justification, of reconciliation, of life not only in the hereafter but already now. In and through the means of grace we hear God's promise becoming for us today. The means of grace take us to the cross, to the hole, the abyss, to that which we cannot remember or capture or contain or explain – they take us to where God suffers in the world. And it speaks to our own suffering by placing that suffering in the light of the Resurrection. The means of grace accomplish nothing less than this juxtaposition – a juxtaposition that sends us out into the world.

# Ordo: Bath, Word, Prayer, Table

## Eucharist and Sending

Sending is as integral to any celebration of eucharistic sharing as are the bread and the wine. The sending is the dissemination of the bread into the world, the scattering of the body, the scattering of our memories, our feelings, our spiritualities as many pieces of bread given for the world. "Do this in remembrance of me" is then not just celebrating the words of institution and the communion, re-enacting a historical moment but it is being sent as living witness of Christ into the world to find Christ already in that world.

The sending becomes a mere dismissal when we adapt the liturgy and its pattern to our lives as *we* have conceived of them, when the lines between culture and Gospel become hazy, when we attempt to dilute God rather than keep God in dialogue with our world, when juxtaposition is leveled and only one voice is heard. The sending, however, as part of the "one law," as part of that singular event, as part of the eucharistic sharing speaks a deep, inner language which can displace our life patterns, prejudices, presuppositions.

The neighbor and the believer are both caught up in the incredible gift of God's continual revelation through Word and sacraments. Luther writes: "So when we eat Christ's flesh physically and spiritually, the food is so powerful that it transforms us into itself and out of fleshly, sinful mortal people makes spiritual, holy, living people."[25] Through participation in the eucharist, believers are made one with Christ and all the saints in their works, sufferings and merit.[26] Union with Christ is not, however, the inception of an individualistic piety (Jesus and me) as it has often become in present-day North American practice. Jesus comes with all the saints – with all the bread scattered over the mountains – with the whole community in its deep diversity. "[B]y the same love we are to be united with our neighbors, we in them and they in us."[27]

The eucharist invites life into the continual pattern of dying and rising in Christ, a spiritual baptism, which has no end until our bodily death and resurrection. This confrontation with dying and rising is not merely an emotional or psychological drama. The equation of religious emotion with a sense that we have "died," that is, that we have given something up for God, is imaginary. The dying of which Luther speaks is a concrete participation in the death of Christ, in the suffering of others. It is not an emotional high. It is not sacrifice. This dying, first realized in baptism, is attached to life – and to the symbols of life in bread and wine – life displaced and reoriented through the promise of forgiveness offered in the "one law," the eucharist.

The believer is sent out into the world: "Go in peace, serve the Lord!" Or, as the old Huguenot liturgy exclaims:[28] "Go in peace. Remember the poor!" Believers go out, sent as the body of Christ. But *in* the world they find the body of Christ already there. They find Christ disseminated in the poor, the suffering, the dejected, the outsider... Christ already in the world. And the one law that is the eucharist embeds within it that juxtaposition that displaces bread, body, knowledge, life, even the holy and in that displacement awakens us to a responsibility. The "service of God" as eucharist – or as Luther puts it "the real fellowship" and "the true significance of this sacrament"[29] – this "real fellowship" engages us through an iterable, that is, repeatable liturgical structure to live out a responsibility. The one law awakens us to this testament, this almost impossible responsibility – continually sent out of the closed circle, out of the community, out of the old law, displaced yet reoriented, to find Christ already displaced, waiting for us outside.

# Ordo: Bath, Word, Prayer, Table

ENDNOTES

[1] The designation "eucharist" will be used in this article. It encompasses the variety of expressions employed in reference to the sacramental "event" such as "Sacrament of the Altar," "Holy Communion," "The Lord's Supper," and "Holy Mass."

[2] Martin Luther, *Eyn Sermon von dem neuen Testament das ist von der heylige Messe*. WA 6:354. [Christus] *"hatt widderumb nit mehr den eyne weis odder gesetz eyngesetzt seynem ganzen wolk, das ist die heylige Mess."* (See also in English: Luther's Works 35:80-81).

[3] "...*ut legem credendi lex statuat supplicandi*" – this phrase, found in the "Official Pronouncements of the Apostolic See on Divine Grace and Free Will" by Prosper of Aquitaine apparently establishes a relation between a rule of believing and a certain rule of supplication. See Prosper of Aquitaine, *Defense of Saint Augustine*, Ancient Christian Writers (London: The Newman Press, 1963), 183.

[4] Michael G. L. Church, "The Law of Begging: Prosper at the End of the Day" *Worship* 73, no.5 (1999) 442-453.

[5] Conversation with Gordon W. Lathrop, March 2004.

[6] Jacques Derrida, *Force de loi* (Paris: Galilée, 1994).

[7] Michel de Certeau, *The Capture of Speech and Other Political Writings*, trans. Tom Conley (Minneapolis: University of Minnesota Press, 1997), 20.

[8] A form of this remembering has been made recently very popular in Mel Gibson's film "The Passion of Christ." It witnesses to an ecumenical curiosity: this controversial example of a deep Catholic piety "remembering" the *Via Dolorosa* and its enthusiastic reception by more right-wing, fundamentalist Christians who relive for themselves the sufferings Christ "as they happened."

[9] The *Didache* was only discovered by Archbishop Philotheos Bryennios in 1873 and published in 1883. For more detailed analysis of this document see Jonathan Draper, ed., *The Didache in Modern Research* (Leiden: E.J.Brill, 1996) and Kurt Niederwimmer, *Die Didache*, (Göttingen: Vandenhoeck & Ruprecht, 1989).

[10] Enrico Mazza, *The Origins of the Eucharistic Prayer* (Collegeville, Minnesota: The Liturgical Press, 1995). See 30, 35, and 38-39.

[11] ibid, 40-41.

[12] "On the night in which he was betrayed, our Lord Jesus took bread, and gave thanks; broke it, and gave it to his disciples, saying: Take and eat; this is my body, given for you. Do this for the remembrance of me. Again, after supper, he took the cup, gave thanks, and gave it for all to drink, saying: This cup is the new covenant in my blood, shed for you and all people for the forgiveness of sin. Do this for the remembrance of me."

[13] See Robert F. Taft, "Mass Without the Consecration." *Worship* 77 (2003), 482-509.

[14] For a discussion of the open shared table of Jesus, see John Dominic Crossan, *Jesus: A Revolutionary Biography* (New York: HarperCollins, 1989), 70ff.

[15] For further discussion of cosmology and its reorientation through the liturgy, see Gordon W. Lathrop, *Holy Ground: A Liturgical Cosmology* (Minneapolis: Fortress Press, 2003).

[16] Is there the possibility that in the remembering that occurs through dissemination, a new definition of ritual is possible?

[17] Martin Luther, *Das diese Wort Christi "Das ist mein Leib" noch fest stehen, wider die Schwärmgeister*. WA 23:64-320. (See also in English: Luther's Works 37:13-14).

[18] "When the reader has concluded, the presider in a discourse admonishes and invites us into the pattern of these good things." Justin Martyr, 1 *Apology* 67:4. Translation by Gordon W. Lathrop. See Gordon W. Lathrop, *Holy Things: A Liturgical Theology* (Minneapolis: Fortress Press, 1993), 31 and 45.

[19] Evangelical Lutheran Church in America, *The Use of the Means of Grace: A Statement on the Practice of Word and Sacrament*, (Minneapolis: Fortress Press, 1997), 6.

[20] Luther — see opening citation.

[21] In English, French and German, the term "means of grace" is ambiguous and cannot be tied down to either singular or plural. This ambiguity I believe must remain as it expresses theologically our inability to pinpoint the means to either one over-riding principle or to a set number of "means."

[22] Gordon W. Lathrop and Timothy J. Wengert, *Christian Assembly* (Minneapolis: Augsburg Fortress, 2004), 25.

[23] Abnormally exceptional memory of the past.

[24] For a discussion of the eighth day, see Gordon W. Lathrop, *Holy Things: A Liturgical Theology* (Minneapolis: Fortress Press, 1993), 39-40.

[25] Martin Luther, *Das diese Wort Christi "Das ist mein Leib" noch fest stehen, wider die Schwärmgeister*. WA 23:205. (See also in English: LW 37:101).

[26] Martin Luther, *Eyn Sermon as diese Wort Christi "Das ist mein Leib" noch fest stehen, wider die Schwärmgeister*. WA 2:749. (See also in English: LW 35:60).

[27] Martin Luther, WA 2:748-749. (See also in English: LW 35:59).

[28] The sending is being proposed by the Renewing Worship Editorial Board for Holy Communion as an option. See www.renewingworship.org

[29] Martin Luther, WA 2:748. (See also in English: LW 35:58).

# SEVEN

# Liturgy: Praising God

*Melva Wilson Costen*

## GROANING IN PRAISE

> She conceived again and bore a son, and said, "This time I will praise the Lord;" therefore she named him Judah. (Genesis 29:35a)

The praise of God begins and ends with God! This is apparently the reason that so many writers overlook this first reference to praise in the Hebrew Bible, assuming it could not come from the mouth of a woman in childbirth. Even the patriarchal society in which Leah was born, lived and died would object to this discovery, because it would be in opposition to the tradition. This is not, after all, a discovery; it is a rediscovery of an often overlooked *anamnesis* – a remembering as if you were there. The use of the word 'praise' from the mouth of a woman has no doubt been listed in every concordance of the Bible since the beginning of published records – or has it? Perhaps the implications of a woman groaning in childbirth limited the inspiration that God would accept groans of praise as evidence of thankfulness.

Leah's groan of praise was not offered in private, for it was the custom among the Israelites for other women to assist with the birth of children. This groan was therefore offered in the midst of an assembly, albeit a small assembly, where at least one among them might have also disliked Leah. "When the Lord saw that Leah was unloved, he opened her womb" (Genesis 29:31a) and gave her the gift of children – four sons, so that the story of Israel could continue. God initiated the praise, and Leah responded, "Praise the Lord," echoing centuries of liturgical offerings of vocal praise!

*Liturgy: Praising God*

The liturgical practices of Israel, initiated by the Almighty, provided the foundation for the *ordo* of Christian liturgy in general and the *ordo* of *praise, thanksgiving and beseeching* in particular. This chapter will begin with evidence of Hebrew praise, flow through New Testament and early Christian practices of praise, and conclude with numerous examples of people groaning in praise into the twenty-first century.

## Ancient Roots of Praise

The concept of praise is older than recorded history. Among the people whose earliest records are transmitted orally, there is evidence of a deity or a pantheon of gods from whom it was believed all of life emanated. Ancient rituals of praise evolved over time from the people who were awed by the power and control of these invisible and imaged gods. It is apparent that *praise* is considered the oldest and most basic element in communal rituals. Rarely is there found a community whose roots are not entrenched in vocal expressions of praise, thanksgiving and sacred stories unique to their survival. A common belief among ancient people was that *praises* offered in a certain manner would provide benefits or favors from the gods: thus praises were offered as a means of soliciting and receiving special favors, special gifts, sanctions, permission and approval. It was believed that all of life was born, survived and died under the awesome power and control of the gods.[1]

All around the world the glorious work of God abounds and was acknowledged through ancient eyes. In cultures and lands long before Judeo-Christian traditions were planted, people acknowledged and praised the Creator upon viewing the overarching and unreachable sky, enormous mountain ranges and lengthy plains, as well as the smallest crawling creature. One need not look beyond the intricacies of human physical structure and ongoing life itself in order to acknowledge that "there is a God who has sovereignty over all, *is good* and *does good* unto all; and is therefore to be praised."[2] Praise of God is also expressed in many languages in acknowledgement that God's love is embodied in the extension of Godself to humankind. Thus, praise of God was at the very core of the life of primal people as an important dimension of existence.

## Hebrew Temple Praise

The book of Leviticus received its title from the Greek and Latin versions of the Hebrew Bible and relates to the persona and duties of the Levitical priests – the sons of the tribe of Levi. The major focus is on the laws that were established for Hebrew worship. It is from First and Second Chronicles that one is able to glean specifics regarding communal praise of the Hebrews. These books chronicle the history of Israel as a community of worshipers whose life centers around praising Yahweh in the Temple of Jerusalem. According to these sources, the kings who founded and maintained temple worship were David, Solomon, Hezekiah and Josiah.

Under the leadership of King David, plans for the ritual praise of Yahweh began to take shape. His intentions were to bring the Ark of the Covenant to Jerusalem and locate it in the Temple, thus allowing it to provide the ritual focus for the people of Yahweh (1 Chronicles chapters 13-16). David's plans and preparations for the building of the Temple which would be the final resting place for the Ark of the Covenant abound with visions of praise to God, a vision that he could never see fulfilled because of God's concern that David was "a man of war" (1 Chronicles, 22:8). David established practices of assembly leadership that speak to every generation with both challenges and new opportunities. David demonstrated the effective use of musicians, vocal and instrumental, who would be in constant preparation to offer praise to Yahweh. He also established a pool of Levites, numbering over four thousand, who would be leaders of worship. Their initial task was to perform certain rituals not handled by the organization of priests. Added to their tasks were the duties of temple musicians, who not only led the musical praises, but also established a professional guild of musicians who maintained a high standard of music befitting the praise of Yahweh.

Public praise within the liturgy of the assembly consisted largely in the immolation and complete burning of lambs: one in the morning, one in the evening. The Temple choir did not sing during the burning of sacrificial offerings, nor during the dashing of the animal's blood at the foot of the altar. Perhaps the exact location of places in the ritual where the choir would sing became the foundation of such practices in the synagogue and ultimately in Christian liturgy. The choir was located in front of the burning altar, so that burning and singing were alternate, therefore complementary acts of worship. It is also of interest that the choir rendered "thanks to Yahweh, for [his] steadfast love endures forever." (1 Chronicles: 16:14; 2 Chronicles 5:13; 20:21)[3]. The texts of the songs were apparently not related to the sacrificial burnings, but were responses to the presence of Yahweh. The singers did not petition Yahweh to bless nor accept the sacrifices offered. It seems that the flames or the ashes invoked the presence of Yahweh.

Solomon, the son of David, is credited with building and dedicating the Temple, thus setting the framework for ritual practices which were later reformed by Hezekiah and Josiah. Under the rule of Hezekiah, a good and enlightened ruler, choirs were reminded of the sacred nature of their task of leading the sung praises of the assembly, and they were required to be cleansed, consecrated and sanctified, along with the worship space (2 Chronicles 29:1-36). Hezekiah also required the singing of praise to God with the psalms of David and Asaph, the choirmaster. An existing collection of psalm settings might have been available enabling the choir to sing from fixed sets of texts.

Josiah, son of Hezekiah, was only eight years of age when he began his reign of thirty-one years. He followed two kings, Manasseh, who is considered to have been the most evil of all kings of Judah, and Amon his son, who continued the evil direction of his father during the two years of his reign. Amon was assassinated. Josiah, in his eighth year, restored Israel to the rightful worship of Yahweh and purged Judah and Jerusalem of the altars of Baalism (2 Chronicles 34:3-7). As he continued the purging process, the book of the law was found by Hilkiah the priest and the workmen as they made repairs to the house of the Lord. During the Passover prepared by Josiah, there was a restoration of praise led by the singers who were the sons of Asaph.

Amid this history are reminders of the importance of praise, joined with the sacrificing of animals, and more importantly, praise as a totally independent ritual act which served as a substitution for animal sacrifices. In ancient Israel and among other primal religious traditions, praise was considered the highest form of prayer.

## PSALMS IN THE HEBREW ASSEMBLY

In the Hebrew texts, the Psalms are titled "Tehilim," a word that means "praises" or "songs of praise." *Halal*, a verb from the same root as *tehilim*, is found more than 160 times in the Hebrew Bible with a large percentage found in the Book of Psalms. Psalms 113 – 118 are traditionally referred to as the *Hallel Psalms* because they refer to the praise to God for deliverance from Egyptian bondage under Moses. These psalms are deeply significant as part of the traditional Passover service. These were probably the hymns sung by Jesus and the disciples on the night of his arrest. *Halal* is the root word for "Hallelujah," most often translated "Praise the Lord," and is perhaps the most familiar Hebrew expression of praise. A more technical translation is "let us praise *Yah*, (or *Jah*)," a shortened form for the spelling of Yahweh. Psalm 150 is the prime example of "Hallelujah praise."

The Psalms have the distinction of being words of humans addressed directly to God, with the psalmist's thoughts and feelings focused entirely on God. Scholars agree that very few of the Psalms reflect the time of tenth-century Israel, BCE. Some have been traced to pre-Israelite days, and others express the life and experiences of early Judaism of at least the third and fourth centuries BCE. In general, the psalms communicate the religion, life and thought of the ancient Hebrews; they reveal how the people experienced and felt Yahweh's presence in their personal lives, in nature, and in their history.

# Ordo: Bath, Word, Prayer, Table

These ancient words have inspired and sustained the faith of generations of worshipers. They represent, as Walter Bruggemann suggests, an articulation of "the gamut of Israel's speech to God, from profound praise to the utterance of unspeakable anger and doubt."[4] It is also apparent that Israel's worship culminated in various forms of praise that reveal the breadth and spiritual depth of the Hebrew worshipers. They were a people who called upon Yahweh in words and songs, especially when they were in distress. After they were delivered, they would sing and dance God's praises interspersed with thanksgiving. Equally important was the praise offered to celebrate Yahweh's sacred story, the story into which they had been called to enter and share with Yahweh and each other. These are often identified as *psalms of glorification*, psalms that venerate the one whom they hold in highest esteem. Yahweh is to be extolled because of who Yahweh is and not because of what Yahweh does. Yahweh is praised as a majestic and powerful being above all other beings (Ps.145:1).

As a form of public ritual, the Hebrew verb *yadah* is an expression of thanks *and* praise. One example is found in the closing doxology of Psalm 7:17, which some scholars contend, is an editorial gloss or commentary added later as a suitable close, suitable for public worship.[5] The four translations that follow provide evidence of different interpretations of the same text. The first is closely aligned with the Hebrew indicating that *Yahweh* is referenced as the object of praise. *Elyon*, the Most High, is named in accordance to his righteous in reference to Yahweh.[6]

> I will praise Yahweh according to his righteousness
> > And I will make melody to the name of Elyon.

The translation of this verse in the King James Version is:

> I will praise the Lord according to his righteousness:
> > and I will sing praise to the name of the Lord most high.

"Praise" in the first line of each of the passages above is translated from the Hebrew word *yadah* or *hodah* meaning "to hold out one's hand toward," "show reverence with extended hands," and confess allegiance to Yahweh. "Praise" in the last lines is translated from the Hebrew word *zamar*, which means "striking the strings of a musical instrument" or "to celebrate in song and with a musical instrument." In the next two translations, *yadah* is interpreted as meaning "give thanks," with *zamar* remaining "to celebrate in song."

> I will give to the Lord the thanks due to his righteousness,
>> And I will sing praise to the name of the Lord Most High (RSV)

> I will give to the Lord the thanks due to his righteousness,
>> And sing praise to the name of the Lord Most High. (NRSV)

From *yadah* comes the noun *towdah* or *todah,* often translated "thanks" or "thanksgiving" in songs of worship (e.g. 1 Chronicles 16:4-7; 29:13; Ps. 95:2 and 100:4). The word is also used occasionally to identify the singing of corporate praise by a choir. Although not an exhaustive list, the following terms for praise are used intermittently throughout the Hebrew Bible.

*berekh* (or *berekah*) – bless or praise the Lord (Neh. 9:5; Pss 103:1; 104:1; 134:1-2)
*shibbath* – praise (Pss. 63:6, 96:3, 145:4)
*romem* – extol, exalt or "lift up" (Pss. 34:3; 99:9; 118:28; 145:1)
*giddel* – magnify the Lord (Ps. 34:3)
*yahav* – ascribe greatness to the Lord (Deut 32:3)
*rinnen* – make a ringing cry; joyful shouting or singing (Pss 33:1; 71:23; 98:4-6)
*rinnah* (n) – joyful shouting or singing (Pss. 304; 47:1)
*rinnah patzah* – break out into joyful celebration (Pss. 9:2; 53:6; 7:12; Joel 2:23)

It is clear that praise was an important part of the life and experience of the Hebrew people.

## Psalms in the Christian Assembly

One element through which praise is offered to God in the Christian liturgical assembly is Hebrew psalmody. Psalms allow the assembly collectively and individually to connect with the dominant liturgical element through which Jesus offered praise to God. They also aid the community in centering itself as an embodiment of praise, offered to the Almighty. Jewish contemporaries of Jesus (who would later become Christians) knew and understood the importance of the psalms as well as the categories of prayers wherein praise was central. In the Jewish liturgy for the weekday, a ceremonial salutation would be followed with an exhortation to prayer, "Praise ye the Lord who is to be praised," followed by the response of the assembly, "Praise the Lord; He is to be praised for ever and ever." These acclamations of praise are followed by the praise of God the creator of all things, especially of light,. This idea is elaborated upon and climaxes in the first *Kedusha* (thrice holy) Two long *berakot* (praises of God, the creator of light and of Godself, who has chosen Israel in love - lead to the *Sh'ma'*(Deut. 6:1-9) This was considered the core of the service, together with the *Amida* (a term that means 'stand.' The opening words are from Psalm 51:17).[7]

These connective links remind us that many of the first Christians were Jews – both by faith and nationality. After the death and resurrection of Jesus, they followed a Jewish cultic ritual, and spoke the Hebrew and Aramaic languages. They later expanded and reinterpreted the Jewish traditions in the light of the message of salvation. The earliest assemblies combined elements from both the temple and the synagogue. According to Werner, the constituent elements were as follows:

Liturgical texts which originated in the temple but were adapted by the early synagogue;
Hierarchy and its function – intrinsically connected with the temple
Ceremonies and ritual – frequently synagogal, but containing elements from the temple, such as
    vestments, rites and *oblationes*
Music – from the synagogue
Organization of the ecclesiastical year[8]

In continuation of the synagogue tradition, psalms were used as a central act of praise in the New Testament Church. Canticles from Luke's gospel later extended the praise repertoire. Christian songs of praise were added as the New Testament age was ending. However, the church primarily sang psalms and canticles until the early fourth century, the era of Ambrose (ca. 340-397), Bishop of Milan, and Hilary of Potiers (c. 315-367) who contributed to the hymnic directions of the church.[9]

The poetic rhythm of the psalms indicates that psalms are designed to be sung. The term *psalmody*, understood to mean a type of musical setting governed by the coordination of syntactic and melodic accents, includes texts of the psalter, as well as any scriptural or liturgical passage. Texts chanted in this manner may follow the flow and the phrasing of the syllables.[10]

There are four main formal schemes in the Psalter: 1) the plain, direct psalm in which strophic arrangement is not apparent;[11] 2) the acrostic psalm, in which the verses are in alphabetical sequence (Ps. 119); 3) The refrain psalm in which each verse ends with the same refrain (Ps. 136); and 4) the "Hallelujah" psalm which begins or ends with the jubilant acclamation – "Hallelujah" (Pss. 145-150).

Although a full review of the use of psalmody in worship is outside the bounds of this chapter, one custom of significance is the opening of the assembly's worship with psalms. Found in particular in the ecclesiastical *invitatorium* (Psalms 95 and 96), this Christian ritual goes back to Jewish practices. A psalm is also usually included in the Sunday Liturgy of the Word. Since the other readings are situated in the history of salvation, the Psalms are considered poetry, even if they allude to historical events.

When describing the evolution of the psalm of the Roman Catholic Mass, Joseph Gelineau notes the different forms or treatments that the psalm assumed as one of the four biblical passages included in the liturgy:

> During the first centuries the psalm might have been treated as another biblical reading in the Liturgy of the Word. During the fourth and fifth centuries, the responsorial form appeared. A psalmist chanted the verses and the whole assembly resounded by a refrain... By the seventh and eighth centuries, the people no longer joined in the songs. Cantors expanded the melodies of the earlier responses while the lone remaining verse was executed in a very ornate form by the psalmist who sang from one of the steps (*gradus*) of the ambo. The rediscovery of the psalms was one of the fruits of the pre-and post-conciliar liturgical renewal.[12]

Gelineau's reference to the post-conciliar liturgical renewal movement's rediscovery of the psalms has also been felt in mainline Protestant denominations where the use of the psalms in worship has seen some rebirth. The inclusion of psalms in a variety of denominational hymnals is one of the recorded evidences of this rediscovery.[13]

## OTHER EXPRESSIONS OF PRAISE

Biblical foundations for communal praise are also found in the Exodus story of Moses, beginning with "The Song of Moses" (Ex. 15:1-18) when Moses and the Israelites sang a song to the Lord, continued on this occasion by "The Song of Miriam" (Ex. 15:20), who was joined by the women who danced as Miriam played a tambourine. Here we find the praise of God expressed through song, movement, and instrumental accompaniment.

Spontaneous responses of praise from the people acknowledge the presence, awesomeness, power and majesty of God. Spontaneity is inevitable when the assembly has a creative encounter with the God of freedom, of love and of power, who, during this time with the Israelites, assured their freedom.

As a noun, praise means being approved, adored, commended or valued.[14] Because praise is a common attribute in the ancient rituals of many cultures, it is generally accepted that praise is a basic or primal form of private and corporate ritual expression. Massey H. Shepherd, Jr. is one of many scholars who align adoration with praise:

> As flowers break into blossom from the warmth and nourishment of sun and rain and fertile soil, so adoration and praise spring from our awareness of the sustaining presence of a God who loves us.[15]

It is in the midst of the assemblage of people that the worship of the Almighty God in and through Jesus the Christ takes place. Gordon Lathrop draws attention to this matter in his observation that "assembly, a gathering of participating persons, constitutes the most basic symbol of Christian worship."[16] Lathrop contends that nothing happens liturgically unless there is an assemblage of holy people who then participate in the reading and hearing of scripture, singing, praying, partaking of the Eucharist, reciting of creeds. During the process of assembling, individuals learn that the church gathers in the first place *for* and *to* the glory of God.

Christianity as a continuation of the Jewish understanding of praise can be confirmed in the syntax of praise. Accordingly, God is praised whenever the mighty deeds – the acts of God – are recounted, as well as in some forms of testimony where "glory to God" is offered in personal and communal testimonies of recent divine interventions. The expression, "let's give the Lord a hand clap of praise" heard in gatherings of varying languages and cultures is indicative of spontaneous "interruptions" of praise offered to God. Worshipers more aligned with formal liturgical gatherings are often shocked, in fact a bit embarrassed, by the "praise clichés" and unbridled "praise eruptions" that punctuate traditional African American and Euro-Charismatic worship. Visitors to these worshiping assemblies are often offended when the "praise team" leaders engender enthusiasm with such admonishments as "you don't know how to praise the Lord!!! Put your hands together and show him [*sic*] that you know how to praise the Lord." We are reminded that praise is not *only* expressing joy but demonstrating praise in action, exuberance surely needs liturgical and pastoral guidance.

Nevertheless, the concept of 'the praise of God' or indeed 'praising God' is recognized as a major event in the life of the assembly that will ultimately shape individuals into a people whose ultimate task is to praise God with their whole beings in every aspect of their lives. If an assembly takes seriously its call and commitment to "glorify and enjoy God forever," the assembly gathered, *kononia*, (κοινονια), as well as scattered in serving, *diakonia* (διακονια) will "never quit praising God" (an expression heard often in African American worshiping communities of faith). According to African griots in the North American diaspora and African American preachers, exhorters, and leaders and conductors in the Underground Railroad Movement, to "never quit praising God," meant that obedience and submission to God was the ultimate and most accurate mode and expression of praise. It was much later in African-American life that this concept of praise could be related to the Westminster Shorter Catechism in response to the first question: "What is the chief end of man [*sic*]? . . . to glorify and enjoy God forever."

As Judeo-Christianity spread around the world and took roots in other contexts and among people who would ultimately become part of the church, we are reminded of Gordon Lathrop's affirmation that "'assembly' constitutes the most basic symbol of Christian worship."[17] The diversity within and among the gathered people reflects long traditions of Christian assemblages that, as Lathrop suggests, "have become linked to the nation or the 'folk.'"[18] During the twentieth century, traditionally unified assemblies, regardless of denominational membership or ethnical composition, have experienced the joy of cross-cultural worship connections. We are grateful that Lathrop included excerpts from "The Nairobi Statement" in *Holy People* as a reminder of the ecumenical movement towards *koinonia* in worship. In this document we are reminded of the challenges to the churches "to give serious attention to exploring . . . contextual elements of liturgy. . . hymnody and other music. . ."[19]

Space will not allow more than one supplemental context. This context is Africa, with a special extension to the African American worshiping community. By so doing we will be drawn, hopefully, toward the practice of liturgical unity.

For ancient African peoples, praise was expressed in deeds and attitudes more than words.[20] Praise, chiefly understood in African contexts as a form of prayer, is often combined with petitions and blessings among some people whose ancient traditions survive in the twenty-first century. Examples of this are provided by the African scholar, John S. Mbiti, who translated these words from the local *Chagga* language . . . : "We praise thee, and pray to thee, and fall before thee..."[21] In rainmaking rites the *Ila* people sing God's "praise-names," which describe the nature and activities of God, rather than literally "praising God" as understood by Western description. To "name" God is to praise God. God is named, therefore praised, as Creator, Giver of Rain, Beyond All Thanks, One From the First, Father of the Placenta, and One Who Carries Everything On His Back.[22] Equally significant is the close relationship between thanksgiving and praise through bodily movements (dance), a concept that has historical continuity in the flow of ancient Africa primal religious practices through to twenty-first century African-American Christian worship practices.[23]

The church in Africa through its various local assemblies demonstrates Lathrop's reminder that "the church is a gathering of people in a particular place who are, together, through concrete means, participating in the mystery of Christ and so are being formed into the holy assembly." [24] One of the many gifts of African experience is the use of the human body in the offering of praise to God. Humans move (physically) toward God, just as God moves toward humankind. Since God is Omnipresent, the movement toward God is not confined to any one particular direction, although cultures might establish certain particularities, based on their interpretation or primal understanding of the rhythm of life in the universe. Bodily motions that are established for "action" occur over a period of time. By so doing, motions join the order or rhythm of interaction in the universe as their local society expresses it. Thus rituals are patterns of action involving stylized bodily motion. The body is a primal symbol that facilitates communication. It is possible for Africans to have motion of the body without speech. However, they are less likely to speak without some observable bodily motion.

Unlike Greco-Roman and Western Christian thought and practices, Africans, both on the Continent and in the Diaspora, experience the human body and physical gestures as one totality – one whole. The body is not understood as a "prison for the soul," and consequently, "an instrument of sin." It is instead the center of the total manifestation of God's gift of beingness. The African liturgical scholar Elochukwu E. Uzukuwu offers helpful insights on how patterns of African ritual assemblies and sacred narratives have merged with Jewish and early Christian traditions to create living communities and liturgies:

> The complexity of the notion of person, instead of a devaluation of the body, reveals itself in bodily gestures. Body motions, whether accompanied by speech or not, embody the group, reveal its universe of beliefs, while not excluding individual responsibilities.[25]

Expressions of praise in African worship across denominations show evidence of the refusal of African people to impose a split between the human world and the spiritual world. Uzukwu notes that this imposes a challenge to African theologians to propose patterns of worship that will integrate the whole world of the African.[26] The active involvement of one's entire body in expressing praise, therefore, is grounded in African ontology which understands the unity in all of life. Contrary to opinions from persons outside of the African context of understanding, African peoples are not simply demonstrating their emotional urgencies or tendencies in their rhythmical offerings of praise. African beliefs and experiences have been merged effectively with Western beliefs. Not only are these gifts available to the universal church; the depth and richness of this heritage is so ingrained in Africans in the Diaspora that new ways of praising continually emerge.

## Praise in Twenty-First Century Liturgy

A twenty-first century theological seminary class gathers to study liturgy, bringing many opportunities and challenges for the professor. A brief visual overview of the newly assembled class reveals much of the same physical diversity as in previous classes over the years. There is an equal balance of females and males, plus or minus a bit in either direction. The variety of young, middle-aged and those more "seasoned" in age are about the same as in previous years. The ethnic diversity is broader than usual. It is always difficult to determine how many are recent college graduates since a few second and third career students return to college in order to complete their undergraduate degrees in response to their call to ministry. Their apparent eagerness to "get to the task at hand" is revealed in the stack of required text books that they retrieve from their back-packs, and the comfortable shoes that they wear for required visits to numerous places of worship. Laptops and tape recorders are in place. Then I notice the headphones and rhythmic bounces of two, no, actually three students, indicating that the headphones are plugged into a CD. The rhythms are different, of course, with students intricately moving and gyrating all over the place! It should have been no surprise for the professor to discover that among those called to ministry are young persons who are part of, or identify with, the "hip hop gospel culture." Each student was listening to praise music in the rhythm of different drummers, offering praise to Almighty God in Jesus the Christ.

These young candidates for ministry may indeed represent the assemblies of many different communities of faith. The teaching – learning process of seminaries will be "differently challenged" to meet the needs of this century. Even the word "praise" occasionally appears to be "up for sale" when attached to the most recently marketed liturgical products. The world is ever changing. Technology and spiraling changes in a technological age bring reminders of the different "beats" that exist in the assembly, gathered and scattered, and offering praise to God in Jesus the Christ.

The concept of change, of course, is not new. Educational systems have coped with new living standards and changes in the society since the beginning of civilization. Professors of liturgy are aware, to some extent, of ways that liturgy has been affected by sound revolutions, software and other technological devices that "facilitate" worship.[27] Aware that many of these originate from the market-driven industry, there is also the reality that some worship committees are drawn into the technological arena without noticing how these inventions affect the meaning of worship.

Following an assignment I gave to a seminary class on "Praise for Sale," it was a relief to discover from discerning students that the *praise and worship* phenomenon is a Protestant approach to worship renewal. From additional research, one is made aware of the Hebrew tabernacle and temple typology that undergirds this approach.[28] The term *praise and worship* was chosen to parallel the logic of the Hebrew typology. Proponents of the 'Praise and Worship' form "make a distinction between praise – usually defined as extolling God by remembering in proclaiming God's character and activity – and worship – usually defined in more relational terms of direct communion with God."[29] It is not clear how Jesus the Christ connects with or is incorporated into this Hebrew worship. Yet, many of the songs used during this portion of worship (in some assemblies) include praise to Christ! The excitement engendered by the leadership team and the sound of percussive instruments apparently establishes memories of Psalm 150, and sets the momentum for praise. The basic movement from praise to worship (as determined by proponents of this form) is accomplished by altering the personal pronouns used for God (the use of 'you' rather than 'he') and slowing the tempo of the music. The intent is to move the assembly in song from an objective remembrance of God to reflections upon God's personhood and the assembly's personal relationship with God.

Praise and worship music has a popular appeal in that the styles of music and the instrumentation (electrical guitars, electronic keyboards, synthesizers, and various percussions) reflect the popular music currently available through the media. The repetitive songs include a minimal number of words, thus, in most instances, a limited amount of theological thought. The words are electronically projected on screens to facilitate viewing by the assembly. The text and music are produced, taped and sold by publishing houses. Although the greatest appeal is designed toward youth, young adults and children, involvement in this form of praise is not limited by age.

The location of praise and worship as the first ritual action of the assembly is similar to the devotional services in African-American congregations, especially in the South. Devotional services were led by the deacons, elders, and mothers of the church and were (loosely) structured around congregational singing, prayers, reading of scripture, and occasionally testimonies, occurring under the leading of the Spirit. The intent of this liturgical structure was to help unify and focus the worshipers who often gathered gradually. The reason why the early portion of the structure did not abound in exuberant praise is that many participants would be too tired to move with any semblance of gusto. The songs and prayers overflowed with words of thanksgiving followed by earnest pleading.

## Praise as Foundational to the Shape of the Liturgy

The chief end of humanity – the main reason for living – is to glorify and enjoy God forever. In the midst of the assembly, the people are at work practicing what they are taught to do forever! The entire liturgy is punctuated with praise. The psalm often sung in metrical form each time the community of faith gathers is an absolute glossary of praise:

> All people that on earth do dwell,
> Sing to the Lord with cheerful voice;
> Him serve with mirth, his praise forth tell,
> Come ye before him and rejoice.

Lathrop reminds us of characteristics "found in the classical structure of Christian prayer itself" and notes that Christian prayer (at the beginning) is modeled after Hebrew prayer with praise in juxtaposition to beseeching.[30] It is no wonder that praise is often defined within the context of the definition of prayer.[31]

> Here too is juxtaposition, one thing set next to another in a mutually interpretative pattern. At dawn and at evening, in the prayers throughout the week, Christians praise the God who is the maker and giver of all creation. They also beg God to hold all things together still, to send light, to be protection in the night of oppression and fear. Their prayer is both praise and beseeching.[32]

An important feature of praise in the Christian tradition is the recital of the great deeds of God in the past followed by praise to God in Christ. For example, the reading of the Gospel in the liturgy is answered with the response "Praise (or thanks) be to thee, O Christ.[33] The hymn of praise that comes to mind is the *Te Deum*, the fifth century hymn of praise that begins with the adoration of God and includes the remembrance of the work of Christ as the ultimate foundation for Christian praise. The assembly gathers and responds to the grace of God, calling God by name, remembering past deeds that hold the world in order, and looking forward with hope toward the future fulfilled in the life, death and resurrection of Jesus the Christ.

New forms or structures of praise within the *ordo*, regardless of their shape, can be evaluated in terms of the liturgical theology articulated by Lathrop. Of particular importance is his reminder that praise in juxtaposition to beseeching is found in the Eucharistic prayer.[34] This prayer, and numerous forms of spontaneous prayer, reflect the close alignment of praise and thanksgiving, most often expressed as synonymous concepts. The need to offer thanks is foundational to the human understanding of relating God with current experiences. Christians are expected to live in constant praise of God. This can be expressed as if one is constantly offering thanks both verbally and non-verbally, both spiritually and in material offerings of thanks.

Gordon Lathrop reminds us that "Jesus Christ is the ground and content of our praise, yet this praise is broken. The grounds of our thanksgiving are found in a crucified man. For Christians, all the suffering with which we are surrounded and in which we participate has been gathered into Christ."[35]

Praises have resounded as groans
- of travail and pain of women in childbirth as they offer praise for the gift of children and new life;
- of an African people enslaved in a strange land as they praised God for impending freedom;
- of native people as they reclaimed their land;
- of AIDS patients who found freedom in approaching death.

Praise of the assembly continually bursts forth under the power of the Holy Spirit
- in the continually singing of the Hebrew psalms of praise;
- in the songs of praise, petition, born of an African people in bondage, and now a part of the liturgy of the global church;
- in gospel songs created for and during nineteenth century evangelical worship;
- in black gospel songs from the nineteenth century through current days;
- in new songs and "raps" of youth who will not be confined inside a prefabricated liturgical box.

Praise of God in the assembly will continue to be carefully honed, under the power of the Holy Spirit
- in prepared prayers throughout the *ordo*;
- in words of the Eucharist;
- in the preparation and delivery of sermons and homilies;
- in old and new songs
- at bedsides as the faithful journey to the kingdom.

## Endnotes

[1] There are a plethora of examples that attest to similarities between the offering of praise to the gods of the people of primal religions and to the God of the Hebrews and Christians. The realities and dangers of cultic praise permeate myths, religious stories and literature in ancient Africa, Greece, Rome, and continued as Christianity took root in primal traditions around the world. One of many examples is found in the first book of Homer's *Iliad* and in *Suppliant Maidens* by Aeschylus. Performances of acts of praise incorporated rituals, the use of music, words and altars.

Practices similar to those adapted for use in Hebrew and Christian assemblies included specific places for the *altar* or places of sacrifice, the use of vocal choirs, instrumentalists, music directors, dancers, and congregational songs with refrains. The ancient Greek *paean* (a joyous, exultant song of praise) must have been a familiar form of praise among early Christians. (Arthur Fairbanks, in *A Study of the Greek Paean* (New York: Macmillan, 1900) notes that the earliest documented musical notations are for Greek paeans, found inscribed on stones dating from second century CE at Delphi.)

Among ancient documented references to the primacy of praise are the writings of the first century Greek philosopher, Epictetus (ca. 50-140), who exhorted the people to offer praise without ceasing:

> Ought we not when we are digging and plowing and eating to sing this hymn to god: 'Great is god who gives us such implements with which we shall cultivate the earth. Great is god who has given us hands, the power of swallowing, a stomach, imperceptible growth, and the power of breathing while we sleep.' This is what we ought to sing on every occasion. (Epictetus, *The Discourse*, Vol. I with trans. By W.A. Oldfather (London: Heinemann, 1925), 16)

An additional example of praise in Greek literature is Homer's *Iliad*, where we read of a thanksgiving sacrifice presided over by Chryses. Following a lengthy ceremony for his daughter who was captured but then returned by the enemy, glad paeans of praise are chanted to Apollo (Homer, *Iliad* I:472-74). The words of Plato in which he expressed his disdain for some of the performances of praise of his day also provide details of acts of praise to the Greek gods:

> A magistrate offers a public sacrifice, and there come in not one but many choruses, who take up a position a little way from the altar, and from time to time pour forth all sorts of horrible blasphemies on the sacred rite, exciting the souls of the audience with words and rhythms and melodies most sorrowful to hear; and he who at the moment when the city is offering sacrifices makes a citizen weep most, carries away the palm of victory. (Plato, *Laws* 800)

[2] Adapted from "The Westminster Confession of Faith," Chapter XXIII, 6.112.

³The role of the choir as a group to minister to the people thus did not develop during Temple worship, but obviously occurs later.

⁴ Walter Bruggemann, *The Message of the Psalms* (Minneapolis: Augsburg Press, 1984), 15.

⁵ Charles Augustus Briggs and Emile Grace Briggs, *A Critical and Exegetical Commentary of The Book Of Psalms*, Vol. I (Edinburg: T. & T Clark, 2nd ed. 1976): 56.

⁶ Ibid.

⁷ This information is taught to students at the Interdenominational Theological Center from lecture notes by Rabbi Zvi Shapiro. It can also be found in Eric Werner, *The Sacred Bridge* (New York: Columbia University Press, 1959), 4-5.

⁸ Werner, ibid., 19-20

⁹ For more details about the music tradition of the Western Church particularly, see especially Paul Westermeyer, *Te Deum: The Church and Its Music* (Minneapolis: Fortress Press, 1998).

¹⁰ Forms of psalm singing are readily available, and will not be included here in detail.

¹¹ Strophic patterns are those in which each stanza (of four to eight lines) utilizes the same music for each stanza.

¹² Joseph Gelineau, *Liturgical Assembly Liturgical Song* (Portland, Oregon: Pastoral Press, 2002), 124.

¹³ See especially John Alexander Lamb, *The Psalms in Christian Worship* (London: The Faith Press, 1962) for a survey of the use of Psalms from Hebrew worship through the various worship traditions. Practices have been the least consistent in African American denominations and congregations, except among some Presbyterians where psalm signing prevailed in the denomination.

¹⁴ *Webster's New Collegiate Dictionary* (Springfield, Massachusetts: G & C Merriam Company, 1980), 896.

¹⁵ Massey H. Shepherd Jr., *The Worship of the Church* (Greenwich, Connecticut: 1952), 26.

¹⁶ Gordon W. Lathrop, *Holy People: A Liturgical Ecclesiology* (Minneapolis: Fortress Press, 1999), 21.

¹⁷ Lathrop, ibid, 26.

¹⁸ Ibid, 28.

¹⁹ Ibid, 236, Appendix 2, #6.

²⁰ John S. Mbiti, *Concepts of God in Africa* (New York: Praeger Publishers, 1970), 217.

²¹ Ibid.

²² Ibid.

²³ See Melva Wilson Costen, *African American Christian Worship* (Nashville: Abingdon Press, 1992), Chapters 1-2.

²⁴ Lathrop, *Holy People*, 49.

[25] Elochukwu E. Uzukwu, *Worship as Body Language, Introduction to Christian Worship: An African Orientation* Collegeville: The Liturgical Press, 1997), 10. This source provides tremendous insights from the African perspective of the experiences of liturgical inculturation in Africa from pre-colonial and colonial times through the adapting of the Zairean liturgy.

[26] Ibid. 33.

[27] See especially Tim Eason, "The Software Driven Church," in *Church Magazine,* December 2000, http:www.church media.net/CMU/article/software/010.shtml.

[28] See especially Lester Ruth, "Praise and Worship Movement" in *The New Westminster Dictionary of Liturgy and Worship,* Paul Bradshaw, ed. (Louisville: Westminster John Knox Press, 2002), 379-380.

[29] Ibid.

[30] Lathrop, *Holy People,* 55

[31] See especially the article by Peter Selby in *The Westminster Dictionary of Worship,* J. G. Davis, ed, (Philadelphia: The Westminster Press, 1972.) 320-321)

[32] Lathrop, *Holy People,* 55

[33] *Westminster Dictionary,* 320

[34] Lathrop, *Holy People,* 57

[35] Lathrop, *Holy Things: A Liturgical Theology*, (Minneapolis: Fortress Press, 1993), 58.

# EIGHT

## Liturgy: The *Ordo* of Liturgical Space

*Gláucia Vasconcelos Wilkey*

On the banks, on both sides of the river,
there will grow all kinds of trees for food.
>Their leaves will not wither nor their fruits fail,
>but they will bear fresh fruit every month,
>because the water for them flows from the sanctuary.

Their fruit will be for food, and their leaves for healing.

(Ezekiel 47: 9-12, NRSV)

### Précis: A Church's Need of a House

The farm in the heartland of Brazil in the interior of Mato Grosso State (now *Mato Gross do Sul*) was lush and lovely. Right in the middle was a grove of mango trees surrounded by gentle hills. Through the grove ran a clear stream born just above it at the foot of one of the hills.

The site was the place chosen by the leaders of a Brazilian Baptist congregation scattered among farms in a wide area of the state in the 1950s. This "scattered congregation" was led by an itinerant pastor—something common in the time and region.

This farm was to become the place that would house the church as it gathered every year for six days.

While "domestic church," centered in this farmhouse and others like it, held weekly prayer services, the distance and the lack of transportation served as barriers for regular gatherings. Eventually the congregation came to designate a site for their meetings. In choosing the place for what was to be the annual gathering place for the church, the leaders focused on some simple criteria:

- the place had to be accessible to all.
- the place for the church had to be close to a living stream, preferably near its source.
- the place had to be rich in trees, preferably mango trees.
- it would be important for the gathering place to be near a village.
- the meeting was to take place during Epiphany, a significant time in the life, faith, and culture of Brazilians.

As all plans around the building of liturgical spaces should be, the set of criteria named was simple and rich in images. As all liturgical spaces should be, this was to become a place designed to house, enable, entice and reorient those who came seeking a home for the church in which to do its doxology and its beseeching, its *kerygma* and its *koinonia*, its delighting and its *pedagogia*. In short,

> [a] place for human interaction and active participation—where the mysteries of God are recalled and celebrated in human history.... Such a place acquires a sacredness from the sacred action of the faith community which uses it. As a place, then, it becomes quite naturally a reference and orientation point for believers.[1]

## A METAPHOR FROM THE WORLD OF MUSIC

A possible metaphor for theology as the foundation for liturgical space comes from the world of music: in a particular musical form known as *passacaglia* one hears a basic theme introduced in the very first bars of the composition. Around and above the theme – always ubiquitously heard – various sets of other phrases, ornaments, rhythms, and tempi are woven into "segments" or variations that begin and end with the restatement of the theme, one movement intrinsically depending on and leading to the other, every note and every silence fully expressing the basic theme yet adding new colors and musical ideas. Unlike other forms, as for example, "theme and variations," the passacaglia is a single unit, with no stopping places between the segments or the restatement of the theme.

In this metaphor it is possible to name the *ordo* of the liturgy, Jesus Christ and his Gospel, as the theme for the *passacaglia*. It is possible to see the movement of the liturgy, the words and the actions of the liturgy around its primary centers, *and* the worship space of the liturgy as the segments of the *passacaglia*. Like that musical form, the *ordo* of the liturgy has no separate or distinct movements that end before the next begins. One does not think of the four basic movements of that pattern as independent one from the other, but as intrinsically woven segments with their own colors yet interdependent,

# Ordo: Bath, Word, Prayer, Table

and deriving their life from the underlying theme. The point of each of the melodies, colors, and rhythms woven in the segments is to make the theme clear and enticing.

In this metaphor the liturgy, its segments and notes, tempi, rhythms, voices, instruments, silences, phrases, and grace notes move in a crescendo of disclosure: the assembly gathers in Christ to go forth into the world. The meeting, says this *passacaglia*, is about the encounter between God and humanity, about God in Christ as the life of the liturgy.

## People and Place as One: A Theme Ancient and New

The idea that a people's theological identity is singularly tied to a particular community's worship environs is far from new. Witness the narratives found in the Hebrew Scriptures telling of encounters between God and people – whether of individuals or whole assemblies. The meeting and the space combine both to forge and to express the very identity of the parties in those encounters, God and God's people.

*From Tabernacle to Early Church Patterns* No one could fail to identify the theme in these directives to the leaders of the people of God from the composer of the tabernacle's *passacaglia*:

> "Have them make me a sanctuary so that I may dwell among them. In accordance with all that I show you concerning the pattern of the tabernacle and of all its furniture, so you shall make it. . . . You shall erect the tabernacle according to the plan you were shown in the mountain. . . . You shall make a table of acacia wood. . . . You shall overlay it with pure gold. . . . You shall make plates and dishes, flagons and bowls. . . and you shall make them of pure gold. . . . You shall make them according to the pattern. . . . And you shall set the bread of the Presence on the table before me always. . . . (Exodus 25-27, NRSV)

A holy place to serve as God's dwelling place called for a holy pattern, "just as the people had been shown in the mountain," (an injunction repeated for every detail in the envisioning of the house for the journeying assembly in the desert). This *passacaglia's* recognizable theme is the holy Presence in the midst of the holy people.

An intentional theological pattern guided the tabernacle's design, repeated and expanded in the plans for constructing the temple many years later. The patterns for all things are those shown in the mountain of the worship of God itself, the patterns speaking of *this* God, *this* assembly, *this* doxology.

We find the same theme and the same meshing of the patterns of worship/space as we come to meet early Christian communities in the New Testament. We know that the word *ekklesia* referred to the assembly gathered on the Lord's Day. But eventually, the use of the word came to identify primarily the building for the assembly, and only later return to refer to the people assembled in the house, as Lathrop reminds us in *Holy People: a Liturgical Ecclesiology*.[2]

*Orientation: The Place of the Dawn* Such weaving of people and space is also manifested in the geographical orientation for the spaces of prayer of the people of Israel and for the houses of the nascent Christian Church. The basic understanding of directing prayer – and thus the house of prayer – to the birthplace of the morning is rich in metaphors. The image of Daniel praying towards the east, expressing both a longing towards "the city of God" and the faith in a God who rises above the dark of the world is a still a present-day hope seen in the faithful orientation of synagogues, temples, mosques, and many Christian churches towards the place of the dawn.

"The rising sun will visit us with healing in its wings," sings the antiphon for a setting of the *Benedictus*, the Canticle of Zechariah at the center of Morning Prayer.[3] The canticle is ancient in theological understanding, sun and stars permeating the language of prayer and praise of Israel and then the Christian faith, giving both faiths a "skyward" geographical and cosmological orientation. The canticle, not unlike Daniel's prayer, gives voice to the hope of fulfillment of the promise of dawn breaking upon God's people. But this Dawn and its accompanying images, Morning Star and Sun of Righteousness, is now Jesus Christ. Though these images and this eastern orientation are metaphors, the life of liturgy and the place for liturgy have been shaped in and through the theological insights such metaphors provide.

As houses became too confining for the growing church, guidelines regarding this eastern orientation soon appeared. Speaking of the first buildings designated as church, Edward Foley quotes an ancient document, the third century's *Didascalia Apostolorum*, a handbook for the liturgy of the assembly: "In your assemblies. . .after all good patterns form your gatherings, and arrange the places . . .carefully. . .for towards the east we should pray as ye know that it is written, 'give praise to God who rideth the heavens of heavens toward the East.'" Foley continues:

> One of the results of moving from borrowed rooms to permanent worship structures was the transference of the name traditionally given the community, *ekklesia*, to the building itself. While this change in terminology did not indicate that the community no longer considered itself the true *ekklesia*, or foundation of living stones, it did anticipate a time when such consciousness would be

# Ordo: Bath, Word, Prayer, Table

lost among the baptized. Eventually, only the building would be recognized by the vast majority of believers as 'the church.'[4]

The space and the church mingling in name and reality say that the life of this new assembly has a definite orientation: eastward, that is, toward God and a Christ-like life in which justice and grace rise as the dawn amidst the darkness of all oppressions and disorientations in the world. Eastern-oriented design reflects specific theology reflects specific mission reflects specific identity, whether that identity is that of the wandering people of Israel, of a large Episcopal congregation in today's New York City, or that of the scattered congregation of Brazilian Baptist farmers.

Don E. Saliers reflects in his volume *Worship as Theology: a Foretaste of Glory Divine*:

> Whole theological histories may be noticed in the arrangement of the space in diverse traditions. A central stone altar speaks of the centrality of sacramental mediation of God, whereas an elaborate central pulpit witnesses to the centrality of preaching so characteristic of many Protestant traditions. A large baptismal font flowing with water located near the entrance or nearby the entrance to a sanctuary speaks of the importance of baptismal theology and the primary symbol of water, whereas a hidden or perhaps non-existent font speaks of the lesser significance of baptismal themes in the community's self-understanding.[5]

## A Room for A View

This is the central affirmation about a Christian liturgical space: this is a *room for a view*. It is a room for a particular way of seeing the Triune God; for a particular way of hearing Christ; for a particular way of reenacting and giving thanks for the mercy of God fully revealed and tasted in Christ; thus, this room enables a particular way of seeing the world – and the life of the assembly after the meeting is over.

Whatever other particularities characterize any given assembly, whether cultural (place in the world) or ecclesial (place in the Church), a Christian liturgical space houses, enables, entices, cajoles, and orients a particular people into the life of the ecumenically embraced movements to *and from* doxology:

- the gathering
- the word
- the bath

- the eucharist
- the sending

This pattern – and so the room for its life – should be simple and clear, uncluttered with things that distort, cover, or ignore those central movements – a room in which everything else is seen as secondary, even the present cultural *or* particular ecclesial context, its simplicity defined as Lathrop describes the church in Dura-Europa, Syria: "Washing next to word next to meal—the *ordo*—was the content of the house." [6] That simple, yet that profound.

In her thoughtful book on Christianity and secular culture, Margaret R. Miles speaks of "visual theology." The writer asks, "How does eyesight become insight?"[7] One answer to the question can be in the constant reiteration, the constant 'seeing,' of patterns, whether of words, actions or meeting spaces, all one single *ordo*. For example, what was seen in this simple Brazilian place of worship could not help but become theological insight for those who cared to see.

As the description of this particular worship space will demonstrate, the question has profound implication for those concerned with the building of the houses of the Church, for such spaces are indeed "for the sake of our communication of Christian meaning."[8] What are those meanings? And how do specific ecclesial lenses interpret and give locality to those meanings? What did the space in the farm in Brazil say? Consider these particularities: First, the church in question was a *Brazilian Baptist* Church; second, members of the congregation lived very far one from the other, and were thus unable to meet more frequently; third, these were people wholly connected to the land, living in full interdependence with the ground and the riches of the soil. For them, the ground was indeed holy ground in a most basic understanding.

Thus the choice of place, the choice of time for the meeting, and the design of the space were more than matters of taste personal or communal. They were matters of viability for the life of the people – and of the land.

*Accessibility* For those who came to the farm field in Brazil, the matter of accessibility was of utmost importance. Farmers and others came in horse or oxen carts, a few in small trucks. All would bring tents, hammocks, cooking utensils, food for six days (including livestock!), and, of course, family and friends. Consideration had to be given to people coming from the east and from the west, from the north and from the south bringing their particular gifts to the meeting. Roads had to be opened in the farm and cleared of anything that could bar the way or make it difficult to maneuver.

# Ordo: Bath, Word, Prayer, Table

But access was also a concern for the people and villages around that farm. Invitations for the Sunday event – evangelism as Justin understood it – were to be a major component of the gathering. As the community gathered, there was indeed a constant flow of people to and from the nearby village and area dwellings. Church members worked through those six days on building projects, and at least one small house for a local family was built by the community every year. Some of the women went to a home near the farm to teach sewing, a basic survival skill for many in the region. Area children and youth came to play with the journeying church's children. Therefore one of the important questions debated in the planning stages was, "How close is this land to the nearest village?" The question implies an invitation: place the church near the centers of human needs beyond the wants and needs of the church itself.

The second year the community gathered on that farm, someone used a piece of wood and on it burned a sign that was placed on the gate to the area. The sign read simply, *Ponto de Encontro*, literally *point of encounter*, or "Gathering Place."

*Water* The need for water was, of course, primary. Water for the life of the church in its gathering place had to be abundant, clear, flowing freely. This water needed to sustain simple life: drinking, cooking, bathing, and all other human needs depend on the presence of living, flowing water. But more, the week was to become the annual baptismal event for that congregation, a place for reorienting life.

A shed was built at the foot of a hill near the stream's source. It was really a shed, built from available trees in the farm, sturdy, open on all sides, with a sloping roof that offered a modicum of protection from possible rainstorms. The design was unique in that the shed was built straddling the shallow stream. On the east side, on the narrower end of the stream, a rough pulpit and a table stood. Across the stream, on the west side, were the pews for the congregation. All furnishings were hewn from the property, the generous gift of the local farmer. To get to the pulpit or the table one had to cross the stream. A small portable harmonium (pump organ) was the only secondary element found in the space, brought in and placed near the front of the pews.

Beyond and below the south side of the shed the water flowed on, widening more and more. On the banks, amid the trees, the community pitched their tents for the week. Looking towards the building from the community's living area, one had the impression that the water flowed from the shed. The metaphors in the design, and the connections to the biblical imagery of water flowing from the sanctuary (Ezekiel 47 and Revelations 22) are evident and were intentional for the Baptist church meeting in that space. This place was to manifest the particular identity of a people. Over a period of time the memory of life in the space was bound to take hold of the imagination of many who experienced the *Ponto de Encontro.*

Such insight comes not in one day, but in the accumulation of days. This is not a space for instant gratification, nor is it a place to make things user-friendly for instant understanding. This sense of identity is forged over a period of time through repeated actions and engagement of heart and body.

Saliers comments on the appropriation of liturgy lived in such places saying, "The sound of song and prayer is internalized in the particular space, and thus the power of association and the emotional depth of memory work to fuse together habits of the body with the present experience."[9] A question for today's church could be, What "habits of the body" do our spaces elicit?

Many years later, one of the sons of the itinerant pastor serving this community became a pastor himself, this time serving a Baptist church in Brasilia, the capital of Brazil. Architects were guided to forge the worship space with the shed's design in mind: the chancel was split in two from one side to the other, forming a large and deep channel through which water flowed quietly, ceaselessly. In this large and very modern building in Brazil's most modern city, the old pattern was adopted. The pulpit and choir were beyond the water, and the table at the level of the people in front of the flowing water. Candidates for baptism came into the pool from one end, were baptized in the center, and went out of the pool on the other end. Death and resurrection were powerfully seen, and living, flowing waters served as visual theology fully expressing the particular sense and understanding of baptism of the Brazilian Baptist Church.

For years, many came to that sanctuary to experience the power and the beauty of the space and the story it told. Recently, however, new leaders and new concepts for worship, particularly in musical ministry, led to the impoverishment of the visual statement the space communicated: the stream was covered with thick planks of wood to hold a band of instruments and electronic gadgets. Only a very small segment of the stream was opened at one end when baptisms were celebrated: potent symbols rendered mute in the presence of that which is unessential.

The place of worship for a particular people is often referred to as a "house for the church."[10] In *The House of Belonging*, a poem by David Whyte, we find this particularly suggestive segment:

> I found myself
> sitting up
> in the quiet pathway
> of light,

# Ordo: Bath, Word, Prayer, Table

>     the tawny
> close grained cedar
> burning round
> me like fire
> and all the angels of this housely
> heaven ascending
> through the first
> roof of light
> the sun has made.
>
> This is the bright home
> in which I live,
> this is where
> I ask my friends
> to come,
> this is where I want
> to love all the things
> it has taken me so long
> to learn to love.[11]

It does take time "to learn to love." It takes many angels ascending and descending before we can awaken to the place where we encounter mercy and find justice. It takes time to see all the *ascendings* of our praisings and our beseechings, and the *descendings* of God's mercy and reorientation as the house of God, Beth-El. When we do see, then we join the Jacob-finding-Bethel song, "How awesome is this place! This is none other than the house of God, and this is the gate of heaven" (Genesis 28: 17).[12] Further, learning to love in the manner of Christ includes questioning all notions of belonging: who in fact belongs? Does the stranger in the midst belong? Do the absent belong? Do the different ones belong? The Gospel faithfully lived – and so liturgy – will make clear that this is a house of prayer to and for *all* peoples, not just the "insiders," in fact, here the outcast belongs, and the not-so-like-us belongs.

## A Second Metaphor: *Semillas Besadas*

For the historical farm church's community there was great significance in the choice of trees, mango trees of a specific kind. The trees found in that property, "Espada" and "Coração de Boi," are often very large. Their foliage is rich, forming wide and hospitable canopies that could offer shelter from the heat. Under those trees the community was embraced by the sweet and inviting smell of mangoes. The sturdy trunks were friendly and strong enough to support the ropes that secured the tents and held the hammocks. And the fruits could literally sustain life with the richness of their vitamins and minerals. Indeed they were equally prized for their nutritional value and taste.

The leaves of the trees were very important. Those leaves were good for tea, and for a variety of health remedies: in a paste, for example, they served as balm for wounds, insect bites, and burns. Those leaves were indeed for the healing of many of the ills in the community. Biblical imagery and all manners of associations between leaves of trees planted by the streams, healing of the nations, theology, and eschatological hope were nurtured, mingling and flowing in the life of the community.

In writer Barbara Kingsolver's novel *Animal Dreams*, the author describes a grove of plum trees. In that fictional grove there is a particular tree, we are led to believe, that is extravagantly lovely. This tree produces more fruit than any other around it. The lovely tree is so rich, so attractive in beauty and so productive that it becomes the tree of choice for birds to build their nests, and of course, the most sought after by humans. What is more, not only is this tree of particular significance for a particular community, it feeds and serves as delight to all around, whether they belong or not. The tree is so loved that people come to place gifts on the tree, family tokens left as symbols of hope for special blessings. The tree itself becomes a place of prayer for all who come.

The name the fictional Spanish-speaking community gave this tree was *Semilla Besada*, or "Kissed Seed." According to those in the know, such a tree tapped into the richest veins of water, and the richest nutrients. It received the best sunlight and it lived longer that any other of the trees. There was no questioning the fact that its fruits were by far the most desirable. The other trees around it, says the author, "merely went on living." [13]

No liturgical thinker has spoken more compellingly about trees and metaphors than Gail Ramshaw. Of her passion for trees in general and the tree of life in particular she writes: "I discovered the tree of life in 1975 in a New York art museum. There for the first time I saw Hannah Cohoon's spirit drawing of her vision of July 3, 1854, 'a beautiful Tree, bearing ripe fruit . . . that grows in the Spirit Land'." [14] As she continues to elaborate on trees as Christian symbols and metaphors, Ramshaw's thoughts enrich the story of the gathering place in the farm of Brazil, a "Spirit Land:"

# Ordo: Bath, Word, Prayer, Table

I came to care for living trees because I first cared for the tree of life.

Metaphor pulled me into matter. The images of mythically magical and psychically extraordinary trees in the art in our house, in the museums I visit, and in the religions I study finally focused my attention on the trees in our yard, the trees by the Maine coast, the rainforests upon which our life depends. Such is the power of metaphor, to make us see newly. Metaphor had accomplished its miracle; it transmogrified the commonplace into the splendid.[15]

Does the liturgy lived in our contexts today and the visual story told by our spaces show the *Semilla Besada*, the Gospel of Jesus Christ, to be "for the healing of the nations?" And *all* nations, not just one? What does a liturgical space that visibly displays national or particular ecclesial symbols say? Do spaces with national or denominational symbols speak of a local God, a local blessedness, a local history to the exclusion of all other nations or all other ecclesial communities? Do these things really say of God's house, "The house will be called a house of prayer for all people?" Or are these houses that speak of a parochial God like trees that "merely go on living"?

If we come to worship and leave with the psalmist's song in our heart, "I was glad when they said unto me, 'Let us go to the house of the LORD,'" then we can say that we have gathered under a fruitful tree, delighted in its beauty, tasted of its fruit, and left a token of our life on it. But that token, an "offering of our life" or the offering of "the gifts of the earth," as our liturgy invites us to do, that token has been transformed.[16] In the liturgical *epiclesis* the Holy Spirit of God is invoked upon those gifts, and there, by grace, they are transformed from ordinary things to the splendid, now becoming "the gifts of God for the people of God." And we go forth in the power and in the hope of that gift, able to "see newly," having become what we have heard, and what we have tasted, the Body of Christ, *Semilla Besada*.

## Sunday: the *Dia da Festa*

*Daily Bread* Communally baked bread was symbolic of the life of the congregation in the *Ponto de Encontro*. Each day one group was responsible for the baking of the bread, but the wheat was gathered from a covered bin into which every family or person poured the grain brought from their own places of life. Grain from many hills and valleys poured into that communal bin, and from the many grains loaves were formed and baked, day in day out, common things truly becoming "compressed goodness."[17]

All week the simple daily fare prepared the community for the *Dia da Festa*, Sunday. On Saturday, preparation day, music was rehearsed, candidates for baptism primed, and the whole community involved in that joyous anticipation. The Sunday meal after church was the best of the week. A lamb, each year provided by a different farmer, was the center of the meal, and it was placed in a charcoal pit very early in the day, smells of bread and lamb mingling enticingly all morning. Smells, tastes, sights and sounds remembered in the bodies of many whose sense of God and Church were forged in that place of loveliness. That week seemed to hold the whole of life and all that mattered for the congregation.

*The Word and Baptism* The Word proclaimed in readings and preaching year after year on that Sunday was rich and faithful – and as local as it was global, the Gospel story of Jesus, John, the River, and the Dove always the central reading for the day. That baptismal event's story was recounted year after year, and then re-enacted in the wonderfully celebrated baptism of many. Dripping wet smiling faces and the singing of "Shall We Gather" combined with all other moments to form memories beyond time, rich and deep as life itself, the *passacaglia's* theme inexorably moving the assembly to its life center.

As the congregation waited for the newly baptized to change into dry clothes, there was a time for the call to discipleship, both invitation to coming to Christ and to *testemunhos*. Giving witness to the faith is a rather significant event in Brazilian Baptist life, so at that time all who wished would recount ways in which God's grace had been particularly manifested in their lives during that year. This was also the moment when the mission of the church as it lived dispersed among distant farms was named for all. The building of a small school that was accomplished by some farm families, help given to the poor as farmers took their carts to villages to sell their products, someone whose crops had made it possible to buy a small truck now used to take children from four farms to school, and introduction of families whose house had been built during the week: these were small and large ways life at the gathering place and daily life merged and flowed.

*The Lord's Supper* After the preaching, the baptizing, and the call to discipleship, the *Ceia do Senhor* (the Lord's Supper) was celebrated, the culmination of the whole of the week. The very smell of bread on Sunday took on new meaning. This was the same daily bread familiar to all, but on this day, among all other loaves, there was the *Pão Sagrado* ("Sacred Bread"), baked last. This was brought into the sanctuary enveloped in a beautifully embroidered napkin used exclusively for that purpose, matching the tablecloth, a distinctly Brazilian "Fair Linen," a thing of beauty on the Communion Table. There was grape juice, rare and expensive, not indigenous to that part of the country, most congregants only tasting it in Communion (wine was not to be had, alcoholic drinks not a choice of most evangelicals in Brazil).

# Ordo: Bath, Word, Prayer, Table

*Contradictions* Another memory that persists is that of the role of the deacons: they were responsible for setting up the daily meal table for the community, and they were responsible for collecting the offerings the people brought on Sunday. They were also responsible for setting the Communion Table, preparing the bread (cutting it in small squares), filling up the tiny cups in the trays, and actually serving Communion. Only *they* could perform those tasks. Alas, only *males* were deacons then. More: they were the first to receive the Bread and the Cup, this while they and the pastor – *and only they* – stood around the Table.

Much has changed in that cultural setting since then. But those actions – some of which are still present in many parts of today's church – could lead one to say: if only *all* would be able to come and stand around the table for communion everywhere the Holy Meal is celebrated, and if only no one was excluded from any ministries in the church on the basis of gender or other perceived differences, then – *and only then* – would our liturgical spaces and actions no longer speak of a table for the privileged few. How sad it is that in the central moment of the encounter, when heaven and earth mingle in "compressed goodness," our very spaces and actions work against the *passacaglia's* theme, with dissonant notes negating the centrality, the hospitality, the inclusion, and the sense of the love feast Eucharist means to convey! When will we be brave enough and hungry enough to say to tables of distinction and exclusion, "*Basta!* [18] This is Christ's Table, and all those baptized in the Triune name belong"?

Amidst the beauty and the good things the *Ponto de Encontro* conveyed, all manners of incongruous visual symbols lived side-by-side. Care and non-care; hospitality and exclusion; tiny bits of pre-cut bread hardly speaking of the largesse of God or the oneness of the Body of Christ: "Because there is one loaf, we, many as we are, are one body; for it is one loaf of which we all partake," says Paul to the church in Corinth (1 Cor. 10: 16-17); small individual cups contradicting the theological claims of the common cup of salvation. Eyesight *is* insight.

*Grace* As the meanings of baptism and communion were repeated around the story of Jesus' baptism, in spite of all contradictions, and utterly by the grace of God, the Word became flesh indeed. If Jesus' baptism was identification with the least of these, if Jesus' baptism was more than a ritual of purification, if Jesus' baptism was not only entrance into a community, but a way of living out of the community and entering into the sufferings and oppressions of human life, then there must be something more to what the *Ponto de Encontro* had to say to those who came to the gathering. Meeting and meeting-place said simply, "Live in the manner of Jesus Christ." Otherwise, the place and the time would mean no more than a lovely exercise in community living, inward-turning, in short, a self-gratifying life.

EPIPHANY: THEOLOGY, CULTURE AND THE STARS

One of the leaders of the congregation in this story was a teacher deeply interested in astronomy. The time for the gathering was decided in part due to this interest: the meeting was to occur when the position of the stars and the dry season combined to give the week the probability of clear skies and cloudless days, and the constellation called the Southern Cross would be at its closest for the region. As the conversation continued, the juxtaposition of these natural factors and the liturgical season, Epiphany, became a joyous idea to all involved. As the now retired pastor tells it, "Natural causes and theological reasons simply came together, this by the grace of God."[19]

The Southern Cross, with its four bright starts visible in the southern hemisphere, is a shimmering gift and sign in Brazilian culture and lore. Seen as a sign of the blessedness of the Southern Hemisphere in general and of Brazil in particular, the Southern Cross is present as symbol in a vast array of places in home and national life in that country, for example, in the flag and the coat of arms of Brazil. The starred cross can be seen in the currency of the country, and is sung in many of its folk songs. Mystical power is attributed to that constellation, the relationship between people and the shape of that grouping of stars holding great power to all. That the symbol was not of anyone's making; that the cross was indeed a celestial gift reaching out to all equally is interpreted as particular grace.

As the scattered-congregation gathered during Epiphany, the Southern Cross added to the locality of the meeting, that is to say, this meeting took place in *this* part of the world, in *this* country, in *this* state, in *this* corner of a farm. But it also took place in *this* season, and with *this* assembly. Like Justin's reference place, the baths of Myrtinus named by Lathrop, the *Ponto de Encontro* served as physical turned spiritual point of reference, identifying the assembly as particular, localized in time and place.[20] For Justin and for that Baptist Church of Mato Grosso these were no mere places, but a way of gathering in a particularly ordered pattern that also ordered life.

The language of heaven and sky, sun, moon, and stars, clouds and light plays a large role in Brazilian culture, and often serves as metaphor for hope and for what is good and beautiful in the prayers and the hymnody of Brazil past and present. Thus Epiphany has always been the central event celebrated in churches throughout Latin America. The powerful symbol of wise ones following a star and the revelation and appearance of Christ as Light continue to be of enormous significance in the popular religion, theology, life and liturgy of Brazilians.

In the country where Liberation Theology (more appropriately, theolog*ies*) found a voice, in fact loudly proclaiming God's option in favor of the poor, eschatological hope and vision are the streams

# Ordo: Bath, Word, Prayer, Table

running underneath that foundational insight. A theology of corporate, communal hope undergirds all of Brazilian theological discourses, whether those insights are named in the familiar writings of liberation theologians like Leonard Boff and Paulo Freire, or of more recent theologians such as Rosângela Soares de Oliveira. Professor Rosângela, reflecting on her experiences in such meetings, and pointing to the connections between human gatherings, cosmos and Brazilian ethos writes,

> I shall begin by mentioning encounters. In Latin America, encounters are places where people build up their knowledge together, where experts and ordinary people exchange knowledge, where experiences are shared, where there is space for spirituality, for experiencing ecumenism and for coordinating political action. Sometimes they give a new direction to people's lives, form small support communities, weave tangled lives into the utopia of a new humankind. . . .The integral relationship of women-men-cosmos is remaking the environment for our survival and spirituality.[21]

In a country oppressed by poverty in the midst of such natural wealth and beauty, it is not surprising that it is in community gatherings that the connections between liturgy and the cosmos build up "knowledge together." It is precisely in community that gift-exchange occurs, this "knowing together" shaping visions of a new world (shades of the Dene peoples of Canada spoken of in Lathrop's rich chapter in *Holy People*, "Knowing Something Together"[22]).

An order for a liturgy for Epiphany in a Brazilian publication is revealing. That liturgy is found in the volume *Manual do Culto* prepared by the *Igreja Presbiteriana Independente do Brasil*.[23] The naming of the four movements of the Christian *ordo* in that publication is profoundly significant in the cultural ethos in which these services are lived: for the Gathering, *Reunimo-nos, Atraidos pela Luz* (We Gather, Enticed by the Light); for the Word, *A Palavra nos Ilumina* (The Word Illuminates Us); the Eucharist, *Agradecemos a Manifestação da Luz* (We Give Thanks for the Manifestation of the Light); and for the Sending, *Seguimos a Luz Para o Mundo* (We Follow the Light into the World).

Speaking of the early church's meetings on the "Eighth Day," the Sunday of Christ's revelation, Paul Bradshaw names this day as "The day of the epiphany of the church," something Brazilians can easily grasp:

> All this suggests that Sunday was seen as the day for the manifestation, or epiphany of the Church. During the rest of the week the Church was dispersed or hidden, as its individual members went about their life and work in different places. But on Sunday the Church came together and revealed

itself in the celebration of the eucharist. . . . In this way, they were also laying claim to their place at the Lord's table in the future kingdom of God.[24]

That the community on the farm had chosen as its meeting time the very season of Epiphany; that baptism was celebrated on the day we came to name as "Baptism of the Lord Sunday;" that the whole of the worship space spoke of hope and mission: these things enabled the people to know their place in God's universe. The assembly stands before God and all of humanity, indeed one with the whole of creation, land and trees, animals and birds, streams and mountains, constellations and worlds unknown. But this assembly also pointed away from the meeting. The very openness of the space, its eastern orientation, and the ever-present sight of the water that ran through and out of the sanctuary – all blessed by the presence of the shimmering constellation, gave the church a sense of direction for its journey, and that direction is, simply, "away-from-here."

Says Lathrop in his recent inquiries in the third volume of his trilogy, *Holy Ground: a Liturgical Cosmology*:

> The triune God is our home in the midst of the earth and our connection with away-from-here. The crucified and risen Christ is our sun that does not go down, our light, our green tree. . . . The risen Christ holds the stars in his hand and shines beyond the sun's light. The Spirit's overshadowing wings and this present assembly in the Spirit are our dark night and our place of refuge. [25]

*Music* Folk songs, guitars, drums, other rhythmic instruments, and Brazilian flutes marked the times around the common fire of the community's gathering. But alas, these were not instruments – or musical styles – seen, heard, felt, nor welcomed into the Sunday gathering in the shed. There, only the portable harmonium would do. Church music and local cultural context were yet sound years apart. It was many years before the indigenous peoples of Brazil found their voice in the singing and the music-making of church, years before Brazilian musical colors voicing faith in the richness of the country's language were deemed as "proper."

In fact, it was a long time before evangelicals in Brazil meshed historical hymnody inherited from other lands to their own, thus giving witness to the Gospel both in context and in the accents provided by the cross-cultural borrowings of expressions of faith. Organ and *Birimbau*, a Brazilian one-stringed instrument, now mesh and sing together of grace in many liturgical spaces. [26]

But here is the "even so" gift. Musical instruments and/or musical styles were not the central elements of the worship life of that community. The singing assembly was. Today one finds many naves visually and audibly dominated by projecting screens, countless sound gadgets, and electronic instruments as in the church in Brasilia. In fact, a pastor in the Pacific Northwest of the United States recently and proudly proclaimed that his church had placed the font in the basement; it was brought up "only on days we need it" for "we need all the space we can get for the band" – a striking lack of grasp of what is essential and unfortunate misuse of musical elements in the liturgy.

At the farm place it was the breath in song from the people, and the humanity and beauty of the voices that gave sound to the faith, the hopes and the visions of the community. No instruments drowned out the voices. No array of microphones and other electronic media dominated or diminished the central symbols of the faith.

### EVERYWHERE THIS RIVER GOES

Not unlike the *kivas*, the holy spaces for the ceremonial life of the Pueblo Indian peoples in the United States, the place on a farm was a space that told a story, and a story-space that identified a people and its mission. That assembly's version of the *passacaglia* in the heartland of Brazil many years ago could do no less than become a "bearer of symbolic meaning" as Lathrop says of the *kiva*:

> The Christian assembly around bread and wine is not unlike the kiva. Here, too, is the domestic – storytelling, a meal – stylized and simplified. Here too, ages of meaning are focused in simple objects – bread and wine – making them a connection to human history (the ancestors) and to a sense of cosmic order (the powers of earth and sky). Before the liturgy even begins, as the food is brought and set out on an offertory table or credence or prothesis, a Christian may rightly behold the loaf and think, 'Here is all human life,' or see the wine, thinking, 'Here is the universe itself.'[27]

Among the many volumes written on liturgical space there seems to be a growing number of publications particularly concerned with the baptismal spaces of the church, revealing a much needed reflection on the nature of baptism. That is only appropriate: it is, after all, baptismal theology and ecclesiology that gives birth to all other understandings of church and mission. In the foreword to *A Place for Baptism*, Mark Searle says, "Assembled together, we *are* a sacrament; and the things we use, the times at which we meet, the places in which we celebrate, all come to share in the value of the sign. . . .This is no ordinary place, but the scene of our being made over in the likeness of Christ."[28] This

*Ponto de Encontro* was, in a deep sense, an ordinary place. But, by the grace of God, that very ordinariness was transformed into an extraordinary space, in fact a room *for* a view, where the baptized were clothed with the likeness of Christ.

The third year of life in the *Ponto de Encontro* compelled someone to write some words on the back of the sign at the entrance gate, *Entrada de Serviço*, literally "Service Entrance." Finally, the *passacaglia* ends where it will begin anew, a never-ending cycle: they came to go. Baptism – and the place for baptism – is the entryway into the exits of life among the poor and oppressed, from death to life, from *here* to *there*, from a gathering to the scattering, from the assembled to the *dis*-assembled.

With these images in mind, let us consider some suggestions for liturgical spaces. These suggestions only address the *ecumenically held essentials* in which the *passacaglia* sounds:

*-Let the space sing of the centrality of the assembly.* Most of our spaces today speak of the assembly as spectators with pews or chairs rigidly set in lines as in a theater. How could we work in existing spaces to reorient that image? Is it possible to change the seating arrangement in some way as to make clear that the assembly is to be gathered around and as integral part of the places for Baptism, the Word, and the Meal? Consider issues of access to all who would come, young or old, and with different degrees of abilities and ways to get there, whether walking or moving through assisting instruments such as wheelchairs. Consider accessibility and hospitality in terms of the assembly and of the *dis*-assembled of the world. Build it near centers of need. Make the space inviting and enticing so that the real source of life of the Church, Jesus Christ, is recognized as the theme and the reason for the gathering and the building. Let us make the assembly's place strong and clear.

*-Let the space sing of the meaning of baptism.* Small fonts covered, invisible, inaccessible, or with minimal amounts of water, or worse, dry, contradict the theology of baptism. Make it as large as possible, with as much water – moving water – as possible. Place it in the entrance and exit place, the narthex (or *Paradisium*, paradise). Think not just of a baptismal font or pool, but of a baptismal *space* around which the assembly may physically gather, even if it has to process to it for baptism. "Shall We Gather at the River?" What a wondrous image! Let it be the place from which charges and blessings are given, and from where Catechumen – and all seekers – are sent. Let it be the place that says "from here we come, from here we go." Place some writing on the exit, and let the exit words or sign say, *Service Entrance*. If a pool that enables immersion or submersion is possible, make it so; consider its shape as revelatory of meaning, death and life, entrance and exit, beginning and reorientation, womb and tomb visually expressed. Let us make the place of baptism strong and clear.

# Ordo: Bath, Word, Prayer, Table

*-Let the space sing of the meaning of the Word.* An ambo/pulpit is the place from which the Word is proclaimed in readings and in sermon or homily. Make its meaning clear. Make its function self-evident and readily grasped: not two places (lectern and pulpit), but one single, simple place. Make it large enough to hold a large Bible. Place it as near the assembly as physically possible, perhaps on a platform, with a visual sense of connectedness to people, baptism, and meal table. In churches where the parity of Word and Sacrament is claimed, make the two places connect in texture, scale, and placement. In churches where pulpits are exaggeratedly elevated, so high as to be the center of the space and the liturgy itself, consider a way of reshaping the space to make it more true to the meaning of the Word read and proclaimed in assembly. Let us make the place of the Word clear.

*-Let the space sing of the meaning of the Eucharist.* An altar/table is simply that: the assembly's meal place, a table. A block of marble or concrete could hardly express that theological meaning. Locate it so that it is at the center of the space, perhaps in the same continuum with the place of baptism and the place of the word. Make it speak of the theology of the Lord's Supper the particular community claims. Make its meaning and place completely present to the whole assembly, visible, accessible, in the same level with the assembly, or, if slightly elevated, build a ramp to it so all can come unencumbered. Leave it uncluttered, unfenced, un-railed, a simple table for a meal to be set in the middle of the gathering space, a table around which all may stand. For Protestants and Free Church gatherings, place Bibles, flowers and other such elements elsewhere, not on the Communion Table. Each vessel and each symbol should speak its own language and its own message. Make the place for the Bread of Life and the Cup of Salvation strong and clear.

*-Let all that is secondary point to what is essential.* That is, let the secondary *be* secondary. Banners and other forms of visual art ought to serve as icons, windows to the divine and the central things that speak of the divine. Pay particular attention to seasonal art, but be wary lest central symbols be distorted. For example, emptying the font or pool for Lent makes the season take priority over the centrality of baptism. But these waters, we say in our ecumenically embraced sense of baptism, never cease to flow, and they are timeless and seasonless in meaning. Instruments ought not to be the visual center of the gathering – nor should they cover the central symbols, or otherwise direct the eyes of those who come away from what matters most. Let us make the things that are secondary serve to strengthen the central things of the liturgy.

The *passacaglia* of the *ordo* moves on. The music is lived outside the assembly's house. And as its tones flow outwardly, wherever they go, wherever they are heard, everything will live.

ENDNOTES

[1] Bishops' Committee on the Liturgy, *Environment and Art in Catholic Worship* (Washington: USCC, 1978), 39, 41

[2] Gordon W. Lathrop, *Holy People: a Liturgical Ecclesiology* (Minneapolis: Fortress Press, 1999), 43

[3] "Canticle of Zechariah (*Benedictus*)" Text: English Language Liturgical Consultation. Music: Howard Hughes, S.M. copyright 1979, GIA Publications, Inc. in *The Psalter: Psalms and Canticles for Singing*. (Louisville: Westminster/John Knox Press, 1993), 160.

[4] Edward Foley, *From Age to Age* (Chicago: Liturgy Training Publications, 1991), 29. *Didascalia* quote translated by R. H. Conolly.

[5] Don Saliers, *Worship as Theology: a Foretaste of Glory Divine* (Nashville: Abingdon Press, 1994), 160.

[6] Gordon W. Lathrop, *Holy Things: a Liturgical Theology* (Minneapolis: Fortress Press, 1993), 107.

[7] Margaret R. Miles, *Images as Insight: Visual Understanding in Western Christianity and Secular Culture* (Boston: Beacon Press, 1985), 3.

[8] Lathrop, *Holy Things*, 114.

[9] Saliers, 158.

[10] See, for example, Marchita Mauck's *Shaping a House for the Church* (Chicago: Liturgy Training Publications, 1990).

[11] David Whyte, *The House of Belonging* (Langley, WA: Many Rivers Press, 1998), 6.

[12] For a glorious interpretation of Jacob's experience in Bethel, the idea of God as a "holy place" for the people of Israel, and the Gospel's Christ as the "holy place" for Christians, see Lathrop's history-making volume *Holy Ground: A Liturgical Cosmology*. (Minneapolis: Fortress Press, 2003), particularly pp. 45-50.

[13] Barbara Kingsolver, *Animal Dreams* (New York: HarperCollins Publisher, 1990), 49.

[14] Gail Ramshaw, *Under the Tree of Life: the Religion of a Feminist Christian* (Akron, Ohio: OSL Publications, 2003), 39.

[15] Ramshaw, 179.

[16] Words of invitation preceding the offertory in the *Book of Common Worship* ( Louisville: Westminster/John Knox Press, 1993), 67.

[17] Lathrop, *Holy Things*, 91.

[18] "It is enough!"

[19] Recorded interview with the Reverend Altino Vasconcelos, Guararapes, São Paulo, Brazil, Summer, 1993.

[20] Lathrop, *Holy Things*, 109-110.

[21] Ofelia Ortega, Editor, *Women's Visions: Theological Reflection, Celebration, and Action* (Geneva: World Council of Churches Publication, 1995), 65-75.

[22] Lathrop, *Holy People*, 101-116.

[23] *Manual do Culto*. Comissão Especial da Igreja Presbiteriana Independente do Brasil, E.G. Faria, Editor. São Paulo, 1998. This volume used as its model the *Book of Common Worship*, the 1993 rich, ecumenically-produced volume published by the Presbyterian Church (USA) (Louisville: Westminster/John Knox Press, 1993). The Brazilian volume includes liturgies that are particular to the context of the liturgical life of Brazilian faith and culture, such as the rich New Year's Eve *Vigilia*, and the liturgy for Epiphany named above.

[24] Paul Bradshaw, *Early Christian Worship: A Basic Introduction to Ideas and Practice* (Collegeville: The Liturgical Press, 1996), 78.

[25] Lathrop, *Holy Ground*, 162.

[26] For further comments on contextualization issues, see excerpts of the "Nairobi Statement on Worship and Culture: Contemporary Challenges and Opportunities" in Appendix 2 of Lathrop's *Holy People*, 233-236.

[27] Lathrop, *Holy Things*, 93.

[28] Regina Kuehn, *A Place for Baptism* (Chicago: Liturgy Training Publications, 1992), iv.

# NINE

## Liturgy: The *Ordo* of Time

*Dwight W. Vogel*

*Time, like an ever rolling stream . . .*[1]

Liturgical time is Paschal time. To understand liturgical time, we must stand in the baptismal waters that, "like an ever rolling stream," mark our identity, our community, and our mission. To live in Paschal time is to participate, in the here-and-now, in the *Pascha* of Christ that centers in his death and resurrection. To be incorporated into that death and resurrection, however, is to include, on the one hand, creation and incarnation (including the life and ministry of Jesus) and, on the other hand, the gift of the Holy Spirit, and eschatological hope. It is the whole story – from creation through incarnation to consummation – in which we participate, a dynamic reality aptly spoken of as *the Paschal mystery*.

For Gordon Lathrop, "time belongs to the core structures of Christian worship."[2] Yet he warns us against understanding liturgical time as "a kind of comprehensive temporal meta-narrative that competes with ordinary experiences of time and draws us into a salvific time-beyond-time."[3] He identifies three forms of this misunderstanding:[4] appealing to *memory*, where liturgical time is understood as an invitation to go back to Bible times in our imagination and find salvation there; appealing to *mystery*, where liturgical time can be seen as incorporating us in a time-beyond-time, a sacred and mythic time that saves all time; appealing to *fantasy*, where liturgical time is experienced as imaginative "play" in which we see the world and ourselves in a way different from the here and now.[5] On the contrary, Lathrop asserts, "classic Christian liturgy is held here and now, inviting us to know where we are and what time it is, as we are gathered before God on holy ground."[6]

# Ordo: Bath, Word, Prayer, Table

In liturgical time, memory, mystery, and imagination all have appropriate roles to play: in paschal time memory does not seek to reconstruct the past. As *anamnesis*, it proclaims the present presence and efficacy of that which the past event also embodied. Mystery points to the *presence* of the Holy One among us, and our relationship with that Presence. Robert Hovda writes of liturgy as "kingdom play" in which we "relax the tight grip of the status quo, so that people can move and breathe and envision alternatives."[7] To these, Lathrop adds *metaphor* as a basic tool for liturgical time. In metaphor, we intentionally use the "wrong" word in order to affirm a present truth in a new way, thus re-characterizing and revealing truth about God and the worshipping assembly.[8]

Liturgical time invites us "to see again the ways in which human beings know something of who they are and where they are by knowing what time it is."[9] In *anamnesis*, something from the past becomes active in the present, transfiguring and transforming it. In liturgical time, Jesus' words from the first century, "This is my body," are experienced as a present reality. In *prolepsis*, the future "invades" the present, transfiguring and transforming it. The way we envision God's future realm becomes embodied in the way we live out our prayer "Your kingdom come." In an *epiclesis*, we pray that the Holy Spirit will come upon us and that which we offer up, so that *anamnesis* and *prolepsis* may happen in us here and now.[10]

Liturgical time is embodied in an *ordo*, a basic pattern of Christian liturgy.[11] The depth dynamic of this pattern is grounded in the Paschal mystery. Lathrop insists that it is also characterized by the way in which the old and familiar is juxtaposed with the new and different so that our usual way of understanding is "broken" and the transforming power of the Holy Spirit comes to "make all things new."[12] We will seek to discern these characteristics in the depth dynamics[13] of the basic pattern of liturgical time in the Church's life.

## LORD'S DAY

Central to the *ordo* of liturgical time is the gathering of the Christian community on the Lord's Day. As the *Constitution on the Liturgy* of Vatican II affirms: "The Lord's Day is the original feast day ...." Indeed, it is "the foundation and kernel of the whole liturgical year."[14] This assembly is perhaps more accurately termed a "convocation," for it has a deep sense of being "called together." Both "gathering" and "being gathered" are juxtaposed in the gathering that takes place on the "first day" of the week, the day of the resurrection in all four gospels (Matthew 28:1ff.; Mark 16:1ff.; Luke 24:1ff.; John 20:1ff.). Adolf Adam notes that

It was also the preferred day for his appearances to his disciples . . ., the day on which he bestowed on them the promised gift of the Holy Spirit . . ., and the day on which he sent them forth, in the power of the Spirit, as the messengers and ministers of salvation. The first day of the week was thus singled out by Christ himself and set apart as the day of the resurrection and the sending of the Spirit. It stood out in the minds of the early Christians as "the day which the Lord has made" (Psalm 118:24). On this day the community gathered . . . "to break bread" (Acts 20:7).[15]

It was an inconvenient time, a work day for the first Christians. Yet, alongside the old Sabbath synagogue services, we find juxtaposed this "new thing," a witness to the presence of the Risen Christ among them. The content of this gathering juxtaposes the *synaxis* (with its readings from scripture, psalms, and prayers), reflective of the synagogue structure, with a meal (broken from its place as a home festival and transformed into a new community context).

This gathering "on the first day" is also understood by the early Church to be a gathering "on the eighth day," layering meanings relating to the completion of the creation and the new creation grounded in Jesus Christ with the eschatological hope proleptically looking forward to and participating in God's ultimate kin-dom. It is a day that human cycles of time cannot capture, yet by its very presence within time, time itself is transposed into a new key, marked by the presence of grace.[16] By its very nature, then, gathering on the Lord's Day juxtaposes past and future, memory and hope, in the context of the whole of the Paschal mystery. So Mark Searle observes, "the baptismal themes of new creation, liberation from slavery, through participation in the death and resurrection of Jesus and being sealed with his Spirit, are precisely those which our tradition has associated with Sunday."[17]

As in the first century it was counter-cultural to gather for worship through word and meal on a workday, so in today's world, liturgical time insists on the Lord's Day as the first day of the week in tension with cultural perception of it as the last day of the weekend. The counterpoint of Christian time is that

after the week is over, before the new week begins, on a day all Christianity has set, at a time my community has determined, I come into church. Just by doing that I am given a rhythm in time, a way to mark change and flow in my days, a simple communal calendar in which to insert my own experience of time.[18]

# Ordo: Bath, Word, Prayer, Table

Because the Christian faith emerged in first century Judaism, a day was understood as lasting from evening to evening. Thus, what we think of as the evening before the Lord's Day, early Christians understood to be part of the next day. Using our current language then, Saturday evening is liturgically part of Sunday. The importance of recognizing this will be seen as we look at both Daily Prayer and the Liturgical Year.

In the *ordo* of liturgical time, the Lord's Day juxtaposes the old and familiar with the new and different so that our usual way of understanding is broken open and the transforming power of the Holy Spirit comes to "make all things new." What was new and unusual for first century Christians, however, may become old and familiar for us. Addressing the obvious so that we become aware of the depth dynamic of the Lord's Day is an ongoing challenge for pastoral liturgical practice. Yet we do well to be reminded that gathering on the Lord's Day is not primarily for the purpose of "producing meanings" but rather, as Nathan Mitchell says, "to produce a ritually inscribed body (both personal and corporate) that knows how, liturgically, to 'do' a redeemed world."[19]

## DAILY PRAYER[20]

The apostle Paul writes: "Rejoice always, pray without ceasing, give thanks in all circumstances; for this is the will of God in Christ Jesus for you. Do not quench the Spirit" (1 Thessalonians 5:16-19). However, we also know that focused times of prayer are essential, for in them we are formed in such a way that we can live into Paul's admonition. Setting aside times for prayer was already part of the spirituality of our Jewish forbears in the faith, for in the psalms we read: "Seven times a day I praise you." (Psalm 119:164a) Patterns for daily prayer were inherited and continued by the New Testament church, and although set patterns took centuries to develop, the punctuation of each day with prayer is present in the Church's life from the beginning. With regard to the experience of the early church, Robert Taft observes:

> Christians by faith had the supreme joy of knowing that they lived a new life in Christ, a life of love shared with all of the same faith. What could have been more normal then, than for those who were able to gather at daybreak to turn the first thoughts of the day to this mystery of their salvation and to praise and glorify God for it? And at the close of the day they came together once again to ask forgiveness for the failings of the day and to praise God once more for his mighty deeds. In this way the natural rhythm of time was turned into a hymn of praise to God and a proclamation before the world of faith in his salvation in Christ.[21]

This manifestation of daily prayer is not a sporadic pattern of prayer dependent on a given cultural and temporal spiritual milieu. It is a form of prayer shared throughout Christian history by East and West, by Roman Catholics and Eastern Orthodox, by Anglicans, Lutherans, Presbyterians, and Methodists among others. Forms of daily prayer that embody this historic and ecumenical pattern can be called the "daily office." As Robert Taft observes, the daily office has been there in one form or another "from the early centuries until our own day. That is a very respectable track record, one that the Church could not ignore and remain true to its heritage."[22]

Yet for many Christians, attention to corporate services of the Church has been focused primarily on services of Word and Table, and largely on those services that take place on the Lord's Day. This relative inattention to the Daily Office is quite different from the experience of the ancient church. Take for example the *Apostolic Constitutions*, written in Greek around 380 by a Syrian living near Antioch, in which we read:

> Do not be neglectful of yourselves nor rob the savior of his members nor divide his body nor scatter his members, nor prefer the needs of this life to the Word of God, but assemble each day morning and evening, singing psalms and praying in the Lord's houses . . . . But especially on the Sabbath and the Lord's Day of the resurrection of the Lord, meet even more diligently, sending up praise to God.[23]

Both daily services of prayer and Lord's Day services were important for the ancient church. But over the centuries, that balance has eroded. While never entirely forsaken by the Church at large, and consistently maintained in one form or another by religious orders, the role of the Daily Office in the life of the whole Church has been severely limited. Current attention to the reclamation of the Daily Office is evident in an article by Arthur Paul Boers in *The Christian Century*: "Reviving an Ancient Practice: The Office of Prayer."[24]

The Daily Office has to do with a daily pattern of prayer, rather than a weekly one focused on the Lord's Day, or a yearly one focused on Christmas, Easter and Pentecost. However, not just any pattern will do. Neither private or personal "devotions" on the one hand, nor corporate "prayer meetings" or "group devotions" on the other, automatically qualify. Rather, the Daily Office reflects the historic prayer of the Church related to "canonical hours" – those specified times which are a measuring stick (a "canon") for our prayer life together. Furthermore, both this historic pattern and the services

# Ordo: Bath, Word, Prayer, Table

within it are spoken of as an "office." An office is a task or responsibility entrusted to us. It is not something we can choose or not on the basis of our preferences and feelings at the moment.

The historical development of the times for, and names of, the various offices is complex and conditioned by many factors. As we look at the *ordo* of liturgical time here, we will follow two cues. One is found in Psalm 119:164, the text cited above, which reads: "Seven times a day I praise you." The number seven is symbolic of completeness, or wholeness. Thus, having seven offices should remind us that all of life is to be prayer.

Our historical cue comes from Basil the Great in the fourth century who lays out the pattern of the seven offices in this way:

> In the morning [we pray] so that the first movements of the soul and mind may be consecrated to God, and nothing else be taken into consideration before we have been delighted by the thought of God . . . Again at the third hour we must stand up to pray . . . recalling the gift of the Spirit given to the apostles at the third hour (Acts 2:15). . . . And we judge prayer to be necessary at the sixth hour, in imitation of the saints who say: "Evening and morning and at noon I will speak and declare and he shall hear my voice" (Ps. 54:17). . . . The ninth [hour] was handed down to us as necessary for prayer by the apostles themselves in Acts where it is related that "Peter and John went up to the temple at the ninth hour of prayer" (Acts 3:11). And when the day is finished, thanksgiving should be offered for what has been given us during the day or for what we have done rightly and confession made of what we have failed to do . . . And again at the beginning of the night we ask that our rest may be without offence . . . And Paul and Silas have handed on to us midnight as necessary for prayer, as the story of Acts proves, saying: "And at midnight Paul and Silas praised God" (Acts 16:25).[25]

Here we have the two offices most often prayed by a gathered community (Morning and Evening Prayer) — sometimes called "cathedral offices" or "people's offices;" three offices during the day (mid-morning, mid-day, and mid-afternoon prayer) and "bedtime prayer" from the monastic tradition, and something already present in the life of the early church, the Vigil. These seven offices, penetrating the day with prayer, form a pattern for the Daily Office:

> Morning Prayer (*Matins* or *Lauds*)
> Mid-morning Prayer (*Terce*)
> Mid-day Prayer (*Sext*)

> Mid-afternoon Prayer (*None*—rhymes with "own")
> Evening Prayer (Vespers or Evensong)
> Night Prayer (*Compline*)
> Vigil

However, when we speak of Daily Prayer as part of the *ordo* of liturgical time, we are not necessarily referring to this particular pattern, but to the underlying experience of the Church that daily prayer, seen as the prayer of the Church and not as individual private devotions, is part of the basic cadence of time kept by the Church. What is more important than the number of offices each day is that these times of prayer be unhurried so that, as Romano Guardini puts it, "that which has been heard or read has time to cease echoing and to sink into the mind."[26]

### EVENING PRAYER

The evening office has three names: evening prayer, vespers, and (because it is frequently sung) evensong. It is the most fully developed of the ancient offices, with the possible exception of a vigil prior to a festival or holy day. For our Jewish forbearers in the faith and hence the early Christian church, a day began at dusk. The Daily Office thus begins with evening prayer, just as we noted above that the week begins with Saturday evening, not Sunday morning.

In the third century Cyprian wrote: "At sunset and the passing of the day it is necessary to pray. For since Christ is the true sun and the true day, when we pray and ask, as the sun and the day of the world recede, that the light may come upon us again, we pray for the coming of Christ, which provides us with the grace of eternal light."[27]

Even before Christian prayer used a service of light, rituals of lighting the evening lamps were already present in the culture. It was necessary, of course, in order to see, and it was not as simple as flipping a switch. Light was received gratefully, and greeted "Hail, good light!" or "Hail, friendly light!" Taft speaks of the entrance of the light as "a baptized pagan rite"[28] but it is clear that even before there was a formal service, family piety in Christian homes would greet the evening lamp with praise for Christ, the light of the world.

By the seventh century in Spain, the light ritual was called the "oblation of light" and involved elevating a lighted candle before the altar. This was accompanied by a proclamation and response which come amazingly close to the dialogue for the Entrance of the Light we use today: "Light and peace in Jesus Christ!" "Thanks be to God!"[29]

# Ordo: Bath, Word, Prayer, Table

The *Phos hilaron* ("joyful light") or evening hymn was also known in ancient times as a *eucharistia,* a thanksgiving for the light. Basil already knew it as an ancient part of the tradition in the fourth century: "We cannot say who was the father of the words of the thanksgiving for the light," he writes, "but the people utter the ancient formula, and . . . were never thought impious by anyone."[30]

The resonance between the service of light and baptism is often overlooked. For those who have celebrated an Easter Vigil, lighting the vesper candle resonates with the lighting of the Paschal candle at the first service of Easter. Indeed, there is good reason to believe that the service of light in the Easter vigil derives from the *lucernarium* of vespers, not, as we might suppose, the other way around.[31] Moreover, in the early Church, baptism was called *phôtismos* or *phôtisma*, that is, "illumination" and those to be baptized were known as the *illuminandi*.[32] At the lighting of the vesper light, we do well to remember our baptism and be thankful! Since the time of the ancient church, there has also been an eschatological dimension here, for we are reminded of the Johannine vision of the Lamb as the eternal lamp of the heavenly city, the sun that never sets.[33]

By the fourth century, vespers was a time to "review and conclude the day, thanking God for graces received, begging pardon for faults committed, and requesting protection from sin and danger throughout the coming night . . . [it] continued to share with the newer compline its original purpose as a service of thanksgiving, examination of conscience, and forgiveness, . . . [incorporating] such classic cathedral elements as the *lucernarium* with hymn, Psalm 141 with incense, and intercessions."[34]

It is interesting to note that somehow the Daily Office escaped the great medieval and reformation fixation on guilt. While bits of confession may appear here and there in the other offices, it is only in Vespers and Compline that Confession and Pardon are an essential part of the office. This is a spiritually healthy approach. It is in the evening, as we reflect on the past day, that we must be honest before God.

There are some who are convinced that preaching is out of place in the Daily Office; it is primarily a service of prayer and contemplation. There is much to be said for such an approach, especially in a Protestant religious culture which places the sermon (and rarely a brief one at that) as the most important element in worship. Yet we must recognize that the Church survived homilies in connection with Vigils, Morning and Evening Prayer, both in the early church[35] and in Anglican practice where "Morning Prayer with Sermon" was a prevalent Sunday morning pattern. A homily can replace or supplement a reading to the benefit of the gathered community, providing the preacher knows that the preaching is to serve the office and our capacity to pray it and not that the office exists for the sake of the sermon, and, one supposes, the preacher! Brevity and relevance to the office determine whether a homily is appropriate or not.

On the evening before or the evening of a holy day or festival, a gathered community may use more scripture, sing as much of the office as possible, and add other appropriate elements to the office. In such circumstances, we speak of "Solemn Vespers." Here the word "solemn" does not mean gloomy or dismal, the connotation it tends to have today. Rather, to use words from *Webster's Collegiate Dictionary*, it means "full," "sumptuous," "splendid," "awe-inspiring," "deeply earnest." Thus, we used to hear of "the solemnization of matrimony." The synonym of "solemnize" is "celebration," so perhaps we would communicate more clearly if we spoke of such services as "The Celebration of Vespers" – but that gets us into trouble because "celebration" has come to be associated with happy joy, and that is not quite right either.

The traditional canticle for Evening Prayer is the *Magnificat* – Mary's song found in Luke 1:46-55. Gail Ramshaw describes it as "that psalm-like praise of the God who turns the established order upside down," while at the same time "asking God to remember the promise of mercy made to our ancestors" and pleading "for all the lowly and hungry of the world."[36] Praise is juxtaposed with lament, memory with hope, thanksgiving with intercession as the evening shadows fall.

### Morning Prayer

In *The Apostolic Tradition* (c. 215 C.E., attributed by earlier scholarship to Hippolytus), morning and evening prayer have a paschal orientation, nightfall and sunrise being metaphors of the dying and rising of Christ.[37] Clement, Origen and Tertullian related this to Christ as the sun of justice and the light of the world.[38] For the Eastern church in the third and fourth centuries, "the rising sun and the new day with its change from darkness to light recalled the resurrection from the dead of Christ, Sun of Justice."[39]

In the twentieth century, Dietrich Bonhoeffer recalls similar themes when he writes:

> The early morning belongs to the Church of the risen Christ. At the break of light it remembers the morning on which death and sin lay prostrate in defeat and new life and salvation were given to [hu]mankind. What do we today, who no longer have any fear or awe of night, know of the great joy that our forefathers and the early Christians felt every morning at the return of light? If we were to learn again something of the praise and adoration that is due the triune God at break of day, God the Father and Creator, who has preserved our life through the dark night and waken us to a new day,

# Ordo: Bath, Word, Prayer, Table

God the Son and Saviour, who conquered death and hell for us and dwells in our midst as Victor, God the Holy Spirit, who pours the bright gleam of God's Word into our hearts at the dawn of day, driving away all darkness and sin and teaching us to pray aright – then we would also begin to sense something of the joy that comes when night is past.[40]

The morning office begins with Psalm 51:15: "O Lord, open my lips, and my mouth shall proclaim your praise." When a time of silence has been kept from the previous office, these words have added significance as we "break the silence" with a prayer for praise. In any event, every morning we break the silence of sleep. Most of the prayers we pray are corporate: we say "we" and "us" even when we are praying alone. Here, however, we are reminded that the Lord breaks our silence and enables us to speak in praise of God and in communion with one another.

From the beginning, the Psalter has been the heart of the prayer of the daily office. The Roman office, following Vatican II, abandoned the monastic pattern of continuous psalmody (praying through the entire psalter from beginning to end) and adopted the cathedral approach of selecting psalms related to the hour of the office.

The morning canticle is the song of Zechariah, known as The *Benedictus*. Indeed, the use of psalms and the evangelical canticles have sometimes been the only scripture used in the Daily Office. Even when that is so, these songs from Luke proclaim the gospel to us day after day, week after week, year after year, in ways that work to incorporate us into the Paschal mystery.

### VIGIL

The Vigil Office joins Morning and Evening Prayer as having been both a people's or cathedral office and a part of the monastic tradition. Even a brief look at the first six centuries makes clear that "vigil" is a term used for not one, but for several kinds of night offices, distinguished by frequency or time of observance, even though the structure remains much the same.[41] Without examining all the variations, let us note the following forms of the Vigil:

1. A midnight office.
2. An all-night vigil.
3. A "resurrection vigil" on the eve before the Lord's Day.
4. A vigil in connection with a holy day.

*1. A midnight office*

By the fourth century, the Cappadocian monastics had a midnight vigil office.[42] The pre-Constantinian church related night prayer to the watch of the virgins awaiting the coming of the bridegroom, as well as the unceasing praise of the angels which we will share.[43] In addition, a text (sometimes in years past attributed to Hippolytus) reads:

> For the elders who gave us the tradition taught us that at that hour all creation is still for a moment, to praise the Lord; stars, trees, waters stop for an instant, and all the host of angels . . . praise God with the souls of the righteous in that hour. That is why believers should take good care to pray at this hour. Bearing witness to this, the Lord says thus, "Lo, about midnight a shout was made . . . saying Lo, the bridegroom comes; rise to meet him."[44]

These themes (the praise of all creation and eschatological expectation) are particularly transparent when the Vigil is observed as a midnight office.

*2. An all-night vigil*

Cassian describes a monastic all-night vigil in Bethlehem on Fridays in commemoration of the passion, beginning with vespers.[45] But it is with Ambrose of Milan that all-night vigils became a people's office. In Holy Week of 385 A.D. the Empress Justina wanted the basilica for the use of the Arians. When Ambrose refused, imperial troops kept Ambrose and his congregation confined for three days. Paulinus writes that "it was in this time that antiphons, hymns and vigils first began to be celebrated in the Church of Milan . . . [a practice] that remains to this day not only in that Church but indeed throughout almost all the provinces of the West."[46] Sometimes this all-night vigil was broken up into little night offices (akin to the little diurnal offices we will examine below) called "nocturns." An all-night vigil, whether kept by the whole community or sequentially by its members, embodies the same basic themes as the midnight office.

*3. A "resurrection vigil" on the eve before the Lord's Day*

By the fourth century, as Egeria and the *Apostolic Constitutions* report, both Jerusalem and Antioch had a weekly resurrection vigil as a people's office before the Lord's Day.[47] These pre-eucharistic vigils consisted of vespers extended by the use of multiple lections, responsories and prayers, with particular emphasis on the readings from scripture.[48] The Lord's Day deserves special attention

# Ordo: Bath, Word, Prayer, Table

in the Daily Office, and we do well to remind ourselves of the resurrection vigils of the early church in our Saturday evening prayers.

### 4. A vigil in connection with a holy day

A baptismal vigil, originating in the Easter Vigil, came to be celebrated on the eve of Christmas, Epiphany and Pentecost when those became occasions for baptism. This vigil was also an extension of vespers, including the *lucernarium* (light ritual) and numerous Scripture lections read in the nave while baptizing was taking place in a separate baptistry.[49] From these great festival vigils has come the practice of preparing for a significant holy day with a vigil.

Whereas in the third century *Apostolic Tradition*, morning and evening prayer have a paschal orientation, symbolic of the dying and rising of Christ, the night hours have an eschatological perspective, looking to the *parousia* and the resurrection of the dead.[50] Cyprian, writing around 250 CE writes:

> So let us who are always in Christ, that is, in the light, not cease praying even at night. This is how the widow Anna, always praying and keeping vigil, persevered in deserving well of God, as is written in the gospel: "She did not leave the temple, serving with fasting and prayers night and day" (Luke 2:37) . . . Let us not be hindered by the darkness which we have escaped, let there be no loss of prayers in the night hours.[51]

The canticle for the Vigil is the *Te Deum Laudamus*. In the middle ages, the *Te Deum Laudamus* was attributed to saints Ambrose and Augustine, along with the legend that it was improvised spontaneously and antiphonally by the two at the time of Augustine's baptism.[52] While that claim remains historically unsubstantiated, it is not difficult to imagine the two of them, both gifted in the use of language and filled with the Holy Spirit, either composing the text on the spot or improvising on an earlier text. Other sources attribute the text to a fourth century Bishop, Niceat (or Nicetas) of Remesiana, and that is probably more historically accurate.

A detailed and thorough study by Kähler concludes that the *Te Deum* originated before the middle of the fourth century as the preface, *Sanctus*, and post-sanctus prayer of an old Latin mass of the Easter Vigil which was, of course, a baptismal mass.[53] Without mentioning any author or source, a number of early texts cite it only as the "Hymn in Honor of the Holy Trinity."[54] St. Benedict directed its use at the Vigil, with special reference to Sundays and festivals, a practice followed by both the Roman and Sarum Brevaries, except that it was to be suppressed during Advent and Lent. The 1549 *Book of Common Prayer* appoints it to be used "daily throughout the year except in Lent." In 1552 that exception was removed, but common practice for most communities of prayer is to "fast" from its use during Lent.[55]

In the *Te Deum Laudamus*, the significance of the Vigil office becomes clear. In this office, the prayer of the Church through all times and places is joined with the praise of earth and all stars, as well as the heavenly host:[56] "... we praise you ... we acclaim you ... all creation worships you;" "to you all angels, all the powers of heaven ... sing in endless praise." The opening lines of this "preface" move us to the great *Sanctus* of the seventh and eighth lines in words which resonate with our eucharistic feasts:

"Holy, holy, holy Lord, God of power and might,
heaven and earth are full of your glory."

Then, lest we assume that only those of this particular time and place are the Church, we affirm the praise of "the glorious company of the apostles, the noble fellowship of the prophets, and the white robed army of martyrs" and "the holy Church throughout the world" before breaking into a great Trinitarian doxology.

As the Great Thanksgiving we pray at celebrations of the Eucharist move to a focus on the person and work of Christ following the *Sanctus*, so the *Te Deum* moves to a celebration of the Paschal mystery, pointing to incarnation, crucifixion, resurrection and ascension, coming judgment, and final consummation, but always in terms of our participation in them, a vibrant affirmation of the paschal mystery:

"When you came in flesh to set us free,
you did not shun the Virgin's womb.
You overcame the sting of death,
and opened heaven to all believers.
You are seated at God's right hand in glory;
we believe that you will come to be our judge.
Come then Lord, and help your people,
bought with the price of your own blood,
And bring us with your saints to glory everlasting."

# Ordo: Bath, Word, Prayer, Table

This invocation for God's help with its eschatological perspective may have concluded the ancient canticle. The prayers that follow were probably originally the *capitellum*, that is an antiphon (usually from a psalm) used at the conclusion of a canticle. In fact, a whole series of these versicles and responses from the psalms have been appended to the *Te Deum*. Since they were always sung with it they came to be thought of as a part of the canticle itself.[57] They serve as a summary of all the prayers of the people we lift up.

The *Te Deum* is a glorious summary containing the heart and soul of our daily prayer, not in some minimalist and truncated form, but uniting us with all creation, with all the Church, and with all the voices of heaven in a great hymn of praise to the Triune God. Such praise is not something we can rush into, however. Its mystery may be out of sight, but it is not beyond our sensing it. The monastic pattern is wise: the Vigil is preceded and succeeded by a great silence in which we are quiet before God in order that we may hear the music of the spheres, the song of the angels, and the hymn of Church praising God in the depths of our souls echoing to the heights of heaven.

### The Diurnal Hours and Compline

People of the New Testament and early church era thought of daytime as involving twelve hours divided into groups of three with the third, sixth and ninth hours being the usual points of reference. This would not have been a matter of "clock time" but rather a reference to mid-morning, noon, and mid-afternoon.

When I worked in the hayfields of Kansas as a youth, we would count on a mid-morning and mid-afternoon "lunch" being brought to the field, and to returning to the farmhouse at mid-day for dinner. It was nourishment that sustained us in the presence of the prairie's searing sun and hot wind. So it is that these became times for the nourishment of prayer, based in the older Jewish times for prayer. In the third century, Cyprian found in them "a sacrament of the Trinity."[58]

In the pre-Constantinian era, the diurnal or day-time offices recalled the passion in Mark 15.[59] At the third hour, Jesus was nailed to the tree; at the sixth hour, darkness fell; at the ninth hour, Jesus died. The third hour was also a memorial of the descent of the Holy Spirit at Pentecost.[60] These were times for private prayer, as they continue to be for many who pray them, and it was not until the fourth century that they became corporate monastic offices.

These "little offices" are intentionally brief and simple, capable of either being "shoe-horned" into a busy day, or prayed in a quiet and unhurried setting. A "little chapter" is provided – only a few verses of scripture on which to center our minds and hearts. A concluding prayer focuses our thoughts on the meaning of the office for the lives we lead. These offices are diaconal in nature, bridges between the Church and the world, between worship and work so that "those who wait on the Lord for help will find their strength renewed." Day by day, O Lord, "hear our prayer and let our cry come to You."

Which brings us to *Compline,* a word coming from the same Latin root as "complete." This is the service that closes the day as we understand it, the last liturgical prayer of the day, unless there is a Vigil. This is the Church's bedtime prayer. The Armenian office of the Christian East speaks of "the hour of peace" and "the hour of rest."[61] The service should end in silence, with persons leaving gradually only as they are ready, when peace and rest have overwhelmed the troubles and concerns of this life, or if that is impossible, when we are able to allow the Savior to bear them with us, thus finding rest for our souls.

Prayer before sleep undoubtedly began as a personal or family devotional practice; it was in the monastic community that gathering to share those prayers in common grew into an office all its own by the fourth century. It would have been prayed in the dark, or very nearly in the dark at least. Its contents were thus extremely stable so they could be easily memorized and prayed without anyone needing to read a book. While contemporary culture allows us additional flexibility in this regard, the basic components of this office continue to remain much the same throughout the year.

The Call to Prayer introduces us to the twin themes of the office: "The Lord almighty grant us a restful night and peace at the last." In order to have a restful night, we will need to have confessed our sins and received the assurance of forgiveness for them. But we also pray for "peace at the last." For the early Christians and, even more so, for the medieval mind, sleep was a rehearsal of death. Compline helps us prepare for death, both the death of baptism and physical death. In both cases, death does not have the last word. The last word is God's and that word is "resurrection." Compline, then is a quiet service of hope and trust in which we give ourselves into God's hands.

The commendation, adapted from the historic Sarum Breviary, provides words of great depth and comfort:

In peace we will lie down and sleep.
*In the Lord alone we safely rest.*
Guide us waking, O Lord, and guard us sleeping,
*that awake we may watch with Christ,*
*and asleep we may rest in peace.*
May the divine help remain with us always.

# Ordo: Bath, Word, Prayer, Table

*And with those who are absent from us.*
    - silence -
Into your hands, O Lord, I commend my spirit,
*For you have redeemed me, O Lord,*
*O God of Truth.*[62]

Here we have the themes of Compline brought into dynamic relationship: trust, hope, redemption, the need for guidance in waking and guarding in sleeping, our need for help, our preparation for death as we join our prayer with the prayer of Jesus on the cross: "Into your hands I commend my spirit."

The Canticle of Simeon, the *Nunc Dimittis,* is not only the evangelical canticle sung at Compline from very early on, but also the words which John Calvin thought should be used after every celebration of the Lord's Supper. And, as I can attest from standing beside my father's deathbed, they speak profoundly of our passover from death to life eternal.

The Daily Office is *a school of prayer,* an ongoing novitiate in which we are taught how the Church has glorified God through the ages, entering into the paschal mystery through the transforming power of the Holy Spirit. From day to day, week to week, season to season, festival to festival, we are plunged into the great mysteries of God's grace. By our continual participation in this rhythm, our lives resonate with it. We begin to understand and embody "Christ in us, the hope of glory" (Colossians 1:27). We are drawn again and again from the peripheral to what is central to the life of faith.

These basic rhythms of day and week and year are grounded in the historic experience of the Church rather than the ebb and flow of our transitory moods. As Taft puts it, this ongoing school of prayer "pulls us out of whatever bourgeois sentimentalism and inverted egoism there may be in our 'private' devotions, and draws us inexorably into the objective spiritual values of a life lived according to the mystery that is Christ."[63]

This school of prayer provides a discipline of learning, which frees us from bondage to our own emotions and preferences. It takes the state of our own soul seriously, inviting us to confession, to lament, to thanksgiving, to supplication, to service. It provides us with core experiences so that in the daily rounds of our existence, we have words and images and patterns so deeply imbedded in us that we learn to see and experience and interpret life in light of that schooling.

The Daily Office is *the prayer of the Church,* part of its *ordo* of time. It is not that my own concerns and prayers and praises are unimportant or irrelevant. Rather they are placed within the framework of the prayer of the Church through the ages and around the world. In the Daily Office, one does not pray alone. When we pray the *Magnificat* at Evening Prayer, we are doing what Christians have done at every evening prayer of every day of every week of every year since the time of the early church. It is an ecumenical act, prayed by an amazing multitude of Christian traditions and denominations from East to West and North to South around the world. In the *ordo* of liturgical time known as the Daily Office, we are part of the "communion of the saints" at prayer.

St. Chrodegang, an eighth century bishop of Metz, provided that "whoever cannot be in church for the hours in common must say them in private."[64] That direction has had far-reaching effects. The Daily Office is always corporate prayer, even when prayed as a solitary office rather than in the immediate presence of a community. Whether we do it alone or in company does not change the nature of the prayer – although if we do not do it together as often as possible, we are not likely to be truthful with ourselves about our belief that it is corporate! Unlike the Eucharist that by its very nature must be done in the presence of others, the Daily Office is prayer, and prayer can be done individually or with others, but that prayer will always be the Church's prayer.

Thus, for Gordon Lathrop, daily prayer "welcomes whoever is able to gather, in the name of the full assembly" as they "bring to expression a communal honesty about the time of day, about the primal joys and fears that do really attend these daily changes in the light . . . [marking] these rhythms with reference to the gospel."[65] As the Song of Zechariah, the Song of Mary, and the Song of Simeon remind us, every day is reinterpreted "as a day for the encouter with the hope-giving, justice-making, rest-giving light of God in Christ."[66]

## Liturgical Year: Times and Seasons in the Church's Life

In addition to the weekly cycle focusing on the Lord's Day and the pattern of Daily Prayer, the liturgical *ordo* of time includes an annual pattern of times as seasons. In terms of the calendar, it starts with Advent. However, both the depth dynamic of the liturgical year and its historical development suggest that it is wiser to start with *Pascha* – the "triduum" of three holy days culminating in Easter.

Already in 1 Corinthians we read: "Christ our Paschal lamb is sacrificed for us; therefore let us keep the feast" (5:7b-8a). As we have seen, this feast is, first of all, the weekly feast on the Lord's Day. When the "first anniversary" of Jesus' last Passover meal with his disciples, his crucifixion and resurrection, came around, it would have been natural for the early disciples to experience that weekly feast with special intensity. As the practice of keeping that yearly feast began to emerge, there was controversy over whether it should be kept on a day of the week determined by the Jewish Passover or on the first day of the week.[67] The practice that won out is that of always celebrating the resurrection on the

# Ordo: Bath, Word, Prayer, Table

Lord's Day.[68] Thus, it resonates with the weekly feast. It is, Lathrop says, "a Sunday to the year, an annual Sunday to our time, all the stories of creation and redemption giving us breath again."[69]

Thus, we would be mistaken if we identified the *Pascha* only with an annual Lord's Day festival of the resurrection. The 1 Corinthians text cited above points to the way in which the "feast" recognizes that "death" and "resurrection" must be linked so as to become one word: death-and-resurrection. Good Friday without Easter is incomplete; Easter without Good Friday becomes superficial. The holy meal Jesus celebrated with his disciples and with us unites the two, as does baptism.

As Thomas Talley concludes: "It is clear that the Lord's passion is not considered an event distinct from his glorification.... Rather, as Melito [of Sardis, c. 165 C.E.] makes clear [in his paschal homily], the primitve Pascha celebrated the memorial of the death of Jesus as a total festival of our redemption in Christ, including not only his glorification but also the incarnation."[70] The services of the *Triduum* from Holy Thursday evening to Easter Sunday are united by the practice of having no "closing rite" – no benediction, sending forth, or postlude in any of the services until the Easter celebrations. It is as though we are saying: "It's not over yet; we must participate in the rest of the story; here-and-now we are plunged into the rich matrix of symbols that includes meal, cross, tomb, fire, story, bath, feast, all reflecting the juxtaposition of death-and-resurrection."

The *Pascha* is full of juxtapositions: death set next to life, meal next to fast, sorrow next to joy, silence next to shout. They are manifested most clearly in the Great Paschal Vigil, observed on the evening before Easter Sunday as "the first service of Easter." A new fire may be kindled outside, the Paschal candle is lighted and carried into the darkened church as we proclaim: "The Light of Christ!" "Thanks be to God!" The *Exultet* is sung – only in this service, never in any other setting. A long series of lessons is read, beginning with creation, continuing through the exodus, and culminating in the resurrection narrative. Salvation history takes a long time; God is faithful. Unless it seems too long, we tend not to get the point! The baptismal covenant is celebrated; the holy meal is shared. Before recorded history our ancestors shared those same simple basic things: fire, story, water, food. Their symbolic potential lies deep in human experience. In the Vigil they are broken open in new ways for new life.[71]

Fifty days after the barley sheaf ceremony during the Passover came *Pentecost* (the Greek term for the Jewish "feast of weeks"), marking the beginning of the offerings of first fruits. According to Acts 2:1, it was "on the day of Pentecost" that the gift of the Holy Spirit was given to the Church. At both Passover and Pentecost, God does a "new thing" at an old festival. The connection with the first fruits given by God and offered up to him resonates with the Pentecost themes of the gift and the gifts of the Spirit.[72]

In between *Pascha* and Pentecost, the *ordo* of liturgical time marks *The Great Fifty Days*. This "week of weeks" can rightly be understood as *the* Pentecost, as can the festival of Pentecost itself. At the same time, they are the weeks *of*, not *after*, Easter. Indeed, Lathrop speaks of it as a fifty-day long feast.[73] For the ancient church, it was a time for *mystagogy*, a time to uncover the implications of "the mysteries" centering on baptism and eucharist as the Church has just experienced them. Mystery and meaning are juxtaposed. Without meaning the mysteries are in-*sign*-ificant (lacking the power of symbolic sign). Without mystery, meaning can be superficial.[74]

The third great festival in the *ordo* of liturgical time centers in a celebration of the incarnation and finds its central text in the *Logos* hymn of John 1.[75] It begins with *Christmas*, extends through the *twelve days of Christmas*, and culminates in *Epiphany*. In cultures that center their attention on either Christmas day or the feast of the Epiphany, a recognition that (like the *Pascha*) this is a multi-day, multi-faceted celebration of the incarnation is counter-cultural, breaking open new meaning in the presence of prevailing patterns. On the one hand, it breaks the superficial sweetness of much of the culture's patterns with reminders of stark and unpleasant realities. On the other hand, it recognizes the lament of many in this holy season, but juxtaposes it with the good news of the Word made flesh who dwells among us.

A walk through the narratives connected with this holy season makes that clear. December 25 (and the vigil preceding it on Christmas eve) points to the nativity as it is told in Luke's gospel with its "no room in the inn" and "manger crib" in a stable, juxtaposed with the proclamation of the mystery of the nativity in the first chapter of John. In the midst of this joy, the *ordo* of liturgical time sets December 26 as the day of St. Stephan the martyr, saying: "Oh yes, there is good news in the birth of our savior, but remember the cost of discipleship!" Lest we be overwhelmed with that cost, December 27 celebrates the feast of St. John the Evangelist who reminds us that "the light shines in the darkness, and the darkness has not overcome it" (John 1:5). Yet the darkness is still very much present in our world, as we are forced to recognize on December 28 as we join our voices in lament for the holy innocents who are killed in this and every age. Eight days after our celebration of Jesus' birth, we remember his circumcision and give thanks for "the holy name of Jesus." And on January 6, we celebrate the festival of *Epiphany*, recalling the visit of the magi and the "showing forth" or "making manifest" of God's presence with us. Such is the depth dynamic of Christmas in the *ordo* of liturgical time, a dynamic often forgotten or ignored.[76]

# Ordo: Bath, Word, Prayer, Table

Liturgical time also includes two seasons of preparation. *Advent* is the season of Christ's coming. It is not an attempt to go back to the time before Jesus was born and live in that time of longing for a Messiah. It is a here-and-now recognition of our longing for Christ to continually come to our lives, especially as we gather in his name, and our eschatological hope for the coming consummation of Christ's kingdom. God's call for works of justice and mercy are set in stark contrast to the commercialization of the culture's observance of these days, yet with thanksgiving that God comes into just such a world with transforming power for new life. Our inns may be full, but by God's grace, in the stable places of our lives, the incarnate one still comes to make all things new. Advent is a time of joyful expectation.[77]

*Lent* has often seemed to be a preparation for Good Friday, marked by penitence and fasting. When we remember that Lent is the time of preparation for the celebration of the whole of the *Pascha*, with particular attention to preparation for the celebration of the baptismal covenant, we are able to set the death and resurrection of Jesus side by side, recognizing that we walk the way of the cross in thanksgiving for the resurrection by the undergirding power of the Holy Spirit.[78]

One additional season in this *ordo* of liturgical time must be recognized, for it includes more time in the liturgical year than any other season. The Sundays in it have sometimes been called Sundays *after* Epiphany, or Sundays *after* Pentecost or Trinity. It is more appropriately called *Ordinary Time*. Just as much of our lives are ordinary, so is much of the liturgical year. Yet, as Laurence Stookey reminds us: "Because of what has been made known in Christ, no time can again be regarded as ordinary in the sense of dull or commonplace. . . . Christ has sanctified all of time, bringing us and the whole of our experience into the orbit of the resurrection. What we deem ordinary, God has transformed into the extraordinary by the power of divine grace."[79]

This pattern of yearly times and season can form the way in which we experience our own pilgrimage as persons-in-community:[80]

- When life seems mundane and we put one foot in front of the other in order to do what needs doing, *we are in Ordinary Time*.
- When we long for things to be different, when we watch and wait, *we are an Advent people*.
- When we recognize the presence of the holy in the ordinary, *we celebrate Christmas*.
- When a sense of the sacramental is broken open to us, and we respond by offering our material wealth, our worship, our lives and our deaths, *we live an Epiphany life*.
- When we wrestle with life and death decisions, seeking to live out our baptism, *we are in Lent*.

- When saving victory and suffering are closely interwoven, *we live in resonance with Passion/Palm Sunday.*

- When death and resurrection become one word, and we are able to dance on the gravestones without ignoring them, *we live as an Easter people.*

- When the dynamics of our mountaintop experiences are uncovered, *we experience the meaning of the Great Fifty Days.*

- And when we are aware that the Holy Spirit empowers us and sends us forth for service, ministry and mission, aware of both the diversity and unity of God's people, *we become Pentecost people."*

The *ordo* of liturgical time participates in one great Paschal unity. Its depth is the paschal mystery; its focus, the presence and work of the Triune God made manifest in Jesus Christ. All its times and seasons interpret one another, and must be juxtaposed with one another if we are to begin to apprehend their mystery and meaning. The *Pascha* provides the focus of the Lord's Day, as well as of the Daily Office and the Liturgical Year. In Lent we learn how to live out our baptism as a Pentecost people. The manger is important because of the cross. Friday is Good Friday because of the resurrection faith that proclaims the good news of Christmas that "God so loved the world that God gave God's only Son." We are a pilgrim people, living through the cycle of seasons with Advent hope that we walk together toward the final consummation of eternal life with God.[81] Lathrop affirms: "Past and future; remembrance and hope; days and nights; weeks, months, seasons and years – all of these have a deep, basic integrity in the practice of the assembly when that assembly makes use of its own heritage."[82] Such is the paschal nature of liturgical time.

# Ordo: Bath, Word, Prayer, Table

### ENDNOTES

[1] Isaac Watts, hymn text fragment from "Our God Our Help in Ages Past," 1719.

[2] Gordon Lathrop, *Holy Things: A Liturgical Theology* (Minneapolis: Fortress Press, 1993), 110.

[3] Gordon Lathrop, *Holy Ground: A Liturgical Cosmology* (Minneapolis: Fortress Press, 2003), 163.

[4] Ibid., 164.

[5] Lathrop notes that the "memory" approach is found in some Protestant views, the "mystery' approach among some Roman Catholic and Eastern Orthodox Christians, and the "fantasy" approach in the work of some twentieth century liturgical "reformers." (Ibid.)

[6] Ibid.

[7] Robert W. Hovda, *Strong, Loving, and Wise: Presiding in Liturgy* (Washington, D.C.: Liturgical Conference, 1976), 20.

[8] Ibid., 166.

[9] Gordon Lathrop, *Holy People: A Liturgical Ecclesiology* (Minneapolis, MN; Fortress Press, 1999), 219.

[10] David Hogue, in his perceptive and provocative book, *Imagining the Past, Remembering the Future: Story, Ritual and the Human Brain* (Cleveland: The Pilgrim Press, 2003), describes how brain research is helping us understand how human beings deal with past, present, and future. It is amazingly close to the way in which sacramental theology has understood *anamnesis, prolepsis,* and the present moment. The role of the Holy Spirit in the *epicletic* prayer of the Church provides additional depth to this understanding.

[11] Gordon Lathrop, *Holy Things,* 33-36.

[12] These are persistent themes throughout Lathrop's work, especially in his *Holy Things, Holy People, Holy Ground* liturgical theology triology.

[13] I use this term to refer to the vital and dynamic underlying matrix of mystery and meaning we discern beneath and behind the immediately observable. Lathrop's use of *ordo* is an example of identifying depth dynamics.

[14] CL, no. 106; A. Flannery, ed., *Vatican II: The Conciliar and Postconciliar Documents* (Collegeville, MN: The Liturgical Press, 1975)

[15] Adolf Adam, *The Liturgical Year: Its History and Its Meaning After the Reform of the Liturgy* (New York: Pueblo Publishing Company, 1981), 36

[16] Lathrop, *Holy Ground*, 167.

[17] Mark Searle, "Sunday: The Heart of the Liturgical Year" in Maxwell E. Johnson, ed., *Between Memory and Hope: Readings on the Liturgical Year* (Collegeville, MN: The Liturgical Press, 2000), 71.

[18] Lathrop, *Holy Things*, 111.

[19] Nathan D. Mitchell, "Ritual as Reading" in *Source and Summit: Commemorating Josef A. Jungmann, S.J.*, Joanne M. Pierce and Michael Downey, eds. (Collegeville, MN: The Liturgical Press, 1999), 178.

[20] Portions of the following section are adapted from articles written by the author that have appeared in the periodical *Sacramental Life* (Akron, OH: Order of Saint Luke Publications).

[21] Robert Taft, *The Liturgy of the Hours in East of West: The Origins of the Divine Office and Its Meaning for Today* (Collegeville, MN: The Liturgical Press, 1986) p. 359.

[22] Robert Taft, *The Liturgy of the Hours in East of West: The Origins of the Divine Office and Its Meaning for Today* (Collegeville, MN: The Liturgical Press, 1986).

[23] *Apostolic Constitutions*, II, 59.

[24] *The Christian Century*, March 21-28, 2001, pp. 14-15.

[25] Longer Rules, *37:2-5. See Migne*, Patrologia Graeca *31, pp. 1012ff.*

[26] *The Spirit of the Liturgy* (first published in 1918; current edition – New York: Herder and Herder, 1997), 21.

[27] For the complete context, see chapters 34-36 of Cyprian's *On the Lord's Prayer*.

[28] Robert Taft, *The Liturgy of the Hours in East of West: The Origins of the Divine Office and Its Meaning for Today* (Collegeville, MN: The Liturgical Press, 1986), 37.

[29] Taft, 161.

[30] *On the Holy Spirit* 29 (73).

[31] Taft, 37.

[32] Taft, 350-351.

[33] Cf. Tertullian, *Apology* 39:18 and *Apostolic Tradition* 25.

[34] Taft, p. 90.

[35] e.g. Ambrose (c. 334-379), *Letter 20*:13-25; Augustine (387-430), *De curia rp mortuis gerenda* 5 (7); St. Caesarius of Arles (c. 503-542), *Sermon* 76:3, 86:5, and 196.2.

[36] Gail Ramshaw, *Reviving Sacred Speech: The Meaning of Liturgical Language* (Akron, OH: OSL Publications, 2000), 143.

[37] Taft, p. 25.

[38] Taft, p. 28.

[39] Taft, p. 56.

[40] *Life Together* (San Francisco: Harper & Row, 1954), pp. 40-43.

[41] Robert Taft, *The Liturgy of the Hours in East of West: The Origins of the Divine Office and Its Meaning for Today* (Collegeville, MN: The Liturgical Press, 1986), p. 165.

[42] Taft, p. 166.

[43] Taft, pp. 29-29.

[44] as quoted in Taft, p. 24.

[45] Cassian, *Institutes,* III, 4:2 and 8-9.

[46] Paulinus, *Life of Ambrose* 13. See Migne, *Patrologia Latina,* 14, 43.

[47] Taft, p. 167, 189.

[48] Taft, p. 189.

[49] Taft, p. 189

[50] Taft, p. 25.

[51] *The Lord's Prayer, chapter 36.*

[52] *The New Grove Dictionary of Music and Musicians* (London: Macmillan, 1980), v. 18, p. 641.

[53] See E. Kähler, *Studien zum Te Deum* (Gottingen, 1958), cited in *The New Grove Dictionary of Music and Musicians* (London: Macmillan, 1980), v. 18, p. 641.

[54] *New Catholic Encyclopedia* (New York: McGraw-Hill, 1967), v. 13, p. 954

[55] W. K. Lowther Clarke and Charles Harris, *Liturgy and Worship: A Companion to the Prayer Books of the Anglican Communion* (London: SPCK, 1932)

[56] On the three parts of this canticle, see Matthew Britt, *The Hymns of the Breviary and Missal* (New York: Benziger Brothers, 1922), pp. 46ff.; *New Catholic Encyclopedia* (New York: McGraw-Hill, 1967), v. 13, p. 954; and *The New Grove Dictionary of Music and Musicians* cited above.

[57] Clarke, pp. 273-274.

[58] Taft, p. 19.

[59] Taft, p. 28.

[60] Taft, p. 28.

[61] Taft, p. 220.

[62] This particular form is found in the Ordinary for Compline in any volume of *The Daily Office: A Book of Hours for Daily Prayer* (Akron, OH: Order of Saint Luke Publications), Dwight W. Vogel, ed.

[63] Taft, p. 369.

[64] Taft, p. 299.

[65] Lathrop, *Holy Ground,* 167-168.

[66] Ibid., 168.

[67] This controversy is called the Quartodeciman [the "fourteenth"] controversy. Those who held the celebration on 14 to 15 Nisan whatever the day of the week seem to have come mostly from Asia Minor

and claimed to reflect a Johannine tradition. This tradition was followed by Celtic churches and was one of the issues at stake between the Celtic and Roman traditions in the historic synod at Whitby, England (664 C.E.).

[68] The power of the Pope and that Church at Rome was a significant and decisive factor in this decision. However, the practice we have inherited has a powerful depth dynamic that we have identified here.

[69] Lathrop, *Holy Ground*, 168-169

[70] Thomas J. Talley, *The Origins of the Liturgical Year* (Collegeville, MN: The Liturgical Press, 1986), 12.

[71] See Maxwell E. Johnson, ed., *Between Memory and Hope*, 99-181; Adolf Adam, *The Liturgical Year*, 57-84; and Thomas J. Talley, *The Origins of the Liturgical Year*, 1-54.

[72] See Maxwell E. Johnson, ed., *Between Memory and Hope*, 232-236; Adolf Adam, *The Liturgical Year*, 89-91; and Thomas J. Talley, *The Origins of the Liturgical Year*, 62-66.

[73] Lathrop, *Holy Ground*, 169.

[74] See Patrick Regan, "The Fifty Days and the Fiftieth Day" in Maxwell E. Johnson, ed., *Between Memory and Hope*, 223-246; Adolf Adam, *The Liturgical Year*, 84-89; and Thomas J. Talley, *The Origins of the Liturgical Year*, 57-70.

[75] Lathrop, *Holy Ground*, 169.

[76] See "From Pascha to Parousia" in Maxwell E. Johnson, ed., *Between Memory and Hope*, 265-348; Adolf Adam, *The Liturgical Year*, 121-158; and Thomas J. Talley, *The Origins of the Liturgical Year*, 85-147.

[77] See Martin J. Connell, "The Origins and Evolution of Advent in the West" in Maxwell E. Johnson, ed., *Between Memory and Hope*, 349-371; Adolf Adam, *The Liturgical Year*, 130-138; and Thomas J. Talley, *The Origins of the Liturgical Year*, 79-80 and 149-153.

[78] See Patrick Regan, "The Three Days and the Forty Days" and Maxwell E. Johnson, "Preparation for Pascha? Lent in Christina Antiquity" in Maxwell Anderson, *Between Memory and Hope*, 125-142 and Thomas J. Talley, *The Origins of the Liturgical Year*, 163-224 and 207-222.

[79] Laurence Hull Stookey, *Calendar: Christ's Time for the Church* (Nashville, TN: Abingdon Press, 1996), 134.

[80] The summary that follows is taken from Linda J. Vogel and Dwight W. Vogel, *Syncopated Grace: Times and Seasons with God* (Nashville, TN: Upper Room Books, 2002), 164-165. For a more complete treatment of this perspective on liturgical time, see chapter 8: "Emmaus Epiphanies."

[81] Ibid., 167.

[82] Lathrop, *Holy People: A Liturgical Ecclesiology*, 221. For Lathrop's treatment of the way in which the time practice of the assembly subverts our time symbols, see 223-226.

# TEN

# Liturgy Reshaping Society

*Cynthia D. Moe-Lobeda*

THE QUESTION: POSED, ANSWERED (OFFENSIVELY), POSED ANEW

"Liturgy Reshaping Society:[1]" the words breed multiple questions with tendrils spreading into all disciplines of theological studies and beyond. Consider in this essay one question: *In the current context, can and how can Christian liturgy play a role in reshaping United States society toward lifeways that allow Earth to flourish and all people to have the necessities for life with dignity?*

Gordon Lathrop, especially in his later works, articulates this challenge and brings ancient wisdom to bear on it. Yes, he insists in a tone of life-savoring hope, word, bath, meal, and prayer may profoundly re-orient us toward earth-honoring, justice-making worldviews and ways of life. His persistent yes, elaborated with grace and spirit, is a profound gift to the church today, to society, and to all who live on this Earth.

This essay responds to Lathrop's resounding yes, and his tenacious exploration of the 'how' portion of the question. The focus is the liturgy's historic centerpiece, the eucharist.[2] My methodological tools reside in the "inter-discipline" of Christian ethics. This inquiry is grounded in two old and widely accepted Lutheran faith claims. First, as articulated by Martin Luther: "The Word of God, wherever it comes, comes to change and renew the world." Secondly, the church is created, called, and sent by God's grace to "to bear witness to God's creative, redeeming, and sanctifying activity in the world...to participate in God's mission...."[3]

How can the eucharist help to reshape United States society toward ways of living that sustain more just and compassionate communities for generations to come? Faith bids the church to enter the question anew for each time and place. Into this mystery, step cautiously. Step gratefully. Move with the humility of knowing that the question defies conclusive, exhaustive answer. The inquiry is into the *mysterion* of God with us and within us. A rich and plentiful body of literature in Orthodox, Catholic, and Protestant traditions poses and responds (directly or indirectly) to the question of how the eucharist shapes and reshapes human society. This contemporary response is indebted to that chorus, building on it both critically and appreciatively.

As commonly confessed, the living Christ comes to us, into us, and among us in multiple and mysterious ways, and in a particular way, in Word and sacrament. The Latin *sacramentum* was used in early Christianity to translate the Greek *mysterion*. The *mysterion* of God, at least in Paul's work, "are the ways of God in getting through to us, in *opening our eyes to face reality*, in *bringing us faith, hope and love.*"[4] Faith, hope, and love, in Christian and Jewish traditions, act. Lutherans speak of "faith active in love." "Faith," writes Luther, "is not the human notion and dream that some people call faith… O it is a living, busy, active, mighty thing this faith. It is impossible for it not to be doing good works incessantly."[5] "Faith . . . is a divine work in us which changes us and makes us altogether different…."[6,7] In the sacraments, the Word of God comes into and through the people called to love and serve God and God's creation with heart, mind, strength, soul.

The sacraments, then, are God's ways of getting through to us in at least two ways. They open our eyes to reality, even when reality may seem too painful to face. And they bring us faith, hope, and love, the ingredients of agency for responding to reality in ways that reflect and serve God's mission to heal and liberate the world. The sacraments "open our eyes" and bring us the capacity to respond as God's "hands and heart."[8]

With these faith claims, confessed and articulated variously throughout the ages, the question – "can liturgy reshape society?" – is answered initially: Yes, Christian liturgy can help to reshape society because in the heart of the liturgy – Word and sacrament – the living God who is creating, saving, and sustaining the world comes to, into, and through us. The God who is liberating and healing from sin, both individual and structural, becomes one with us in this sacrament. That inbreaking Word of God changes the world. *Society is not exempt from that transforming love.*

This claim that the eucharist shapes how we live is an ancient faith claim. It is life-giving, yet offensive, because it reveals the opposite. North American Christian communities in sites of relative economic privilege regularly and sincerely celebrate the eucharist. Yet our lives are not regularly transformed toward social and ecological justice. We do not love neighbor by resisting economic arrangements that buy our luxury at the price of others' blood.[9] Instead, we share "generously" from our wealth, fail to ponder its connections to others' impoverishment or to Earth's distress, and carry on with life as usual. History deepens the offense. Christians who celebrated the eucharist also practiced chattel slavery, plundered Africa, and killed entire peoples in the Americas. What was and is missing or distorted in our practice of the eucharist, that we can so readily and blindly deal death?[10]

The question, a matter of life and death, has haunted me for years. Sri Lankan theologian, Tissa Balasuriya, O.M.I. puts it well: "Why is it that in spite of hundreds of thousands of eucharistic celebrations, Christians...who proclaim eucharistic love and sharing deprive the poor people of the world of food, capital, employment, and even land... inequities grow... [and] the rich live like Dives in the Gospel story?"[11] He is talking about caring, compassionate Christians like you and me who unwittingly benefit from and comply with economic arrangements that enrich some, including many of us, by impoverishing many and consuming Earth's natural capital. The transfer of wealth from the impoverished nations to the rich is mind-boggling. For many of the poor, notes a Salvadoran Jesuit priest, "poverty means death."[12] How is it possible that a people gathered and fed by God to spread the truth of God's healing, liberating, justice-making love could go forth from the eucharist into a "life as usual" that contributes, albeit unintentionally, to life-shattering poverty?

Any claims about the eucharist – if they are to be valid, faithful, and fruitful – must be accountable to that tormenting question and must confess that unholy historical and contemporary context. The question addressed herein must shift. *Given the role of United States society in the global economic and environmental story, how are we to receive, perceive and practice the world-changing gift of Christ's body and blood such that we repent, change direction[13], and take our place as God's "rusty tools"[14] in God's work to save this generous and broken planet?[15]*

In this essay, the path into this query is the teaching, both ancient and contemporary, that the eucharist is school for living and for morally empowering seeing: seeing what is, what could be, and the power and presence of God "fill[ing] all things."[16] I will argue that through the sacrament of the body and blood of Christ, God offers morally empowering vision for reshaping society, and that we receive this gift when we practice the sacrament both as communion (*koinonia*) and as eucharist (*eucharistia*) in their fullest senses.

## A School for Morally Empowering Seeing

Since at least the time of Irenaeus of Lyons, the eucharist has been known by some as a school for seeing and for Christian living.[17] Cyril of Jerusalem, in his teaching on the eucharist, admonishes participants to "hallow your eyes by the touch of the sacred Body, and then partake... After partaking of the Body of Christ [and]... receiving also the Blood of Christ... while It is still warm upon your lips, moisten your fingers with It and so sanctify your eyes, your forehead and other organs of sense."[18] Thirteen centuries later, Martin Luther insisted that vision of how we are to live in accord with faith is obscured when sacramental practice is ignored or distorted.[19] In a contemporary Lutheran baptismal rite drawing upon this heritage, the cross is traced on the eyes with the words "receive the cross on your eyes that you may see the light of Christ, illumination for your way."[20]

It is no wonder that sharing in the body and blood of Jesus Christ would enable seeing. Jesus constantly opened peoples' eyes, pushing and prodding them to see the world around them differently (what is), to see how to live (what could be) and to see God present and saving. In first century Palestine, according to the authors of Mark, Jesus queried his disciples, "Are your hearts hardened? Do you have eyes, and fail to see?" (Mk 8:17-18). Today Jesus asks his followers the same.

To what will the sacrament open our eyes if, through it, God is enabling Her people to see differently so that they may live differently, "reoriented" (the term is Lathrop's) toward the healing of the world? What vision will evoke the wisdom and courage to struggle toward society re-shaped along contours of compassion, economic justice, and sustainability? The *sacramentum*, the *mysterion* of God are, we have said, "the ways of God in getting through to us, in opening our eyes to face reality...."[21] Consider three realities entailed in morally empowering vision for contemporary North American Christians who are relatively economically privileged: the reality of what is happening on this fragile planet, the reality of what could be (understood as more just and ecologically sound ways of being human), and the reality of God's power and presence coursing through all of creation, "even the tiniest leaf."[22] Together, these three constitute what I refer to as "critical mystical vision," gift of the eucharist.

### Seeing What Is: Where Evil Masquerades as Good

Vision for reshaping society requires that we dare to see the social and ecological conditions in which we swim and, in particular, to unmask social structural evil where it parades as good. Theologian Douglas John Hall underscores the peril of failed vision. "[Western] Christianity in the modern epoch," he writes, "gave itself over to a vision that promised the imminent emergence of a better world within history... manifest in daily demonstrations of progress... The nonrecognition, minimization, and resolution of evil formed an integral part of this new world view from its inception. So long as the ideology of progress could seem to be sustained by experience it did not require so great an effort to *close ones eyes to the evils that were present*, always, even at the height of the age of progress... In these decades [the vision of progress] can be maintained only at the expense of *shutting ones eyes* to experience altogether. The nonrecognition and minimalization of evil, which was part of this enter-

# Ordo: Bath, Word, Prayer, Table

prise from the outset, has assumed the proportions of a way of life." Modern Christianity, Hall asserts, has *"shut its eyes to the data of despair."*[23]

Feminist and womanist voices long have demanded that ethics reveal systemic and ideological arrangements whereby the privilege of some requires the dispossession of others. Christian ethicist Mary Hobgood puts it well, "To act justly in the world, we need to know how the world works."[24] Domination and subordination are "constantly reproduced when unequal power relations *are hidden* within 'commonsense' assumptions about class, race, and gender. We *do not notice* how the patterned behaviors we engage in daily, either as individuals or as affiliates of institutions, exploit, silence, disable, or marginalize some as they confer status, profits, and other benefits on elites."[25]

The realities – of ecocide and economic violence – however, are brutal. They are the "data of despair," and they invite it. From acknowledging realities like these, we flee. Not seeing them – moral blindness – is far more bearable. Blindness failing, numbness sets in. Where numbness thaws, despair makes sense. We retreat into denial and defensiveness, privatized morality, or overwhelmed exhaustion. Holy outrage and lament are stillborn, and we hide our hopelessness regarding systemic evil under the comforting cloak of virtue in private life.

### Seeing What Could Be

Where reality is brutal and we (not by intent, but by social structure) are implicated in it, to see seems far too dangerous. Eucharistic vision, if it reveals the devastating impact of economic life as we know it – on the Earth itself and on neighbors who are dispossessed by our possession – is perilous unless simultaneously that vision reveals another reality. It is the vast array of more just and sustainable alternatives already in existence or in the making.

The church, of all bodies on Earth, is equipped for seeing what could be. Gordon Lathrop says it well: The church is charged with seeing that "the oppressive structures [truly surrounding us] ... are not eternal; they should be challenged and changed."[26] In baptism we are born into an alternative reality, nay, the true reality ... an everyday life in which we resist the principalities and powers that thwart abundant life for all. Friends, this includes economic practices, policies, and presuppositions that cast some into death by poverty and the earth into mortal distress. In the eucharist we are fed to live into that true reality of challenge and change.

We know little of the visionary and practical organizing of groups throughout the world aimed at surviving, resisting, and transforming global economic arrangements that endanger Earth's life-systems and the lives and dignity of those who are impoverished. Including farmers and fisherpeople, economists, labor unionists, ethicists, scientists, students, business people, activist coalitions, and others throughout the globe, they develop and live toward alternative visions of a global economic order in which the wealth of a few is not bought by the degradation of many and of the Earth.[27] Existing alternatives encompass concrete principles, public policies at all levels and practices.

The church can bring to this work of crafting alternatives the wisdom offered by millennia of teaching and learning ways of economic life that cohere with God's will of abundant life for all, as that will and way are revealed in Jesus Christ and the faith tradition in which he lived, died, and rose. In Word, Bath, and Meal, we have, in fact, been placed into alternative relationships ... relationships of "living justly with neighbor."[28] We are charged with perceiving and then embodying those relationships! We are charged with seeing what it looks like to live according to the right relations that God has given us in the gracious gift of justification. What a splendid charge: it is to shape our daily lives, our searching the scriptures, our prayer, our building of church structures, our evangelism and stewardship.

Gordon Lathrop would have us believe that the eucharist, set with Word and prayer, may thus "reorient" our vision. The meal with Word may "heal our eyes," drawing participants to "see a new order in the cosmos itself." That order includes human life as God would have us live it – earth-honoring and justice-making ways of being human.

### Seeing the Power and Presence of God "Fill[ing] All Things"[29]

The forces lined up against that re-oriented way of life are indescribably powerful and agile. Human agency alone has not the strength to confront them. And so God provides. Encounter with Christ in the elements of Earth – water, wine, grain – assure this: we face the powers of death and destruction neither alone nor by our power alone. Humans are sensual creatures. We know through visible, flavorful, touchable signs, through our senses. In the meal, we taste, see, touch, smell that the Creator and Liberator of all that is, is with and *within* this good creation, we human creatures included. Perhaps it is God's sage response to the human mammal's pernicious proclivity to create God in our own image: "Remember me and receive me in *the elements of Earth, in grain eaten and wine taken into your bodies* am I present. Touching, tasting, smelling, seeing them, know that I am with you."

"Those who eat my flesh and drink my blood abide in me and I in them" (Jn. 6:56). Luther's commentary on this passage speaks for countless voices in Christian traditions that claim that the living Christ comes as pure and utterly unearned gift to dwell in the believing community. "In Hebrew,"

# Ordo: Bath, Word, Prayer, Table

Luther writes, "the word 'abide' denotes 'to remain' or 'to dwell' in a person... Now this is a precious dwelling place and something to glory in, that through faith in Christ and through our eating, we... have Christ abiding in us with [Christ's] might, power, strength, righteousness, and wisdom."[30] "[T]his is... one of the exceedingly great promises granted to us poor miserable sinners, that we should become partakers of the divine nature, and should be so highly honored as not only to be loved by God through Jesus Christ... but should even have the Lord Himself dwelling completely in us...."[31] According to Luther, that indwelling Christ presence *is* the moral-spiritual power with which the faith community lives out its call to serve the well-being of those in need, a vocation expressed today as justice-making earth-honoring neighbor-love.[32]

Scholarly debates have raged through nearly two millennia regarding the way in which the risen Messiah is present in the eucharistic celebration. Paul's eucharistic theology, the accounts of the Synoptic gospels, John's testimony, and the extracanonical early Christian writings vary. Patristic, medieval, reformation, post Tridentine, post Vatican II, and modern Protestant interpretations of the early writings develop and defend varied positions (to understate the conflict) on *how* Christ is present in union and communion with the communing community.[33] Undisputed is *that* in the sharing of bread and wine, the first generation Christians experienced the presence of the risen Lord in whom they were united.[34]

The ancient Hebrews and Luther (along with much of Orthodox tradition and mystics throughout the ages) join the sacraments themselves in teaching that the "us" in and through whom God is working extends beyond the human. In the Psalmist's wisdom, God calls upon the creatures and elements of Earth to "testify," "witness," "minister" (Ps.104:4); convey God's message (Ps. 104:4); and praise God (Ps. 148). Luther insists that Christ actually is present not only in believing communities, but in all created things. "Nothing can be more truly present and within all creatures than God himself with his power."[35] "God ... exists at the same time in every little seed, whole and entire, and yet also in all and above all and outside all created things."[36] "[E]verything is full of Christ through and through ... "[37] "[A]ll creatures are ... permeable and present to [Christ]."[38] "Christ ... fills all things... Christ is around us and in us in all places... [H]e is present in all creatures, and I might find him in stone, in fire, in water, or even in a rope, for he certainly is there...."[39]

This morally-empowering vision requires a third form of seeing, as well. This seeing offers us ever-greater glimpses of the life-giving, life-saving, life-sustaining, life-savoring Mystery that we so lamely call God, indwelling flesh and earth and working toward abundant life for all. Only at great peril will we face the powers of structural sin without an awareness of this Mystery indwelling us and all the created world.

*School for Seeing: Sacrament of the Meal as Communion and as Eucharist*

Failure to recognize reality, notes mathematical cosmologist Brian Swimme, means failed living. "We are six billion humans and we need to learn to live with one another and with all the other ten trillion species of life in a mutually enhancing way. We fail at the present time precisely because we fail *to see* and understand what it is that surrounds us...."[40] In an era when life-destroying ways of living parade as normal and good, re-shaping society calls for opening eyes to three realities: social causes of unnecessary suffering and of Earth's distress, more equitable and ecological alternatives, and the indwelling presence of God "luring us to choose life rather than death."[41] Christian living in the United States today has at its heart the task of holding together these three (what is, what could be, and the indwelling Mystery) in order to discern where and how God is working to heal Her splendid creation, how the church may serve that mission, and wherein lies its moral-spiritual power to do so. That this critical mystical vision is inevitably and monumentally fallible and partial, and that we gravitate toward sacralizing our version of it, is no excuse to evade it as both gift and obligation.

Christ in the eucharist may open eyes to all three. "Tasting enables seeing," contends Lathrop with characteristic elegance.[42] How? *How will the church receive and celebrate the meal in a manner that opens our eyes to see what is, what could be, and the power and presence of God "compassioning"*[43] *the world, so that we may participate in God's work "to change and renew the world?"* How will receiving the body and blood of Christ reorient our vision, unleashing our vision and power for reshaping society toward justice, compassion, and Earth-care?

An inquiry is shaped not only by its questions, but also by its sources. Here, I call upon two sets of sources integral to Christian ethics: contemporaries speaking from the underside of power and privilege, and faith forbearers. The selected voices herein are Christian communities of the first two centuries suffering under persecution by the Roman Empire, Martin Luther, Christian communities of Chile tortured by the brutal regime of Pinochet, and finally the early Hebrew communities addressed by the prophet Joel. Together, this cloud of witnesses draws us into the sacrament of the supper, first as communion (*koinonia*) and then as eucharist (thanksgiving).

# Ordo: Bath, Word, Prayer, Table

## Eucharist as *Koinonia*

### The First Two Centuries: Sacrament of the Eucharist as Sacrament of Koinonia (Solidarity)

With good reason, Christians throughout the ages have referred to the sacrament of Christ's body and blood as communion, the English translation of the Latin *communio,* which in turn translates the Greek *koinonia* of the New Testament. According to Paul, what we know as the eucharist and as communion is just that, *koinonia*. New Testament scholar Barbara Rossing notes that "one of the earliest and most powerful Christian proclamations of *koinonia*" is the body of blood of Christ shared by the community gathered in Christ's name:[44] "The cup of blessing that we bless, is it not a sharing (*koinonia*) in the blood of Christ? The bread that we break, is it not a sharing (*koinonia*) in the body of Christ?" (1 Cor. 10:16).

What are the implications of Paul's claim and ours that the Lord's Supper is communion, *communio, koinonia*? First is a clue in the shift Paul makes from the implications of *koinonia* in ancient Greco-Roman culture. There *koinonia* used religiously was understood as participation with the gods or with a god through the eating of a sacrificial meal. Paul takes this cultic notion of participation with the gods and renders it anew. In Paul, the *koinonia* is with God in Christ *and* is within the body of Christ on earth, the church. "Because there is one bread," he writes, "we who are many are one body, for we all partake of the one bread" (1 Cor. 10:17). While in this particular context, Paul's appeal to *koinonia* is a call to unity within the fractured church of Corinth, the implications of *koinonia* in Christ as also *koinonia* within the community gathered in his name are more extensive. Those implications appear as we dig further into the rich and multi-layered Second Testament understandings of *koinonia*.

In the Hellenistic world, *koinonia* originally referred to financial partnership, partnership in work, friendship with a willingness to share material possessions, mutually shared obligation, and other relationships of sharing. In the Second Testament and other Christian writings of the first two centuries, the word means "to share with someone in something." As a noun, *koinonia* retains this meaning and is used to express other dimensions of the communion created by God in Jesus Christ and the Spirit. Those dimensions include the following:

- Believers' communion and union with Christ, or participation in Christ, by the power of the Holy Spirit and through faith. In this sense, *koinonia* is both in the present and more fully realized in the future.[45]

- Union and communion among believers, manifest as sharing in sufferings of another/others, or being companions of those who are suffering.[46]
- Union and communion among believers, manifest as economic sharing ("giving a share"). Paul writes: "When I left Macedonia, no church shared (*koinoneo*) with me in the matter of giving and receiving except you alone" (Phil. 4: 15). The *Didache* instructs "You shall not turn away the needy, but shall share everything (*syg-koinoneo*) with your brother or sister, and shall not say that it is your own. For if you are sharers (*koinonoi*) in the imperishable, how much more in perishable things (*Didache* 4.8).[47]
- Communion and union with Christ and among believers that is experienced in the Lord's Supper. Paul says *that* this communion happens but not *how* it happens.[48]
- Communion with the Holy Spirit.[49, 50]

Communion, then, is multi-dimensional and may not be reduced to a single aspect. To live the eucharist only as a mystical moment with Christ, or simply as a sign and promise of forgiveness, or even as a shared moment of union between the community and Christ, is a tragic reduction having monumental, even life and death implications. The communion with Christ that is experienced in the Lord's supper, also is a communion of being with and being for[51] those who are in need by becoming Christ's love for them and receiving Christ's love from them or from others.[52] In this essay, the term 'solidarity' signifies this sacramental practice of being with and for. The sacrament of the body and blood of Jesus Christ inherently entails the sacrament of solidarity.[53] The eucharist as solidarity "re-members" the body of Christ on Earth.

### Martin Luther: Sacrament of the Eucharist as Sacrament of Koinonia (Solidarity)

Martin Luther, the theologian, was grounded in Martin Luther, the biblical scholar. It should come as no surprise that for him economic ethics and eucharistic theology are intricately intertwined and interdependent.[54] His economic ethics, radically oriented around serving the well-being of the economically vulnerable, are most vivid in his eucharistic writings.[55] In "The Blessed Sacrament of the Holy and True Body and Blood of Christ, and the Brotherhoods"[56] Luther writes (italics mine):

- "Christ has given his body for this purpose, that the one thing signified by the sacrament – the fellowship, *the change wrought by love – may be put into practice*."
- "The sacrament has no blessing and significance unless love grows daily and *so changes a person* that he is made one with the others."

# Ordo: Bath, Word, Prayer, Table

- "Thus by means of this sacrament, all self-seeking love is rooted out and gives place to that which *seeks the common good of all.*"
- "When you have partaken of this sacrament, therefore, or desire to partake of it, you must in turn share the misfortunes of the fellowship… Here your heart must go out in love and learn that this is a sacrament of love. As love and support are given you, you in turn must render love and support to Christ's in his needy ones… See as you uphold all of them, so they all in turn uphold you; and all things are in common, both good and evil."
- "In times past this sacrament was so properly used, and the people were taught to understand this fellowship so well, that they even gathered food and material goods in the church, and then… distributed among those who were in need… this has all disappeared, and now there remain only the many masses and the many who receive this sacrament without in the least understanding or practicing what it signifies… They will not help the poor, put up with sinners, care for the sorrowing, suffer with the suffering, intercede for others, defend the truth…"

The import here is not one of obligation. It is of transformation. Luther primarily is describing, not prescribing. He is describing the transformative power of Christ with us and in us in the eucharist. The sacrament changes the communion community into a people who create a different economic world.

Luther, I think, would be delighted with Gordon Lathrop's "eucharistic economics."[57] "The eucharist," Lathrop writes, "makes an economic proposal, its house-ordering idea for house-hold Earth."[58] Practiced in a liturgical context of Word and prayer, the feast reorients and forms its participants into a worldview that includes a love for the earthy and embodied conditions of life on Earth. That reorientation leads the community to serve the well-being of those who are in need and to care for the Earth.

*COMMUNITIES RESISTING TORTURE: SACRAMENT OF THE EUCHARIST AS SACRAMENT OF KOINONIA*

William Cavanaugh's *Torture and Eucharist,*[59] an account of resistance to torture systematically imposed by the Chilean regime of Augusto Pinochet, echoes the claim that the eucharist is world-changing. Cavanaugh grounds the claim in his experience with Chilean *communidades de base* (base Christian communities) who were victims of that torture. Torture, Cavanaugh argues, dismembered not only bodies but also the social bodies/bodies politic capable of resistance. The eucharist, re-membering the body of Christ, re-membered those social bodies. The incarnate Christ, incarnate in the communing body, was capable of resisting the social strategies and actions of the repressive regime. Eucharist – as for the early Christian communities theorized by Wayne Meeks and those addressed by Luther – was a public action that did something. It "re-membered" the body of Christ incarnate in the church. In the words of Orthodox theologian Alexander Schmemann: "...the original sense of *liturgia* was 'an action by which a group of people become something corporately which they had not been as a mere collection of individuals.'"[60]

In the eucharist, Cavanaugh writes, a body was formed, the body of Christ, a body of "social practices, the true body of Christ capable of resisting... worldly power" where that power bred injustice. It was a political body, a body of evangelical defiance, defiance of humanly constructed systems that thwart God's intent of life abundant for all. Yet again, in faith communities of Chile suffering persecution by torture two millennia after the first Christian communities, the eucharist entailed solidarity; it re-membered the body of Christ.

*These Voices, in Sum*

We asked: *How will the church receive and practice the eucharist in a manner that opens our eyes to see what is, what could be, and the power and presence of God "compassioning" the world, so that we may participate in God's work to change and renew the world?*

In Christian communities of the first two centuries, in the movement of evangelical defiance inspired by Martin Luther, and in torture-wracked Chile, solidarity with those marginalized by structures of power or wealth was claimed as an *integral dimension* of the eucharist. The eucharistic community practiced re-membering the body of Jesus Christ on Earth in their time and place through *koinonia*, solidarity. The eucharist was *koinonia* in the full sense of the word.

Could it be that the power of the eucharist as school for seeing lies here: Because the eucharist ontologically places the sacramental community *with* those who suffer from the unjust exercise of power and the unjust distribution of what is needed for life with dignity, eyes are opened to life from that perspective? The postmodern turn has taught that knowing and seeing are perspectival. We know and see from standpoints. In Christian ethics, one of the most significant dimensions of this epistemological revolution is the claim that moral wisdom for a human future, if there is to be one, will be learned by listening to the underside of power and privilege,[61] putting those perspectives into conversation with other critical analyses of the Earth crisis and of social injustice.[62]

Practicing solidarity opens eyes and hearts to see differently. It enables vision of three realities: 1) what is going on from perspectives of those who are denied life's necessities, even where that vision

# Ordo: Bath, Word, Prayer, Table

seems too brutal to bear; 2) what could be, that is, pathways toward more just and sustainable ways of living; and 3) the presence of Jesus Christ with, within, and among the creatures and elements of this good earth, hastening there toward the healing and liberation of all. These three, held together, are a critical mystical vision for reshaping society. Could it be that the eucharist shapes society to the extent that it is practiced also as the sacrament of solidarity, inroad to morally empowering vision?

### SOLIDARITY SUSPECT AND RECLAIMED

This response, although promising, is perilously flawed. Theological claims by people of privilege must pass through the refining fires of scrutiny by those who stand to lose life or dignity from those claims. In this essay, solidarity itself is suspect and then is refined by the constructive critique of postcolonial theology and the emerging awareness of the other-than-human world as bearing moral agency.

Today, the term 'solidarity' is used readily, but often is inadvertently *depleted of content*, and thus misused. Tissa Balasuriya adds four crucial insights into the content of solidarity, the first of which I have argued already. He claims that the eucharist is "in captivity" and will be freed to serve God's work of justice-making and peace-making when the church: 1) seeks truly to see from perspectives of people historically and contemporarily on the underside of colonizing power, 2) takes "into account what is happening to these peoples and the causes of their worsening situation," 3) repents for the role that Christianity has played in varied forms of oppression, and 4) "makes a fundamental choice to struggle against contemporary forms of oppression."[63, 64] These challenges, held together, sketch the contours of solidarity that bears transformative substance and power.

The Sri Lankan priest suggests yet another dimension of solidarity, using the tools of theology and social theory in dialogue. We are to probe how and why it was possible for Christians of conscience to be so conditioned that the celebration of the eucharist could go hand in hand with history's worst plunder and genocide, the colonial expansion of the tribes of Europe over most of earth's continents.[65] Questioning what prevented colonizing Christians from hearing the cries of the millions that they oppressed, Balasuria suggests, "may be the beginning of wisdom"[66] for eucharistic communities in positions of privilege today.

To these, I would add a sixth "content of solidarity," pertaining to method in liturgical theology.[67] Where interpretation and norms of eucharistic practice are established by a society or social sectors that benefit – albeit unwittingly – from structures of privilege and domination, danger looms. Eucharistic theology and practice curve almost magnetically, though not intentionally, toward serving the interests of those social sectors or that society.[68] Where that is the case, the sacrament's socially transformative power is "captive." It will be loosed when historically subjugated peoples are the *subjects of eucharistic theology and norms,* and when we dare to ask if and where those norms and theology re-inscribe the social evils of our day. Both are tasks of liturgical theology in our day.

Finally, solidarity as commonly conceived is truncated by anthropocentric boundaries. Thus limited, it will not enable the breadth and depth of vision called for by the Earth crisis. Solidarity that assumes human mammals can survive without an all-encompassing commitment to the health of Earth's life-systems and life-support systems is tragically mistaken.

These prescriptions for the content of solidarity, if taken seriously, are daunting. The invitation to practice *koinonia* as substantive solidarity along these lines *as an integral dimension of the Lord's supper* borders on the ludicrous without acknowledging the barriers to doing so and pointing toward the moral-spiritual power for moving beyond them. To do so is beyond the scope of this essay. Here I simply suggest one wellspring of that moral-spiritual power: the communion as *eucharistia* and as true body and blood of Christ.

## COMMUNION AS *EUCHARISTIA* AND AS TRUE "BODY AND BLOOD OF CHRIST"

By the early second century, the celebration of the Lord's Supper became known in many Christian communities as *eucharistia* (thanksgiving), because the prayers surrounding the sharing of the bread and wine were characterized by praise and thanks.[69] If eucharist (thanksgiving) is a "school for Christian living and for morally empowering seeing," then we learn how to live and are enabled to see by giving thanks to God. Said differently, how we live – including in what directions our lives are to reshape society – is taught by the liturgical practice of giving thanks to God. Our power to see what is and what could be for the sake of moving toward the latter lies in giving thanks.

### *FOR WHAT WE GIVE THANKS MATTERS*

Are the people gathered around the table giving thanks to God for saving me for eternal life after death? For saving all believers for eternal life after death? Or are we giving thanks for the entirety of God in God's fullness as creator, savior, and sustainer of all that God is creating? That is, do we offer gratitude to God for creating this magnificent world; for saving it from sin in all forms, be they systemic or individual; and for creating, gathering, and sending the church to "participate in God's mission?"[70] Do we give thanks that God in Christ has freed us from *esse incurvatus in se* ("being turned in on oneself") as persons and as societies? Is our thanksgiving for the *life* of Jesus – including his willingness to challenge the powers of exclusion, violence, and domination of his day – and our call to follow

# Ordo: Bath, Word, Prayer, Table

his way as well as for his death and resurrection? Are we thanking God for having revealed Godself in earth's elements and creatures, for being so intimately present with us, that we may touch, see, taste the incarnate God? Do we truly give thanks to God for the incarnation, for giving – in Word, bread, wine, and water, through the power of the Holy Spirit – the living Christ to abide in us? Do we sing out in gratitude that God has called human creatures to be God's hands and heart on earth... that "through faith in Christ and through our eating, we... have Christ abiding in us with [Christ's] might, power, strength, righteousness, and wisdom"?[71]

If our thanks is for this plentitude, then the eucharist is nothing less than the celebration of all creation's redemption[72] and of our calling to "dedicate ourselves to the care and redemption of all that God has made."[73] Few things could be more profoundly transforming than that dedication actually lived by the church in United States society with its "dedication to" keeping the major part of Earth's bounty in the hands of a very few. To thank God for "abiding in us,"[74] for "mak[ing] habitation"[75] in a particular way in the mud creatures who place their trust in God so that they may be God's "rusty tools"[76] in "striv[ing] for justice and peace in all the earth,"[77] is to receive God's gift of the indwelling Christ as moral-spiritual power to heed our society-reshaping call.

### *Who Is Giving Thanks Matters*

According to the United Nations Human Development Program, basic health care and adequate nutrition for all people in "developing countries" would cost $13 billion. $12 billion a year is spent on perfumes in the United States and Europe.[78] "The average greenhouse gas emissions of one US citizen are equal to that of 500 Nepalese."[79] In this historical moral crisis of inequity, argues theologian Sallie McFague, "who we are should be understood in terms of how much we consume of the planet's bounty, both in terms of its health and of justice to other inhabitants."[80]

Given *who we are* in that sense, giving thanks has a less-recognized sister: communal lament.[81] In a powerful sermon on the book of Joel, Christian ethicist Emilie Townes claims that, for people living in covenant relationship with God, social healing begins with communal lament. Lament was integral to the ancient Hebrews' covenant relationship with God, suggests Townes, drawing on the work of Walter Brueggemann. A loss of lament meant "also a loss of genuine covenant interaction with God."[82] Where the assembly praises God but does not lament, "covenant is a practice of denial and pretense."[83] Communal lament, as Townes explains it, is the assembly crying out in distress to the God in whom it trusts. It is a cry of sorrow by the people gathered, a cry of grief and repentance and a plea for help in the midst of social affliction. Deep and sincere "communal lament... names problems, seeks justice, and hopes for God's deliverance." Lament, as seen in the book of Joel, she says, forms people; it requires them to give name and words to suffering. "[W]hen Israel used lament as rite and worship on a regular basis, it kept the question of justice visible and legitimate."[84] Perhaps for us too, lament is integral to thanksgiving, to *eucharistia*. Could it be that the eucharist will empower the people of God for social and ecological healing where thanksgiving for God's boundless love includes profound lament for the ways in which our lives unwittingly endanger Earth's life-systems and vulnerable neighbors far and near?

The crucified and risen Christ present in bread and wine in the gathered community reminds the people why they can lament without drowning in despair: In the sacrament of the supper, we taste and we see that the only power that can heal this beautiful and broken world is present with, among, and within the stuff of earth. That saving presence is incarnate – abides in the earthy and earthly – and flows instinctively to life's broken places, there nurturing power for reshaping society in the contours of abundant life for all.

## In Sum

The church throughout the ages has claimed that the grace of God comes to save through Word and sacrament. In an age which finds a portion of one species designing ways of living that destroy a beloved planet and impoverish many, all of creation groans for salvation. All of creation groans for human society to change. How, in this context, will the eucharist help us to reshape society in contours of social justice and ecological health? In this essay, the path into this mystery has been the wisdom, both ancient and contemporary, that the eucharist is school for living and for morally-empowering vision: seeing what is (especially evil where it parades as good), what could be, and the indwelling power and presence of God. Asking how we are to perceive and practice the eucharist in ways that enable such seeing, we sought the wisdom of faith forbearers, both ancient and recent. They hint at this: The sacrament of the body and blood of Christ offers morally empowering vision for reshaping society where the eucharist is communion (*koinonia*) in the fullest sense of the word – profound solidarity – and where communion is eucharist (thanksgiving) in all its plentitude.

The role of a public Christian theologian is to speak a word of life-saving truth about the God whom Jesus loved and about what it means to live as the body of Jesus Christ on Earth today. That includes disclosing and subverting worldviews where they betray God's justice-making love. Gordon Lathrop's remarkable work in constructive and critical liturgical theology is fertile public theology. He challenges the people gathered in the name of Jesus Christ to live as though baptism, eucharist, and

# Ordo: Bath, Word, Prayer, Table

Word are indeed life-altering and society-shaping realities. His tenacious and spirited quest is for liturgy that nurtures justice-making, earth-honoring Christianity. Lathrop, as poetic public theologian, bids us re-enter the mystery of "God with us" in the liturgy, enabling us to see the cosmos and our place in it so that we might live differently, reoriented toward the healing of the world.

## ENDNOTES

[1] For an inquiry into this issue that puts liturgical theology in conversation with the political theology of Johann Baptist Metz, see Bruce T. Morrill, *Anamnesis as Dangerous Memory: Political and Liturgical Theology in Dialogue* (Collegeville: Liturgical Press, 2000).

[2] I have explored the same question, but centering on baptism in Cynthia Moe-Lobeda, *Public Church: For the Life of the World* (Minneapolis: Fortress Press, 2004), Introduction and chapter 2.

[3] *Constitutions of the Evangelical Lutheran Church in America*, 4.01–02.

[4] Christopher Morse. *Not Every Spirit: A Christian Dogmatics of Disbelief.* (Valley Forge: Trinity Press International, 1994), 43, italics mine.

[5] Martin Luther, "Prefaces to the New Testament," LW 35:370. Luther goes on to say: "[This faith] does not ask whether good works are to be done, but before the question is asked, it has already done them and is incessantly doing them."

[6] Martin Luther, "Prefaces to the New Testament," LW 35:370–71.

[7] What this means has been open for debate for centuries. An interpretation that I find convincing holds that the faith and love that we receive in the eucharist are the actual faith of Christ and the love of Christ coming to "abide in" us (John 17). Elsewhere I have argued that this interpretation is found also in Luther (see Cynthia Moe-Lobeda, *Healing a Broken World: Globalization and God* [Fortress Press, 2003], chapter 4 and 5), and in Bonhoeffer (see Cynthia Moe-Lobeda, *Public Church: For the Life of the World* [Minneapolis: Augsburg Fortress Press, 2004], 53).

[8] Martin Luther.

[9] This claim, I make not lightly, but with deep grief. It has been articulated by countless voices. Hear, for example, Bishop Bernardino Mandlate of the Methodist Church of Mozambique in a presentation to the United Nations PrepCom for the World Summit on Social Development Plus Ten, New York, February, 1999. The international debt of the most indebted nations, he declared "is covered with the blood of African children. African children die so that North American children may overeat." So too spoke a Mexican strawberry picker addressing a delegation of U.S. elected officials that I led on a fact-finding delegation to Mexico: "Our children die of hunger because our land which ought grow food for them, is used by international companies to produce strawberries for your tables."

[10] Sri Lankan theologian, Tissa Balassuriya, asks a similar question: "Why is it that in spite of hundreds of thousands of eucharistic celebrations, Christians ...who proclaim eucharistic love and sharing deprive the poor people of the world of food, capital, employment, and even land...inequities grow,...[and] the rich live like Dives in the Gospel story" (xi-xii)? His concern and response resonate strikingly with Luther's. He responds that in "hundreds and thousands of masses"...the dynamism flowing from the Lord's Supper has been suffocated by ritual formalism and conformity to the prevailing power system" (xii). He attributes this to "a domestication of the sacraments within the colonial system," (5) claiming that the eucharist has been distorted by the "powerful official controllers of the eucharistic its" into a "very supple instrument for the domestication of believers," (3) an efficacious way of personal sanctification..." (3).

[11] Tissa Balasuriya, *The Eucharist and Human Liberation* (Maryknoll: Orbis, 1979), xi-xii.

[12] Jesuit priest, Jon Sobrino, in conversation.

[13] The New Testament Greek word for "repent " in fact means "to turn around and walk the other way."

[14] Luther, W.A., 2, 413, 27, cited by George W. Forell, *Faith Active in Love* (Minneapolis: Augsburg Publishing House, 1954), 92.

[15] "We" and "us" are loaded words, fraught with ambiguity both evident and concealed. In this essay, the words refer very generally to Christians of the United States who have more than enough material

wealth and have income sufficient to enable concerns beyond survival. Space precludes elaborating the problems with the terms and with a specified referent this broad and heterogeneous. For more coverage, see Moe-Lobeda, *Healing a Broken World: Globalization and God* (Minneapolis: Fortress, 2003), chapter 1.

[16] Martin Luther, "The Sacrament of the Body and Blood of Christ – Against the Fanatics," in *Martin Luther's Basic Theological Writings,* ed. Timothy F. Lull (Minneapolis: Fortress Press, 1989), 321.

[17] Timothy Gorringe, *The Education of Desire* (Valley Forge: Trinity Press International, 2001), 104.

[18] *The Works of Saint Cyril of Jerusalem,* vol. 2 of *The Fathers of the Church,* trans. Leo P. McCauley, S.J. and Anthony A. Stephenson (Washington, D.C.: Catholic University Press, 1970), 203. Gordon Lathrop introduced me to this particular work of Saint Cyril.

[19] As Caryn Riswold points out, for Luther, to erase the practice and memory of sacramental communion with God is to erase knowledge both of who we are and of how we are to live. Luther condemned Rome's doctrine of the mass as sacrifice offered rather than gift received, because that doctrine "quench[ed] the power of baptism...in adults, so that now there are scarcely any who call to mind their own baptism....so that they might know what manner of men they were and how Christians ought to live." Luther, "The Babylonian Captivity of the Church," *LW* 36:58. See Caryn Riswold, "From a Babylonian Captivity to the Otherworld: Martin Luther and Mary Daly." Paper presented at the ELCA's Lutheran Women in Theological Studies Conference, November, 1996.

[20] *Holy Baptism and Related Rites* in *Renewing Worship* series (Minneapolis: Augsburg Fortress Press, 2002), 27.

[21] Morse, *Not Every Spirit,* 43.

[22] Martin Luther, "That These Words of Christ, 'This is My Body,' etc. Still Stand Firm Against the Fanatics," *LW* 37:57.

[23] Douglas John Hall, *Lighten Our Darkness: Toward an Indigenous Theology of the Cross* (Philadelphia: Westminster Press, 1976), 113, all italics mine.

[24] Mary Hobgood, *Dismantling Privilege: An Ethics of Accountability* (Cleveland: Pilgrim Press, 2000), 14-15.

[25] Ibid., 5-6, italics mine.

[26] Gordon W. Lathrop, *Holy Ground: A Liturgical Cosmology* (Minneapolis: Augsburg Fortress Press, 2003), 111.

[27] Delving into that vital story must await subsequent work.

[28] Martin Luther, "Two Kinds of Righteousness," *LW* 31:297.

[29] Martin Luther, "The Sacrament of the Body and Blood of Christ – Against the Fanatics," in Lull, 321.

[30] Martin Luther, "Commentary on the Gospel of John," *LW* 22:76.

[31] Martin Luther, "Third Sermon on Pentecost Sunday," in Lenker, 3:316-7.

[32] This assertion regarding Luther is argued in Moe-Lobeda, *Healing a Broken World*, chapter 4.

[33] Arguments range from seeing the bread and wine as the actual bodily presence (i.e. Ambrose) to a strictly symbolic presence. For excellent account of these debates in the Latin church, see Edward J. Kilmartin, S.J., *The Eucharist in the West*, ed. by Robert J Daly, S.J. (Collegeville: Liturgical Press, 1998).

[34] Cf. Joseph Martos, *Doors to the Sacred: A Historical Introduction to Sacraments in the Catholic Church*, rev.ed. (Liguori, Missouri: Liguori Publications, 2001), 215.

[35] Martin Luther, "That These Words of Christ, 'This is My Body,' etc., Still Stand Firm against the Fanatics," *LW* 37:58.

[36] Martin Luther, "Confession Concerning Christ's Supper," in Lull, 397.

[37] Ibid., 387.

[38] Ibid., 386.

[39] Martin Luther, "The Sacrament of the Body and Blood of Christ – Against the Fanatics," Lull, 321.

[40] Brian Swimme, *The Hidden Heart of the Cosmos* (Maryknoll: Orbis Books, 2000), 26, italics mine.

[41] Sigurd Gottesdottir at a meeting of the Society of Anglican and Lutheran Theologians.

[42] Lathrop, *Holy Ground*, 3.

[43] Irenaeus of Lyons, *Against the Heresies*, trans. Dominic J.Unger (New York: Paulist Press, 1992).

[44] Barbara Rossing, "Models of Koinonia in the New Testament and Early Church," in *The Church as Communion* (Geneva: Lutheran World Federation, 1997), 71. The following two paragraphs are derived from this article by Rossing. Any mistakes in my interpretation of her fine work are my fault alone and should not be attributed to her.

[45] See, for example, 1 Cor. 1:9, and 1 Jn.1:3 and 6.

[46] See, for example, Phil.1:7; Heb. 10:33.

[47] See also 1 Jn. 1:3,6; Rom.15:26-27; Rom. 12:13; Phil: 4:15-16; 1 Cor.9:11; 2 Cor. 9:13.

[48] See, for example, 1 Cor.10:16ff.

[49] See, for example, Phil. 2:1.

[50] *Koinonia*, in the second testament may also be interpreted as meaning participation in the detailed phases of the life of Christ (Christ's life, suffering, and rising). Finally, *koinonia* is used at least once (Lk. 5:10) to mean partnership in work.

[51] The words are Dietrich Bonhoeffer's.

[52] Wayne Meeks, in his seminal inquiry into the morality of Christian communities of the first two centuries, concludes that the moral sentiments and behaviors of early Christian communities were shaped by

their practices which, in turn, expressed or taught those values and mores within the faith communities and to outside observers. Baptism, for example, frequently is referenced in early writings as a reminder to people of how they are to "walk" in the world. The Lord's Supper was practiced in such a way that it refigured awareness of self in relationship, proscribed ways of living that shamed the have-nots, and rendered people concerned for and committed to those who were in need (96-98). (Meeks presupposes Alasdair MacIntyre's theory – itself grounded in Aristotelian notions of "practice" forming virtue – that social practices shape moral inclinations. Meeks, however, emphasizes the social dimension of this dynamic over the individual.) While evidence is insufficient to determine "how much baptism really changed behavior of people who were baptized," the evidence "does at least help us to understand the horizons of expectation that baptism established" (92). See Wayne Meeks, *The Origins of Christian Morality: The First Two Centuries* (New Haven and London: Yale University Press, 1993). Other recent research argues that, indeed, the distinguishing feature of early Christian communities was their profoundly counter-cultural practices of caring for the sick, poor, persecuted, and otherwise vulnerable people, not only within the Christian community but also outside its boundaries. See, for example, Rodney Stark, *The Rise of Christianity*, (San Francisco: HarperSanFrancisco, 1997). Early Christian communities were enormously varied in practice and belief. What seems relatively constant were the convictions that: 1) the moral life – to walk in the way "worthy of the God who has called you" (1 Thes. 2:12) – was to behave in accord with the character and action of God as revealed in the person of Jesus of Nazareth, the Christ; 2) character and behavior was a character and behavior of solidarity with those who were in profound need, including material need; and 3) the sacramental community understood itself to be giving social form to the body of Christ, re-membering the body of Christ on Earth. The communion and union with Christ and among believers that was experienced in the Lord's Supper, also was a communion of profound solidarity – taking on the burden of the others' suffering and need, be it material or otherwise.

[53] I first use this term and develop it somewhat in *Healing a Broken World*, ch.5.

[54] This point is elaborated in Moe-Lobeda, *Healing a Broken World*, chapter 4 and pp. 114-132. This paragraph and the following are drawn directly from that work. See also Carter Lindberg, *Beyond Charity* (Minneapolis: Fortress, 1993).

[55] Consistent with the economic ethics in these writings are Luther's three treatises focusing on economic life ("The Short Sermon on Usury," *Weimar Ausgabe* 6. 1 ff; "Trade and Usury," *LW* 45:244-308; and "Admonition to the Clergy that They Preach against Usury." *Weimar Ausgabe* 51. 325ff) and his treatment of economic life in the following works whose primary focus is not economic life:

- "The Ninety-Five Theses."
- "The Blessed Sacrament of the Holy and True Body and Blood of Christ, and the Brotherhoods."
- "Address to the Christian Nobility of the German Nation."
- "Ordinance of a Common Chest." (This contains Luther's biblical rational for social welfare and his descriptions of how a congregation ought organize its social welfare efforts).
- The "Large Catechism" comments on first, fifth, sixth, seventh, and ninth/tenth commandments. (The comments on the seventh contain fierce denunciations of acquiring wealth in ways that burden or oppress the poor.)
- The "Large Catechism" comments on the fourth petition of the Lord's Prayer.
- "On Temporal Authority."
- "Treatise on Good Works."

[56] The following five statements are from Luther, "The Blessed Sacrament of the Holy and True Body and Blood of Christ, and the Brotherhoods," in Lull respectively on pages 255, 251, 260, 247, and 250.

[57] The similarity in the eucharistic economic ethics of Luther and of Lathrop is, of course, only partial. For example, while both see eucharist as forming the assembly into people who love and express that love in meeting the needs of people who are impoverished, Lathrop's claim that this happens through re-oriented worldview is not shared by Luther (at least explicitly), and Luther's theology of the indwelling Christ as the love with which Christians love neighbor is not integral to Lathrop's eucharistic economics. Lathrop, *Holy Ground*, 148.

[58] Lathrop, *Holy Ground*, 152.

[59] William Cavanaugh, *Torture and the Eucharist* (Oxford: Blackwell, 1998), 279. Cavanaugh's theorizing of eucharist as power for resistance is similar to mine, but distinct in many ways, one of which is the locus of dominating power that he describes as confronted by the eucharist and solidarity. His work discusses power in the form of the repressive state, and mine power in the form of unaccountable global economic players. My agreement with Cavanaugh's weaving together of solidarity and eucharist (and with his political ecclesiology) does not signal agreement with all of his christological presuppositions.

[60] Cited in Cavanaugh, 12.

[61] Perspectives all too often unheeded in the dominant discourse.

[62] That valid and vital claim also is complex and messy. Feminist philosopher of science, Donna Haraway says it well. "To see from below is neither easily learned nor unproblematic, even if 'we' 'naturally' inhabit the great underground terrain of subjugated knowledges." [Donna Haraway, *Simians, Cyborgs, and Women: The Reinvention of Nature* (New York: Routledge, 1991), 192.] The problems

are countless. I begin to identify them in Moe-Lobeda, Cynthia, "Christian Ethics toward Earth-Honoring Faiths," in *Festschrift* in honor of Larry Rasmussen. *Union Seminary Quarterly Review* 57:1-2 (2003).

[63] Lutheran diaconal ministers from around the world, gathered in South Africa, iterate the last of these: "We acknowledge with gratitude the many kinds of diaconal work that the Church has carried out through the centuries, and which necessarily continues in our own day. This work is now challenged to move toward more prophetic forms of *diakonia*. Inspired by Jesus and the prophets who confronted those in power and called for changes in unjust structures and practices, we pray that God may empower us to help transform all that leads to human greed, violence, injustice, and exclusion." "While *diakonia* begins as unconditional service to the neighbor in need, it leads inevitably to social change that restores, reforms and transforms." "An Epistle form the LWF Global Consultation on Diakonia," 7 November, 2002: 1.

[64] The claim made in this essay, and made by Gordon Lathrop and Luther before him – that the eucharist may change people toward a form of neighbor love that leads to earth care and to heeding the needs of the vulnerable – has at least one great fault. It is the problem of classic virtue ethics when not accompanied by social value based ethics: Character shaped into the form of love, even at its best, is not adequate to lead people into lives that actually ameliorate poverty because it does not account for its systemic causes. These "contents" of solidarity go far in resolving that problem. They are one try at a necessary complement to the ethic of character/virtue.

[65] Balasuriya, 59. Whereas Jesus gave his life for others, and the eucharist is a memorial of that self-sacrifice, in the colonial expansion, Tissa asserts, the roles were reversed. "The 'Christians' were the robbers and plunderers. They murdered in the name of the expansion of western civilization and of the religion of Christ… the eucharistic community was in the main oblivious to its obligation of love of neighbor."

[66] Ibid., 61.

[67] Here I refer to theological method in its many modes: theology of worship, theology of liturgy, liturgy as theology, theology from liturgy, theology and ethics.

[68] Lathrop, in *Holy Ground,* highlights a powerful example of this "curve:" where liturgy nurtures an interior or privatized orientation to the world, it leaves largely untouched the public realties of social injustice or ecological degradation.

[69] Martos, *Doors to the Sacred*, 218. Actual rituals centered in the bread and wine varied, of course, depending upon time, location, theological community, cultural, political influences. Developed over years, and developed differently in different regions and under influence of different leaders, and in

context of different cultural roots. For excellent description of that development in highly accessible language and form, see Martos chapter 8. For an account of that development in the Latin church, see the work of Kilmartin.

[70] *Constitutions of the Evangelical Lutheran Church in America*, 4.01–02.

[71] Martin Luther, "Commentary on the Gospel of John," *LW* 23:146.

[72] The phrase is taken from Larry Rasmussen's reference to the "drama of all creation's redemption," in "Drilling in the Cathedra" *Dialog: A Journal of Theology* 42:3 (Fall 2003), 206.

[73] Offertory Prayer in the *Lutheran Book of Worship,* pages 68, 88, and 109.

[74] John 6:56 and Martin Luther in comments on John 6:56, *LW* 23:144-148.

[75] Martin Luther, "Third Sermon for Pentecost," in John Nicholas Lenker, ed., *Sermons of Martin Luther* (Grand Rapids: Baker, 1983), vol. 3: 321.

[76] Luther, W.A., 2, 413, 27, cited by George W. Forell, *Faith Active in Love* (Minneapolis: Augsburg Publishing House, 1954), 92.

[77] *Lutheran Book of Worship,* 201.

[78] The United Nations Development Programme, *Human Development Report 1998* (New York and Oxford: Oxford University Press, 1998).

[79] "NGO Matters: Newsletter of the South African NGO Coalition" 3:3 (April 2000), 9.

[80] Sallie McFague, *Life Abundant* (Minneapolis: Fortress Press, 2001), 128.

[81] This paragraph regarding lament is taken from Moe-Lobeda, *Public Church: For the Life of the World* (Minneapolis: Fortress Press, 2004), 68-9. See it for more extensive inquiry into the role of lament in the life of the church.

[82] Townes, 24, drawing upon the ideas of Walter Brueggemann, "The Costly Loss of Lament," *Journal for the Study of the Old Testament* 36 (1986), 60.

[83] Ibid.

[84] Ibid.

# ELEVEN

# Violent Death, Public Tragedy, And Rituals Of Lament: An Interfaith Agenda

*Herbert Anderson*

Loving and healing God, we pray for everyone whose death was violent. Shower with your sustaining grace all those who mourn one slaughtered by the violence of our fallen world. Do not hide your face from us in our anger and despair over death without meaning or sense. Help us to fashion sturdy souls and safe environments. Reweave the fabric of our lives and renew us in the hope that your justice will roll down like mighty waters and joy will spring up from broken ground into a living stream. Amen.[1]

How shall we mourn our losses in a toxic world in which random violence dominates our daily lives and darkens our hope? How shall we fashion sturdy souls and safe environments in which to foster hope that endures and dreams that flourish? What kind of rituals will reweave the social fabric, renew our visions of hope and be the source of joy? My proposal is that we combine the recovery of lament with the renewal of ritual in order to fashion public rituals of lament that will sustain individuals in their grief and refashion communities shattered by the public tragedy of violence so that together we might hope again.

## THE PROXIMITY OF DEATH WITHOUT MEANING OR SENSE

Violence is an old and troubling dimension of the human story. Although the origins of violence are ambiguous and debatable, the consequences of violent death are clear and pervasive. Families and friends have always struggled with complex thoughts and feelings in the aftermath of a violent death from suicide, homicide, or accident. In our time, the spread of indiscriminate violence not only destroys innocent lives, it challenges our notions of invulnerability and threatens to destabilize societies. As individuals and as communities, we need to mourn the death of "one slaughtered by the violence of our fallen world" and then reweave the fabric of our lives and renew our hope for justice, as the opening prayer suggests.

The proximity of the world's suffering from violent death "without meaning or sense" is the new feature of our time affecting how we mourn. In *Suffering and Hope,* written in 1986, New Testament scholar A. Christiaan Beker defined this time in history as a "global, apocalyptic climate" of tragic and meaningless suffering. Beker's analysis is still relevant. However, in contrast to former times, "modern technology and the media bring these world events and their attendant suffering into the inner sanctuaries of our homes."[2] Because we can watch bodies fly and buildings crumble and children burn on television, suffering anywhere in the world invades our homes and becomes our own. The proximity of suffering is also the result of societies being more porous: stress from anywhere in the outside world is more likely to penetrate the inside. The scope and intensity of irrational suffering is therefore simultaneously public and personal. This leads to one of the conundrums of modern, pluralistic, urbanized societies: *while we are more vulnerable to outside forces, we have fewer commonly shared beliefs and practices with which to cope with the consequences of violence and terror as individuals and as communities.*

Because the distinctions between public and private grief are less and less clear, we mourn for suffering not our own and discover personal sorrow often attached to public loss and displayed in the public sphere. Communal lament for a recognized hero, for example, allows for personal mourning otherwise not permitted. It is not surprising, therefore, that people around the world attached their personal grief to the tragic death of Princess Diana. That accumulation of personal grief in turn intensified the public despair over her death. As with Princess Diana, the death of President Ronald Reagan prompted spontaneous, makeshift displays of shrines that appeared at his boyhood home, at his presidential library, and on the Hollywood Walk of Fame. Those *de rigueur* shrines included jars of jelly beans, President Reagan's favorite candy, as well as flowers and flags. When the death is a public tragedy, it is increasingly likely that the places where death occurred are not only shrines of remembrance but places where people actively mark a death with ritual activities such as lighting candles, tying ribbons, displaying pictures and writing messages in memory of those who has died.

# Ordo: Bath, Word, Prayer, Table

## Public Tragedy and Communal Grief

Every death has a communal dimension. Families, the organization of the workplace, neighborhoods, and religious congregations are all affected by the loss when one of its members dies. The grief that a community experiences is more than the accumulation of individual pain; it is a systemic loss that must be acknowledged fully and mourned publicly in order to form a common memory and rebuild a community. Violent death that becomes a public tragedy shatters carefully constructed worldviews and threatens to fracture the stability of a community. It challenges assumptions of an ordered universe and undermines a community's presumptions of invulnerability. Because modern societies are more porous and the boundaries between private and public grief more fluid, systemic loss and communal grief will be more frequent. After violent death, communities will ask the same question individuals ask: *will the world be safe again?* One of the reasons we tell stories and form rituals after violent death is to make the world feel safe again.

According to Kenneth J. Doka's definition, a traumatic event or violent death becomes a public tragedy "when there is a collective definition of that event as a significant calamity."[3] The more pervasive the consequences and the more extensive the suffering caused by the violent event, the more likely it will be experienced as a public tragedy. The social value of the victims and the duration of events surrounding the death or deaths also contribute to defining violent death as a public tragedy.[4] Not all violent death is a public tragedy and not every public tragedy is the result of violence. The sudden or premature death of a beloved public official may also be regarded as a public tragedy because of the social consequences of the loss. The dissolution of a rural town or the disruption to a community when a major employer leaves are public tragedies warranting lament.

When a public tragedy occurs, Lawrence E. Sullivan has observed, diverse histories are brought together carrying meanings that may collide with one another. Forming rituals of lament in response to public tragedies in a pluralistic society is therefore both necessary and complex. It is necessary because of the ability of ritual "to *compress* experiences and evaluations of existence in time into terse symbolic shorthand."[5] And yet, forming ritual response to public tragedy is complex because any ritual is "full of contradictions, paradoxes, and rough edges, because it stylizes, in a brief time, competing forces spread over a life-time of perceptions."[6] Tragic events, Sullivan argues, have a peculiar way of fusing diverse histories with one another. The rituals we fashion about public tragedy therefore need to be able to encompass those diverse narratives.

This essay focuses on those violent deaths that are also a public tragedy. A natural disaster or catastrophe is a public tragedy because the death or destruction is extensive. Some public tragedies, like the Columbine High School shootings in 1999 or the explosion of the Columbia space shuttle in 2003, cast long shadows of pain and evoke questions of meaning not easily resolved. Violent death becomes a public tragedy because of its significance and wide-ranging consequences. The expression of communal grief is seldom easy because there are competing emotions about the same loss and conflicted beliefs about how the violent death shall be mourned by the community. *In modern, pluralistic societies, finding common language that will transform mute pain into a shared experience is necessary but not sufficient. Rituals in response to public tragedy must also embody the diversity of the mourning community.*

## RESTORATIVE STORIES AND RITUALS

Stories of grief demand ritual. Without rituals to shape our stories of grief, we may be overwhelmed by its chaos or trapped in a private cul-de-sac of inexpressible sadness. Rituals express our darkest fears and our deepest pains in order to find enduring consolation. There is almost always a ritual context to telling and hearing stories of loss that could be as simple as lunch with an old friend or as complex as retirement celebrations for famous public persons. When the grieving moment is a personal conversation with one or two people, the ritual can be quite spontaneous and unpredictable.[7] When grief is communal, a public, patterned, symbolic, dependable action is needed to insure an environment in which to mourn together for our individual and communal grief.

Ritual fosters community reorganization for the sake of continuity in the midst of chaos. Rituals fashion common meaning and remake the world into a hospitable and habitable place after a public tragedy. If diverse and complex communities are to grieve together, a careful, collaborative process is required to insure a ritual structure that gives expression to their common and very separate grief. That ritual structure needs to be supported by a public sphere hospitable to strongly held, and yet radically diverse, religious beliefs. The planning for such a ritual must attend carefully to conflicting interpretations of a violent death and the equally diverse and often conflicted understandings of evil and justice as well as well as culturally formed patterns of mourning. The desire for the safety that commonly held beliefs and practices provide is in tension with the need for a pluralistic ritual that seeks to hold together a diverse community suffering from a common tragedy. While the first commitment of any community that has suffered violent death must be to honor difference in so far as that is possible, there is always a limit to how much diversity one ritual can bear. Public tragedies nonetheless demand public ritual.

# Ordo: Bath, Word, Prayer, Table

The purpose of a ritual after public tragedy is to structure communal lament and show solidarity with the victims. Kenneth J. Doka has proposed that the public ritual reaffirms community and "offers an opportunity for the different strands of a community, potentially fragmented by a crisis, to stand together and publicly demonstrate their fundamental unity."[8] Doka's vision of a single narrative response to public tragedy is an understandable goal for the sake of communal or national unity. It is not likely, however, that a single ritual will be able to reconstruct a common narrative or interpret a violent death in a single philosophical or spiritual framework. There will be many interpretations and many responses to a single tragic event. Weaving together diverse threads of communal grief and rage with differing interpretations of a public tragedy is a complex task, fraught with deep tensions between particular cultural or religious responses and the longing for a common narrative about a public tragedy that will hold together those diverse threads.

Narrative and ritual are distinct but complementary processes by which we individually and collectively express and maintain or recreate a vision of life. This connection between story and ritual is a major theme in *Mighty Stories, Dangerous Rituals*.[9] "Whether we are conscious or not of this need, it is nonetheless true that our search for meaning is a search for an appropriate narrative for life. In this quest, ritualization becomes indispensable, for it provides time, space, symbols, and bodily enactment for disclosing, entering, and interpreting the many stories that comprise our individual and communal narration and give shape and meaning to our lives." This connection between narrative and ritual is never more necessary and seldom more complex than after public tragedy.

## Planning a Public Ritual Response to Public Tragedy

Every community facing public tragedy will need to design a ritual response that is appropriate to the context in which the public tragedy occurs. Religious communities will be expected to exercise leadership in fashioning such a public ritual. The details of such a public ritual will be a combination of deliberate choice, random chance, and routine precedent. In this time of global violence and irrational suffering, ecumenical organizations and/or interfaith structures need to be planning for a ritual moment before such a public tragedy occurs. There will be more deliberate choice if religious leaders have an established working relationship. When religious leaders are brought together for the first time by the tragic event, random choice (because of the people who happen to gather) and routine precedent (because under stress we revert to traditional patterns) will dominate the planning process. What is at stake is more than the ritual product: the planning process is itself a way to make the world feel safe again after violent death.

Whether it occurs prior to a public tragedy or in response to a tragic moment, the planning process needs to attend to several questions. 1) Are all the religious voices represented in both planning the ritual and participating in it? 2) Is there any ritual gesture or action that would exclude a religious community/tradition from participation? 3) From their tradition, what must they be able to do in a public gathering in order that it might be ritually meaningful to participants from their tradition? 4) What is the distinct contribution of each religious tradition to a shared ritual moment? Beyond these preliminary questions, there are four foci that should inform planning the ritual moment: the context; the ritual aim; ritual honesty; and embodied juxtapositions.

*The Context* When people gather for a ritual after a public tragedy, basic orientation to the world God has created has been shaken. At the same time, a tragedy may fuse together diverse narratives into a deeper awareness of the communal dimension of all life. Gordon Lathrop has used "geography" as a metaphor to invite our awareness of the location, direction, time, and physical interdependence of an assembly at worship. Many human communal rituals, Lathrop argues, contain a "geography:" dreams of a land or community as it was or as it will be. Planning rituals of lament after violent death will need to include careful attention to "geography" so that the ritual will connect "to the past, to the future, to all the surrounding communities of creatures, even to the cosmic and geologic location of the earth itself."[10] Violence disrupts our common care for one another as creatures in the community of creatures. The "geography" metaphor reminds us of the need "to wait confidently amidst all things for the healing of all things"[11] as part of our ritual response when violent death occurs.

Because geography matters, more and more public ritualizing occurs at the place of the tragedy. Simple, almost spontaneous, rituals happen as large numbers of people place flowers at the sight of a road accident, often marking the anniversary of an event. With visits to graves now less common, the 'sacred place' associated with a dead person may be the site of their sudden and violent death, not their last resting place. The specific location for a public ritual of lament should be in response to those places that the community has identified as significant markers of the public tragedy. It may include a procession to several places where violence has occurred in order to heal the physical places where we remember the tragedies of our lives.

When ritual occurs in the public sphere, it cannot concern itself only with the gathered community. Lathrop again: "Worship is not just for us. Lines of connection and meaning run out from the worship gathering to the very contours of ordinary daily life, to the structures of our societies, to the commerce and communication between peoples, to the earth itself and all its animals and inanimate inhabitants."[12] Planning such an event is, according to Edward Foley, Capuchin, an exercise in public

# Ordo: Bath, Word, Prayer, Table

theology. This perspective of public theology, he argues, enables communities to discern what kind of theology they are making when they worship.[13] What kind of commentary on world events is implied in the ritual action? How is the public ritual a community's interpretative act of their relationship or their hopes for neighborhood, society and world in which they pray? What sort of "ordered world" does the public ritual imply? Does the "geography" of the ritual embrace all the dimensions of human life shattered by the public tragedy? These questions will help the planning process move toward a deeper, more inclusive ritual that will begin to reorder a worldview shattered by violence.

*The Ritual Aim* The effectiveness of a public ritual after violent death is determined in part by the clarity of the ritual aim. Rituals that are political, in so far as they seek to re-establish the values of the body politic, are sometimes in tension with rituals that seek to heal, exorcise, and protect. Catherine Bell makes a useful distinction between these two ritual aims. *Rites of affliction,* she suggests, demonstrate "people's persistent efforts to redress wrongs, alleviate sufferings, and ensure well-being"...and... "redefine the cosmological order in response to new challenges and new formulations of human needs."[14] *Political rites* seek to order a community around shared values and invite people to trust political leadership in their exercise of power for the common good. In a political ritual, one must provide a simplified interpretation of what is going on in the world that can help those involved make sense of a tragedy. "It is through ritual that those claiming power demonstrate how their interests are in the natural, real, or fruitful order of things."[15] On the other hand, rites of affliction acknowledge and deepen the ambiguity of a situation in order to identify the complexity of grief after violent death. While both ritual forms are necessary for social order and the common good, rites of affliction are more effective in response to public tragedy. Rituals of lament, as one expression of rituals of affliction, provide an opportunity to refashion a view of the universe in response to new challenges and new forms of human need without oversimplifying the deep underlying issues too ambiguous or awkward or painful to address in political rituals and without diminishing human pain. Anger and the desire for revenge, issues of truth and justice, and the need for reconciliation are more effectively expressed in a ritual of affliction until they can become the community's political agenda as well.

Religious leaders may have the difficult task of insisting that a political rite should not be the primary response to a public tragedy. The need to accommodate diverse and sometimes competing political agendas may in fact diminish the capacity of the ritual action to give expression to communal sadness. On September 11, 2001, I was on the staff of St. Mark's Episcopal Cathedral in Seattle, Washington. By the time we gathered as a staff to plan a ritual for that evening, the major political leaders in the community had agreed to participate in the service at St. James Roman Catholic Cathedral. Their presence moved that gathering toward a political rite. The singing of "God Bless America" at St. James Cathedral was broadcast widely on National Public Radio and then replicated at many similar gatherings. Because the participants in the service at St. Mark's were religious rather than political leaders, we were able to fashion a ritual of affliction. Instead of "God Bless America," we heard Samuel Barber's *Agnus Dei* and sang "We Shall Overcome." Although the difference was quite by random choice, it is a reminder of the importance of fashioning public rituals after violent death that keep the focus on expressions of affliction and lament.

*Ritual Honesty.* Authentic rituals provide the occasion, the language, and the gestures for people to encounter realities and truths that most of us would choose to avoid. Rituals enable us to tell, to hear, and to act out the truth about ourselves and our world, and the truth about God whose ways are not our ways. For that to happen, rituals must be honest. If the stories we tell conceal more than they reveal, they foster dishonesty. When the stories we tell our children about our lives do not include instances of vulnerability, we fashion a mythic view of reality that is finally false. When they are honest, the stories we tell and the rituals we enact both express and create community.

Rituals that are honest will unlock secret pain. We cannot fashion a restorative narrative or ritual without visiting the moments and memories that are most painful. Consolation for both individuals and communities depends on the freedom to attend to the wounds that hurt most. Reconciliation will only begin when people are free to tell the stories of violence in the context of a community narrative of care even if there is more than one version of the story. "Ritual is a privileged place for appropriating [God's] redeeming narrative because it honors diverse stories within a community of shared values. It also provides a setting in which to explore the darkness and name the demons without mythologizing or secret keeping. Such communal gatherings have a particular capacity for embracing personal tales of violence and destruction."[16] Not all injustice can be addressed before prayers for justice must be prayed. Ritual honesty does not mean that all secrets must be publicly revealed but it does mean that the ritual is not used to hide the truth. Ritual honesty is, however, mandatory if the lament is to identify topics that a community must address in order to heal.

*Juxtapositions.* The complexity of honesty and the inevitability of ambiguity inherent in public tragedy are maintained in ritual form through paradox. Paradox embodies the necessary contradictoriness of life and faith in the light of God. The paradox of *kenosis* and *plerosis*, of power and powerlessness, fulfillment and struggle, brokenness and wholeness is a way of challenging triumphalistic and elitist certainty or arrogance on the one side and immobilizing pessimism on the other. Contradictions are inherent in human nature, in human community, in the circumstances of life, and in some religious belief systems. Public tragedy is inescapably ambiguous. Therefore contradictions need to be part of any public response to violent death in order for quite different visions of the same reality or competing interpretations of death and suffering to coexist in the same ritual moment.

Only by saying two things, Gordon Lathrop has observed, may we avoid being immediately misled. Lathrop uses the word 'juxtaposition' to identify a liturgical paradox: thanksgiving next to lament, judgment alongside grace, speech with silence, the presence of absence beside the absence of presence. Paradoxical liturgy is a way to avoid absolutizing. In the face of so much fear and uncertainty – so much violence and senseless suffering – so much diversity – so much change and flux, there is the human tendency to look for absolutes. For that reason, idolatry stalks the same terrain as anxiety. Ritual that embodies paradox will deepen our pain and at the same time draw us out of ourselves before the living God. These juxtapositions are essential because they help to fashion a worldview without arrogance or pessimism, acknowledging "that we do not know everything of the mysteries and powers that surround us."[17]

There are other issues in the present climate of this culture that make it difficult yet mandatory to give public shape and form to our grief. The individualism of this society has made it more and more difficult to find common cause except perhaps in our grief. And yet our common grief is difficult to express because we lack a shared symbol system. We return at the end to the question posed at the beginning of this essay. What kind of rituals will help us mourn our losses in a toxic world in which random violence dominates our daily lives? My proposal is that we form rituals of lament to give voice to our shared and separate affliction. There is an urgency to lament because it is a way of responding to the permeability of irrational suffering and violent death without apathy or cynicism. The great enemy of hope is cynicism and the alternative to cynicism is the recovery of lament.

### Rituals of Lament

Every community's response to a public tragedy will be different when it reflects the diverse cultures and religious traditions of its context. If the community's planning process follows some variation of a ritual of mutual affirmation, as Rabbi Lawrence Hoffman has proposed, then each religious tradition will be invited to make its best contribution to the ritual moment. In a service of mutual affirmation, Hoffman suggests, "religious traditions represented are given the opportunity to worship side by side, as it were, alternately speaking in their own particular way and then silently witnessing to their co-worshippers doing the same."[18] The advantage of this model for public ritual is that it honors particular beliefs and invites all participants to learn from each other. The challenge of this model of mutual affirmation is that some religious traditions will face the difficult task of setting aside ritual invariability in order to fashion a common response or simply being present for a differing or even unorthodox ritual action for the sake of community healing. If, however, the chronological priority of the human story and public tragedy is respected, then there will be room enough to embody the whole story without leaving anything out. And when there is general agreement that a ritual is an embodied, contextual, social and strategic experience, it will be easier to plan a service with sensitivity and respect for others and for one's own faith tradition.

The prayer of lament is deeply rooted in the psalm tradition shared by Jews and Christians. Until recently, however, lament has been a hidden dimension of Christian piety and ritual practice. The recovery of lament, Billman and Migliore suggest in *Rachel's Cry: Prayer of Lament and Rebirth of Hope*, "keeps prayer anchored in real life experience and prevents it from drifting off into make-believe and empty phrases. Israel's faith and hope are all the more remarkable for refusing to stifle the voice of anger, pain, and despair."[19] The presence of lament keeps ritual honest. When our prayers do not include protest, it is too easy to overlook the deeper pain and hidden ambiguities of public tragedy. When the community laments, it demonstrates with its tears that suffering is not without meaning and that suffering is worth weeping over. For these reasons and more, I believe lament is the best contribution of Christians and Jews alike to developing a service of mutual affirmation.

The practice of lament and arguing with God is an unsettling tradition of prayer because it includes the expression of complaint, anger, and protest to God. The psalms of lament are filled with terror and hurt, confusion, anguish and bewilderment about the absence of God when life is not going well. Lament psalms presume that life is not going well because God is absent. The argument of a lament psalm is that a public tragedy has occurred because God was not paying attention. Lament is a prayer of protest that expects God's active engagement in human affairs. The lament psalms regularly promise that God will not be permanently absent. Our prayer of protest is in fact possible because we believe God will not be absent permanently. The covenant with God, in which we live and argue and lament, is marked by the permanent promise of presence but not the promise of permanent presence.

J. Frank Henderson has outlined several liturgies that include lament psalms and that follow the psalm form of lament: address to God; complaint; confession of trust; petition for help; vow of praise. The introductory actions of greeting, call to worship and invocation address God. The complaint, confession and petition segments include appropriate psalms, relevant stories of violence and public tragedy and hymns. The blessings or benedictions and sending return the community to the mystery of God's promised presence in the midst of the experience of God's absence.[20] Words are balanced with silence, stories with song, light with darkness, individual pain with communal suffering, despair with hope, symbolic action with personal reflection in order to create an environment in which suffering is validated and hope is restored. The use of a lament psalm in an interfaith context still requires sensitivity and respect for all involved because there are religious traditions in which arguing with God is not acceptable behavior.

Rituals of lament reflect the belief that consolation will be found where our wounds hurt most. We cannot fashion restorative narrative or healing rituals without visiting the moments and memories from the past and the present that are most painful. Lament is a cry that gives voice to the dread of abandonment and the terror of emptiness that often accompanies deep loss. It provides a language for our pain that makes it possible to share what we might otherwise hide. Lament diminishes isolation by making sorrow public. In rituals of lament, the community is formed into a safe container for the chaos of grief. Communal lament helps to make the crisis manageable in part because people refashion themselves into a community of the suffering ones. Public rituals of lament also help a community maintain continuity in a chaotic time of grief by integrating past experience, present circumstances, and future hope.

Lament in an apocalyptic time of meaningless and irrational suffering is not without hope. It is a hopeful form of prayer because it juxtaposes the present horror with a future unknown. Lament holds pain and hope in respectful tension. The existing order of things is not the final reality. What is happening in the world can be named and described clearly because it will not be forever. Rituals of affliction in apocalyptic time can be fiercely honest because they nourish the hope that things can and will be different. As long as we keep lamenting, the need for justice is never out of sight. Lament rituals foster hope by calling evil, injustice, violence and irrational suffering by their proper names. Communal lament names problems, seeks justice, and hopes for God's deliverance. It is a prelude to justice.

The possibility of authentic hope for individuals and communities after violent death is determined by the way we connect suffering to hope. For that reason, for this time, we need to fashion souls sturdy enough to live with vulnerability without being overwhelmed by it and endure the presence of irrational suffering both in public and private spheres without becoming cynical. For that reason, for this time, and through the power of hope, we don't give up, and don't give ourselves up; we remain unaccepting of and unreconciled to an unjust and violent world. For that reason, for this time, we need rituals of lament that will renew our communities and strengthen our resolve to stand together in hope. For this time, we need honest rituals that will reweave the fabric of our lives and renew in us a hope that endures and joy that springs forth from broken ground.

## Endnotes

[1] Prayer by Herbert Anderson after prayers from *Enriching Our Worship 2*, (New York: Church Publishing Incorporated, 2000), p 143.

[2] J. Christiaan Beker, *Suffering and Hope: The Biblical Vision and the Human Predicament*, (Philadelphia: Fortress Press, 1987), 16.

[3] Kenneth J. Doka, "What Makes a Tragedy Public?" in *Living with Grief, Coping with Public Tragedy*, ed by Marcia Lattanzi-Light and Kenneth J. Doka (New York: Brunner-Routledge, 2003), 10.

[4] Ibid., 6-10.

[5] Lawrence E. Sullivan, *Histories and Rituals: The Case of a National Rite of Mourning* (Arizona State University: The University Lecture in Religion, 1991), 2.

[6] Ibid.

[7] Kenneth J. Doka, "Memorialization, Ritual, and Public Tragedy," in *Living with Grief, Coping with Public Tragedy*, ed by Marcia Lattanzi-Light and Kenneth J. Doka (New York: Brunner-Routledge, 2003), 180.

[8] Herbert Anderson and Edward Foley, *Mighty Stories, Dangerous Rituals: Weaving Together the Human and the Divine* (San Francisco: Jossey-Bass Publishers, 1998), 27.

[9] Edward K. Rynearson, *Retelling Violent Death* (Philadelphia: Brunner-Routledge, 2001). Rynearson has outlined in a compelling fashion how the violence, violation, and volition of unnatural dying give a different meaning to death and necessitate distinct modes of immediate *and* long-term care over the duration of "violent death bereavement." Work on this essay began while collaborating with Rynearson and Fanny Correa, MSW, on a "Protocal for the Development of Community Grief Centers" for the Office of Victims of Crimes, U. S. Department of Justice.

[10] Gordon W. Lathrop, *Holy Ground: A Liturgical Cosmology* (Minneapolis: Fortress Press, 2003), 44.

[11] Ibid., 53.

[12] Ibid., 102.

[13] Foley, Edward, Capuchin, "Worship as Public Theology," in *International Journal of Practical Theology* 8 (2004) pp 1-13.

[14] Bell, Catherine, *Ritual: Perspectives and Dimensions* (New York: Oxford University Press, 1997), 119-120.

[15] Ibid., 129.

[16] Anderson and Foley, *Mighty Stories, Dangerous Rituals*, 172.

## Ordo: Bath, Word, Prayer, Table

[17] Lathrop, *Holy Ground*, 218.

[18] Henderson, J. Frank, *Liturgies of Lament* (Chicago: Liturgy Training Publications. 1994), 92. Rabbi Lawrence Hoffman suggests three different types of interfaith services: 1) An *Indigenous Service with Guests* in which one religious tradition hosts a service to which others are invited; 2) A *Service of Highest Common Denominator* in which the ritual practice draws on what the traditions hold in common without excluding; 3) *Service of Mutual Affirmation* in which each participant offers the best from his or her tradition as a response to a public tragedy.

[19] Kathleen D. Billman and Daniel Migliore, *Rachel's Cry of Lament: Prayer of Lament and the Rebirth of Hope* (Cleveland, Ohio: United Church Press, 1999), 33.

[20] Henderson, *Liturgies of Lament*, 33.

# TWELVE

# Liturgy: Many Becoming One

*Anscar J. Chupungco*

LITURGY: A SIGN THAT UNITES AND DIVIDES

Worship of God, which is regarded as the noblest of human activities, is like a double-edged sword. It can rally Christians toward "becoming one" or it can divide them into splinter groups. The experience of some religious groups and parish communities in matters referring to common worship is emblematic: often it is not the theology behind worship that provokes people to dispute but the observance of the liturgical *ordo*. On the other hand, worship has the rare power to unite warring parties and calm their anger or to strengthen the peace and harmony that exist among family members and friends.

Time and again the Church of Jesus Christ has suffered the pain of division brought about by doctrinal, socio-cultural, political, and liturgical differences. Although the question of *Filioque* was uppermost in the debate that led to the separation of Rome and Constantinople in 1054, liturgical questions as minor as the singing of *alleluia* in Lent were irritants. Martin Luther's (+1546) program of church reform contained substantial liturgical issues that took the Roman Church to task for abuses in matters pertaining to indulgences, private Masses, exaggerated veneration of saints and their relics, rubricism, denial of the chalice to the laypeople, use of Latin (already a dead language), and the doctrine of the sacrifice of the Mass. More recently the Roman Church experienced another division caused by the objections of Marcel Lefèbvre, a Vatican II Council father, against the revised Roman Missal of Pope Paul VI.

Against this backdrop of dissension and division among Christians we are privileged to witness the many efforts of theologians, pastors, and liturgists who work for unity. Ecumenical dialogues have produced such remarkable documents as *Baptism, Eucharist and Ministry* (1982) and *One Baptism: Towards Mutual Recognition of Christian Initiation* (2001). For its part the Roman Church published as early as 1967 an *Ecumenical Directory* that dealt with several liturgical concerns. Ecumenical liturgies are frequently held in small communities and a good number of churches devoutly observe the annual Week of Prayer for Christian Unity. These are comforting signs that the Spirit of unity is at work in the Church.[1]

## Liturgical *Ordo*: A Road to Unity

This small contribution to the *Primer* in honor of Gordon Lathrop takes inspiration from Lathrop himself who is both a liturgical and ecumenical theologian and a friend in the Lord. The aim of this writer is to elaborate, if that is at all possible, the thesis Lathrop enunciated in his classic book *Holy Things: A Liturgical Theology*, namely that the liturgical *ordo* is an instrument of unity among Christians. In the preface to that book, Lathrop informs the readers "the book itself arose out of a years-long reflection on the ecumenical significance of the meaning of the *ordo* in the liturgy." A liturgical theologian who is zealous for the unity of the Church, he enjoins all to study the liturgy and to discover in its *ordo* the elements that affirm the fundamental unity of all Christians. "Against all the current forces of disintegration, we need reflections on the liturgy that are ecumenical, not so much explorations of our differences as quests for the patterns and symbols and faith that unite us."[2]

Liturgical *ordo* plays a significant role in the ecumenical thinking of Gordon Lathrop. His study of liturgical *ordo* in Christian antiquity, especially in the writings of Justin Martyr, and his reading of classic authors such as Anton Baumstark, Gregory Dix, and Alexander Schmemann led him to the conclusion that the ritual ordering, pattern, or basic shape of the liturgy "has united Christians throughout the ages."[3] Despite the centuries-old division among churches, there is a core *ordo* of liturgical worship that defines them as Christian and unites them beyond their particular liturgical traditions. In this sense the foundational liturgical *ordo* is indeed one of the many roads to becoming one. The science (or art) of comparative liturgy initiated by Baumstark reveals that beneath the diversity of liturgical traditions among denominations, especially those that belong to the mainline, one can discover a common *ordo* that defies confessional divisions. Comparative liturgy allows us to look beyond the differences and to identify the points of convergence. Churches celebrate baptism with varying formulas ("I baptize you" as against "This servant of God is baptized") and ritual (immersion as against infusion). Some churches practice elaborate pre-baptismal and post-baptismal rites that include exorcism, blessing of water, anointing, vesting, and presentation of lighted candle. Others have trimmed the celebration to the minimum: proclamation of the word of God and immersion in the name of the blessed Trinity. What Lathrop wishes his readers to realize is that underlying the confessional differences in liturgical traditions there are "root elements of an *ordo*" that safeguard the fundamental unity among Christ's churches in matters of worship.

The *ordo* is sometimes regarded almost exclusively as the format of a worship service. Thus we commonly name our service books "Order:" the Order of Baptism, the Order of the Eucharist, the Order of Daily Prayer, and so on.[4] However, Lathrop rightly understands liturgical *ordo* as a pattern encompassing not only the format of worship service but also the church calendar of feasts and the liturgical environment.[5] Here we also find points of convergence among various traditions, especially in the observance of Sunday and the annual feast of Easter as well as in the arrangement of the liturgical space and its furnishings.

## A. The *Ordo* of Worship Services

The road to becoming one should start with the useful exercise of identifying the core elements of the liturgical *ordo*. Two criteria may be used for this exercise. The first is the antiquity of the elements, which can be safely dated from New Testament times to the late patristic era, and the second is the connection they have with the commonly accepted belief of Christians regarding the service in question. It is important to note that the core elements cannot be confined to what the New Testament offers as ritual data. The subsequent interpretation and elaboration of such data by the churches, especially during the first eight centuries, constitute what Lathrop calls "root elements of an *ordo*."

### 1. The Baptismal Ordo

To appreciate this point it is helpful to recall that in the New Testament the celebration of baptism centered on the bare essentials. Ephesians 5:26 mentions only the "washing of water with the word." On the other hand, the references in Romans 6:4 ("when we were baptized we went into the tomb with him") and Acts 8:38 ("Philip and the eunuch went down into the water") seem to imply the rite of immersion. At any rate, washing (bathing) and the word (a ritual formula) would appear to have made up the core or nucleus of the New Testament baptismal *ordo*. Churches have maintained that the baptisms Jesus charged his disciples to perform consisted basically of the act of washing in natural water accompanied by an invocation of the name of the blessed Trinity, as Matthew 28:19 indicates. In fact, in cases of emergency all that is required is the washing with water and the recitation of the Trinitarian formula, or in other words, the bare essentials of the New Testament baptismal liturgy. Yet,

## Ordo: Bath, Word, Prayer, Table

it would be unwise to simply ignore the ritual embellishments included after the biblical period, even if some of them, like the washing of the feet of neophytes and the cup of milk and honey offered to them at Communion, did not endure the test of time.

Lathrop's treatise on the basic baptismal *ordo* relies heavily on the information offered by Justin Martyr before the middle of the second century. One cannot agree more with Lathrop's choice of Justin. It is from Justin's *1 Apology* 61-66 that we receive "a report of the baptismal *ordo*, the scheduling of teaching and bath leading to the meal in the community" or, in other words, the *ordo* of Christian initiation.

Surrounding Justin's data are other sources that practically complete the core elements of the baptismal *ordo*. Around the year 90 CE, the *Didache* informs us that baptism was administered "in the name of the Father, and of the Son, and of the Holy Spirit".[6] Whether this was the actual formula or was meant to define the Trinitarian character of baptism as presented by Matthew 28:19 is difficult to determine. All that we are allowed to conclude is that three divine Names were invoked at baptism. Later patristic writings mention the use of the more elaborate creedal formula. The third-century *Apostolic Tradition* attributed to Hippolytus of Rome uses the form of question and answer before each of the threefold immersion: "Do you believe in God, the Father almighty? I believe. Do you believe in Jesus Christ, the Son of God, who was born by the Holy Spirit and the Virgin Mary, was crucified under Pontius Pilate, died, was buried, and on the third day rose from the dead, ascended to heaven, sits at the right hand of the Father, and will come to judge both the living and the dead? I believe. Do you believe in the Holy Spirit, the holy Church, and the resurrection of the body? I believe."[7]

The *Didache* mentions living water (that is, the running water of springs and rivers) or, if this is not available, also such bodies of water as pools and reservoirs where water does not flow. Is this an indication of an early preoccupation with the symbolism of baptismal water as life-giving water? It is evident that the mode of washing was immersion, or was it submersion? A later interpolation to the text directs the minister to "pour water three times on the head" in case water was scarce. The rite of infusion, which has become common practice in several churches, would appear to have been exceptional in the primitive baptismal *ordo*.

A century after Justin Martyr we witness an unprecedented elaboration of the baptismal *ordo*. In Tertullian's book *On Baptism*, written toward the year 200, appears for the first time the practice of blessing the water to be used for baptism. The prayer of blessing includes biblical types of baptismal water (water of creation, the Red Sea, and River Jordan) and an invocation of the Holy Spirit who makes the water holy so that those immersed in it may in turn receive holiness. Also for the first time we come across the practice of anointing the neophyte, which Tertullian likens to the anointing of Aaron as priest. We learn that Easter and Pentecost are the preferred days for the celebration of baptism.[8] All these items have profoundly influenced the baptismal *ordo* of the succeeding centuries. At the same time, they have solidly contributed to the theological thinking on the sacrament of baptism. Such theological reflection comprises the following topics: baptism as the sacrament of new creation and salvation in Christ Jesus, the sanctifying and transforming role of the Holy Spirit through washing in water and word, the common priesthood of all the baptized, the paschal character of baptism, and the connection between baptism and confirmation or the outpouring of the Holy Spirit of Pentecost.

In the fourth and fifth centuries other significant elements were introduced into the *ordo* of baptism. Ambrose of Milan, Gregory of Nyssa, and Cyril of Jerusalem mention the white garment and the lighted candle that were given to neophytes. The white garment was explained as symbol of Christian dignity or baptismal innocence. In *The Mysteries,* Ambrose writes: "You received the white garment as a sign that you had put off the covering of sins, and had put on the chaste robes of innocence."[9] Historians of liturgy are not unanimous in interpreting the meaning of this practice. It could have been inspired by the *toga candida* of the Roman citizens. In this sense the white garment could very well symbolize membership in the "heavenly city" that is the church. There was also the white *toga virilis* worn by Roman boys at the end of their fourteenth year of age, but its similarity to the baptismal garment is not immediately clear. A more likely source is the initiatory white garment used in the Mithraic mystery rites to express new life and membership in the religion of Mithra. On the other hand, the use of candles, which Christians until the fourth century had associated with pagan worship, was introduced into the baptismal *ordo*, probably to illustrate Justin's teaching of baptism as *photismos* or enlightenment.

A word of caution: not all of the above elements of the ancient baptismal *ordo* have the same importance for the celebration of the sacrament nor are all of them to be considered "root elements." This is especially the case with such ritual elements as anointing, vesting, and giving of a lit candle. Today they are referred to as "explanatory rites," because they illustrate the meaning of the baptismal act. The fact that other ritual elements of similar nature (facing west at renunciation and east at profession of faith, foot-washing, and offering a cup of milk mixed with honey) disappeared in the course of time demonstrates that these so-called explanatory rites need not be a measure of a church's fidelity to the traditional *ordo* of baptism. Nevertheless as churches of different confessions become ever more conscious of the role liturgy plays in the process of "many becoming one," a more careful attention to

# Ordo: Bath, Word, Prayer, Table

these ancient elements of the baptismal *ordo* is a desirable thing. Being one in the bare essentials of baptism is a reality that confessional division did not and could not eradicate. Becoming one in the long-standing tradition of the baptismal *ordo*, even if not every part of it is essential, is a goal still to be achieved.

## 2. THE EUCHARISTIC ORDO

Regarding the eucharistic *ordo* as point of convergence among churches, Lathrop has written one of the finest treatises. He speaks of the *ordo* of Word and Table which constitutes the core of the eucharistic celebration. Basing himself on Justin's *1 Apology* 65 and 67, Lathrop proposes the core elements of the Sunday Eucharist: "One could better say that the community meets around the scriptures and the ritual meal. Gathering, hearing the readings, preaching, and praying – these belong to a simple description of the flow of a meeting around the scriptures, a *synaxis*. Setting the table, giving thanks, eating and drinking, and including absent others – these belong to a simple description of a ritual meal."[10] Translated concretely in current liturgical terms, the eucharistic *ordo* can be said to consist of the Liturgy of the Word (biblical readings from Hebrew scripture and New Testament, homily, and general intercessions) and the Liturgy of the Eucharist (presentation of gifts, Eucharistic Prayer and the people's assent, and Holy Communion). Four important elements complete the eucharistic *ordo* described by Justin: Sunday, the gathering of the faithful in one place under the *proestos* or president of the assembly, regard for those who were absent, and concern for the material welfare of the needy.

Justin's binomial *ordo* of word and meal celebrated by the Christian community gives ritual expression to Luke 24:13-35. Biblical scholars see in this Emmaus episode the basic shape of the early Christians' Eucharist, which consisted of the preaching of the word and the breaking of bread. Underlying the account is the church's belief that when the word was proclaimed it was Christ himself who spoke to the assembly (Luke 24:27) and when bread was broken it was Christ himself who took the bread, broke it, and gave it to his gathered followers (Luke 24:30). Thus Luke 24: 13-35 can very well be considered the New Testament core of the eucharistic *ordo* that later evolved into what we call today the Order of Mass. It would be quite disturbing to celebrate the Eucharist without reference to this biblical outline.

It is useful to note here the development of the Order of Mass as recorded in the early Sacramentaries, which were altar books that contained the rites and formularies of Mass. The 6th - 7th -century Sacramentaries known as the Veronese, Gelasian, and Gregorian include euchological formulas, namely: collects or opening prayers, prayers over the gifts (*oratio super oblata*), prefaces, prayers after communion, prayer over the people (*oratio super populum*). On the other hand, the Gregorian-Hadrian Sacramentary makes a brief description of the Order of Mass with the title *Qualiter Missa romana caelebratur*. The Roman Order of Mass according to *Qualiter* has the following elements: Introit or entrance song, *Kyrie eleison*, *Gloria* (said by the bishop on Sundays and feast days; by the priest only at Easter; in Lent neither the *Gloria* nor the *alleluia* is said), collect, Apostle (New Testament reading), gradual (responsorial psalm) or *alleluia*, Gospel, offertory, prayer over the gifts, Eucharistic Prayer, Lord's Prayer, embolism ("Deliver us, Lord"), breaking of bread, and Lamb of God. Although *Qualiter* does not mention the homily, general intercessions, and Communion, one can assume that in the 7th century these core elements were part of the Roman *ordo*.[11]

As one can readily see, the eucharistic *ordo* began to be decked with elaborate rites during the middle ages. The added rites gave to the *ordo* a more solemn form, though in the process some of the core elements were relegated to a lesser status or simply lost their rightful place. Such was the case of the Hebrew scripture reading, the homily, the general intercessions, and the communion of the gathered faithful. When we are not able to identify what is basic, we lose sight of the original *ordo* that defines the Eucharist of the churches. Nevertheless, the road to "many becoming one" through the Eucharistic *ordo* entails more than the core or root elements. Being one in the basic *ordo* of word and meal is surely a divine gift for which the churches should thank the Lord. However, the basic *ordo* alone will not sufficiently make the unity of the churches visible. While we should leave enough margin for confessional differences, we need to work for a common *ordo* of the Eucharist that incorporates some of the better features of ritual development in the course of the centuries. Churches should not settle for unity in essentials; they should strive for unity on a larger scale. After all, the Eucharist is more than word and meal, but encompasses the ritual elements whereby the church concretizes and illustrates the word of God and the meal of Jesus Christ.

## B. THE *ORDO* AS CALENDAR OF LITURGICAL FEASTS

In liturgical tradition the *Ordo*, such as the *Ordo Romanus 1*, was a book that generally described the format of liturgical celebrations. In Roman Catholic usage today, the *Ordo* stands for the calendar of liturgical feasts that occur in the course of a year. Rightly, Gordon Lathrop speaks of the *Ordo* of Seven Days and the Eighth Day and the *Ordo* of the Year and *Pascha*.[12] Christians mark the passing of day and night, of weeks and months, and of years and seasons with appropriate liturgical worship. For Lathrop "this key characteristic of Christian scheduling has become a common and

# Ordo: Bath, Word, Prayer, Table

presupposed ecumenical inheritance."[13] Indeed unity is expressed by shared observance of feasts and festivals. The family of nations observes international days to commemorate world events. National holidays foster the unity of citizens. People gather to celebrate their family days.

The common observance of the liturgical *ordo* of feasts and seasons should thus be regarded as another road to "many becoming one." History tells us, however, that this has not always been the case. The second-century Quartodeciman controversy on the date of Easter exemplifies this type of disunity occasioned by the *ordo* of liturgical feasts. The Quartodeciman Christians, who lived in Asia Minor, kept Easter on the 14$^{th}$ day of Nisan, which was the full moon of spring, regardless of whether or not it was Sunday. Underpinning this observance is the theology of the Paschal Lamb slain for us on the 14$^{th}$ day of Nisan. Rome, on the other hand, insisted that Easter had to be kept only on Sunday as profession of belief in Christ's resurrection. In 196 Pope Victor I threatened to excommunicate all the Quartodecimans because of the Easter date controversy.[14]

## 1. THE SUNDAY ORDO

Sharing a common *ordo* of liturgical feasts should not, however, be confined to the calendar. Almost all the Christian churches keep Sunday and, in the West, they celebrate together the Easter festivals and such feasts as Pentecost and Christmas. Sharing a common *ordo* involves sharing the same doctrinal beliefs on which the liturgical feast is founded.

Sunday plays no small role in the spiritual life of Christians. It is the day when the faithful experience more profoundly what it means to be church. Many religions consecrate a day in the week to gather the members in worship and fellowship as a community. The Jewish people observe the Sabbath and Muslims keep Friday, but most Christians the world over set Sunday apart as the Day of the Lord. The New Testament records that Christ rose on Sunday, the first day of the week, the third day after he was crucified. After his resurrection Christ appeared to his disciples, and the gospels of Luke 24 and John 21 mention Sunday as the day of his apparitions. In the consciousness of the first disciples, Sunday was the day not only to commemorate the resurrection of the Lord, but also to meet him in the gathered assembly, in his word, and in the breaking of the bread. Justin Martyr reports: On Sunday "we all gather in a common meeting, because it is the day on which Jesus Christ, our Savior, rose from the dead... and appeared to his apostles and disciples."[15]

The apparition of Christ that has a lasting effect on our observance of Sunday is the one recorded by the gospel of Luke in chapter 24: 13-35. Two disciples, discouraged by the events of Good Friday, left Jerusalem, and headed home to Emmaus. But Christ, joining them incognito, explained the words of Scripture concerning him. It was evening when they reached Emmaus and the disciples invited him to join them for supper. At table he took the bread, said the blessing, broke it, and gave it to them. Their eyes were opened, they recognized him in the breaking of bread, and they exclaimed: "Did we not feel our hearts on fire as he talked with us on the road and explained the Scriptures to us?" The story is an image of what would have been a typical Sunday eucharistic *ordo* of the first disciples: it consisted of the reading of the Scriptures and the breaking of the bread. From the beginning, then, the observance of the Lord's day has been intimately joined to the celebration of the Eucharist, so that Sunday as the Lord's day could not be properly observed without it. It is the eucharistic celebration that defines Sunday as the Lord's Day.

The road to "many becoming one" through the common *ordo* of liturgical feasts implies the celebration of a complete Eucharist on Sunday, not only the preaching of the word but also the common sharing in the Lord's Supper. Christians of different confessions, having consulted historical sources, have become increasingly aware of the eucharistic character of Sunday. Speaking of the Sunday meeting or assembly, Lathrop writes: "The meeting is called a meeting on the Lord's Day because the content of the meeting is, as Christians believe, the encounter with the risen Lord in the interpretation of scriptures and in the keeping of the Lord's Supper."[16]

Another aspect of Sunday that can be an instrument for closer ties among Christians is the day of rest. We know that in the year 321 by Emperor Constantine introduced the Christian observance of Sunday rest, in order to encourage the faithful to participate in the solemn celebration of the Eucharist. Up till then Saturday was kept as holiday in the Roman Empire, and Christians, like the others, worked on Sunday, though they set aside the early morning hours of Sunday for the eucharistic celebration. Today in developed countries and among the middle class, Sunday has become part of the modern phenomenon called weekend. In situations of poverty, however, the observance of Sunday rest can become difficult. For the parish community, Sunday rest should not mean rest from works of love and social concern. The professional service of doctors, lawyers, and teachers offered freely to the poor of the community should become a distinguishing mark of the parish Sunday observance. The Sunday assembly does not end in church but continues on in parish clinics and community halls. Community representatives visit the sick and the aged to share with them Holy Communion and the community's spiritual comfort. In the early Church the collection given at Mass in cash or kind, as Justin Martyr informs us, was set aside for the community's poor, widows, and orphans. The Sunday Eucharist is incomplete unless it overflows into community service.

# Ordo: Bath, Word, Prayer, Table

Works of love and concern for those in need typify the observance of Sunday rest. Through them Christians become a united sign of Christ's enduring presence in the world. The world at large should be able to witness, regardless of confessional affiliations, the love Christians have for each other and for any person in need. The road to "many becoming one" requires the concerted effort of Christians to alleviate human suffering. Sunday as the day of Christ's Supper and of weekly rest is the privileged time to extend to others the meaning of Sunday as the Day of the Lord.

*2. The Easter Ordo*

As regards the festival of Easter, Gordon Lathrop has provided us with solid theology.[17] The festival of Easter ranks highest in the calendar of yearly feasts in the same way as Sunday in the weekly cycle of seven days. The parallelism between Sunday and Easter is noteworthy. The preaching of the word, sharing at the Lord's Table, celebrating the sacrament of rebirth while recalling the passion and resurrection of Jesus are vividly present in both Sunday and Easter observances. But while Sunday compresses all these elements of the *ordo* in one day, Easter spreads them out in several days which constitute the Easter Triduum. A brief review of the Easter *ordo* can help pave the road to greater liturgical harmony among churches.

"On the third day he rose again from the dead." From this article of faith the church developed the observance of the Easter Triduum. St. Ambrose (*Letter 23*) writes: "It is necessary that we observe not only the day of Christ's passion, but also the day of his resurrection, so that we may have a day of bitterness as well as day of joy. This is the holy Triduum in which Christ suffered, was buried, and rose again." Hence, Friday, Saturday, and Sunday. St. Augustine (*Letter 55*) explains: This is "the most holy Triduum of the Savior crucified, buried, and risen again." Toward the seventh century, the memory of the Lord's Supper was introduced with an evening Mass on Holy Thursday. Thus the Lord's Supper fittingly began the Easter festival.[18] On Good Friday Christians recall the passion and death of the Lord in a solemn celebration that often takes place at about three o'clock in the afternoon, the hour when Christ died on the cross. The liturgical *ordo* of the Western church originally consisted only of a liturgy of the word that centered on the proclamation of the passion according to John. This was followed by general intercessions. In the 7th century the West adopted the veneration of the cross, which had been observed in Jerusalem from the fourth century after Empress Helena discovered the wood of the cross. Thus in the Good Friday *ordo* the word of God and the cross of Jesus Christ are the two significant ritual elements. Holy Saturday commemorates the time Christ stayed in the tomb. It signifies his "rest" after the weeklong work of creating the human race anew. Silence, gravity of demeanor, and recollection are the characteristic traits of Holy Saturday. These are external expressions of our awe and admiration of what Christ did for us. In churches the only sound that can be heard is the chanting of the divine office. The altar is left bare and the Eucharist is not celebrated. Holy communion is given only as *viaticum* to the dying.

On Holy Saturday night Christians hold a solemn vigil as they await the return of the Lord from the tomb. The traditional liturgical *ordo* includes several readings (as many as twelve after the 6$^{th}$ century) that review the major works of God in the history of salvation, namely: creation, sacrifice of Abraham, passage through the Red Sea, the new Jerusalem, salvation offered to all, fountain of wisdom, a new heart and a new spirit, the meaning of Christian baptism, and the announcement that Christ is truly risen. In this sense the Easter Vigil is the compendium of God's work of creation and redemption. After the readings catechumens are baptized and the Christian assembly renew their baptismal commitment. Finally all sit around the table of the risen Lord to partake of his Easter meal. Thus the Easter Vigil *ordo* revolves around Word, Baptism, and Eucharist. Liturgically it culminates the season of Lent, Holy Week, and the Easter Triduum.

Several elements that comprise the Easter Triduum may be rightly considered "root elements" of the Easter *ordo*. Most come from the patristic times and they ritually illustrate the belief of Christians regarding the saving work of Christ. On the road to "becoming one" the *ordo* of Easter can play a significant role. The reality of "becoming one" goes deeper than a universal agreement among Christians on the Easter date. In consideration of the centuries of disagreement between Western and Eastern churches regarding the Easter calendar, insistence on this type of unity is moot and academic or at best an exercise in futility. The Easter *ordo* exhorts the churches to discover the rich doctrinal and spiritual content of the celebration of *Pascha*, regardless of the time of the year when it is celebrated. This festival, like many church festivals, is grafted on the season of the year, but its doctrinal content is rooted in the mystery of Christ and the Church. This mystery is what the core elements of the Easter *ordo* have ritually conveyed to Christians for many centuries.

## C. The *Ordo* for Liturgical Environment

Gordon Lathrop relates the story of Justin Martyr's trial. When the Roman prefect asked Justin where he and his companions met, he answered "above the baths of Myrtinus" where he lived. With this information the prefect concluded with this simple question: "You do admit then that you are a Christian?" Lathrop gives us fresh insight on the dialogue between Justin and the prefect: "Being a Christian and having a place of meeting went together."[19] If Christians must gather weekly and on

# Ordo: Bath, Word, Prayer, Table

special occasions in the course of the year in order to celebrate the liturgical *ordo*, they need a place where they can meet, a house where they can worship as God's family. The liturgical *ordo* needs a liturgical space. The space can be a public building or a private house; it can even be an open field, a gymnasium, or amphitheatre. Liturgical tradition, however, has preferred a building that has been set aside for the purpose of community worship.

The building, which is called house-church (*domus ecclesiae*), is the figure of the worshiping community called Church, the *Ekklesía,* whom God "assembled out of darkness into his marvelous light" (1 Peter 2:9). This community is made up of "living stones" with which the spiritual house is built as a holy priesthood offering up spiritual sacrifices to God (cf. 1 Peter 2:5). There is a certain identification of the sacred building with the community that worships within it. This would seem to be the underlying reason why the prefect concluded that Justin was a Christian. To belong to a church is to belong to a particular community of worshipers meeting together in a specific place.

> Since the body of Christ is the true temple where God dwells in the Spirit, our chief justification for building churches and other places of worship is that the community assembled in them expresses the presence of Christ among the two or three gathered together in his name (Matthew 18:20). In this sense the community gathered in worship is the 'extension' and presence of Christ's glorified body; it is the visible form of Christ who is the temple of God. The liturgical assembly is thus the liturgical "space" *par excellence*. Wherever it gathers in worship, there is the place where God encounters his people.[20]

When we speak of the *ordo* for liturgical environment, the worshiping community should be our fundamental consideration and point of reference. This applies to the construction, arrangement, and furnishings of the space. Other considerations that have no regard for the worship requirements of the Christian community are alien to the nature and purpose of the church building. The church is not meant to be a monument to the everlasting memory of its builders and sponsors; it is not meant to be an artistic monument (although it must project good taste), but a place of gathering for the worshiping community. Its primary purpose is to house or provide suitable shelter to the community as it celebrates the liturgical *ordo*, particularly the Eucharist. For this reason the art and furnishings of the church should all relate to the community and its act of communal worship. On the other hand, a church building that lacks essential furnishings such as baptismal font, table for the Lord's meal, lectern for the preaching of the word, presidential chair, nave or a suitable space for the assembly, and liturgical books falls short of the requirements of the *ordo* for the church as a house for worship. In the final analysis, ecclesiology, that is, a theology of the church as a worshiping community, should be our primary consideration.[21]

The foregoing considerations offer some basic elements that could very well constitute the *ordo* for liturgical environment. What is important is that Christians are aware of the theology of the liturgical space and its function as a house where they gather for worship. The architectural design and appearance of church buildings (people are wont to identify churches as Roman Catholic, Orthodox, or Protestant by their external appearance) are of little or no consequence to our common goal to become one in Christ Jesus. What counts for unity in matters related to liturgical environment is the *ordo* that requires us to make the church a suitable space for preaching the word, celebrating baptism and eucharist, and welcoming all the members of Christ into the house.

## Conclusion

The quest for unity in the Church's liturgical *ordo* can, like the liturgy itself, be a double-edged sword. It can come about that in the name of a common liturgical *ordo* some Christians might infringe on the freedom of others to remain liturgically different or to conserve the received ritual patterns of their church. In this regard there is much we can learn from the wisdom of Martin Luther. While in Wittenberg in December 1521, to his dismay he saw armed students and townspeople invade the parish church, jeer at the friars, prevent them from offering private Masses, break sacred images, and carry away the Latin missals. In March of the following year, dressed in his religious habit, he was daily in the pulpit of Wittenberg directing his anger not at the pope but at the hotheads who used physical force to fight abuses.[22]

For Luther such things as liturgical formularies, vestments, and vessels were "neither prescribed nor forbidden." To prescribe such matters meant to restrict the freedom of Christians. The Latin Mass was not necessary for salvation, but neither was the German Mass. As humanist and teacher, he wanted the Latin language to be preserved because of its cultural value. He had great attachment to the traditional *ordo* of the liturgy and hence believed that the correct shape of worship must grow organically from its roots.[23] His pastoral sense dictated that priests be allowed to simply omit any reference to sacrifice in the prayers and Canon of the Mass, so that they could celebrate "according to the Gospel," while the common people "would not notice anything to cause scandal." He allowed time for the simple folks with "weak consciences" to gain purity of faith and did not want "to burden their consciences through precipitate changes not adequately prepared by preaching."[24]

# Ordo: Bath, Word, Prayer, Table

The topic "Liturgy: Many Becoming One" is a tall order and a challenge addressed to churches, especially those with serious reflection possible on their liturgical *ordo* in the light of a more universal tradition. However, Martin Luther's pastoral wisdom should temper any excessive zeal that borders on uniformity in the observance of a common liturgical *ordo*. In the final analysis, several components of the received liturgical *ordo* that are not of divine institution should, strictly speaking, be regarded as "neither prescribed nor forbidden." Unity in the *ordo* of worship does not negate the fundamental freedom of any church to determine its pattern of worship under the guidance of the Holy Spirit and in keeping with the liturgical principle of "sound tradition and legitimate progress."[25] The adage often attributed to Saint Augustine, for whom Luther had the greatest respect, sums up and concludes these pages of reflection in honor of the ecumenical liturgist and theologian Gordon Lathrop: *In necesariis, unitas; in opinabilibus, libertas; in omnibus, caritas.*[26]

## Endnotes

[1] P. Lyons, "Liturgy and Ecumenism," *Handbook for Liturgical Studies I* (Collegeville 1997), 81-92; D. Heller, "Ecumenical Worship," *The New Westminster Dictionary of Liturgy and Worship* (London 2002), 163-165.

[2] Gordon Lathrop: *Holy Things. A Liturgical Theology* (Minneapolis: Fortress Press, 1993), x.

[3] Idem, 33.

[4] The typical edition of the liturgical books of the Roman Catholic Church is called *Ordo* (*Ordo Baptismi Parvulorum, Ordo Missae, Ordo Matrimonii*, etc.) to indicate the sequence of the various elements of celebration. The English translation of *Ordo* as "Rite" (Rite of Baptism, Rite of Marriage, Rite of Penance, etc.) expresses the components that make up the celebration.

[5] Lathrop, *Holy Things*, 36-43, 68-79, 104-115.

[6] *Didaché*, ed. W. Rordorf-A. Tuilier, *Sources Chrétiennes* 248 (1978) 7, 170-71. W. Rordorf, "Le baptême selon la Didaché," *Mélanges liturgiques offerts a Dom Botte* (Louvain 1972), 499-510.

[7] *La Tradition Apostolique de Saint Hippolyte*, ed. B. Botte (Münster 1989) no. 21, 48-50.

[8] *De Baptismo, in Corpus Christianorum* I/1 (1954) pp.277-95. Tertullian explains the meaning of anointing in the context of the anointing performed by Moses on Aaron, namely unto priesthood. Perhaps he was thinking of this when he wrote in his Exhortation to Chastity, "are we of the laity not also priests?" (*De Exhortatione Castitatis in Corpus Christianorum* I/1, 1954) 7, 1024.

[9] "De Sacramentis/De Mysteriis," ed. B. Botte, in *Sources Chrétiennes* 25bis (1961) 6, 117.

[10] Lathrop, *Holy Things*, 43-53.

[11] M. Metzger, "The History of the Eucharistic Liturgy in Rome," *Handbook for Liturgical Studies III* (Collegeville 1999), 119-122

[12] Lathrop, *Holy Things*, 36-43; 68-79.

[13] Idem, p. 36. W. Rordorf, *Sabbat und Sonntag in der Alten Kirche* (Zürich 1972).

[14] A. Chupungco, *Shaping the Easter Feast* (Washington, D.C. 1992), 43-59.

[15] *Apology*, c. 67.

[16] Lathrop, *Holy Things*, 40.

[17] Idem, pp. 68-79. Lathrop prefers the old term *pascha* to the English *Easter*. By doing so he underlines the historical ties of Christian Passover with the Jewish *pesach*. This writer himself expressed the same preference in his book *The Cosmic Elements of Christian Passover* (Rome 1977).

[18] Holy Thursday is also called Maundy Thursday. Maundy is derived from Latin *mandatum* (command) and recalls the Lord's command at the Last Supper to wash each other's feet. This gesture has been interpreted to mean mutual service, but in John's gospel it can carry the interpretation of what the Lord's Supper is all about.

[19] Lathrop, *Holy Things*, 109-110.

[20] Paul VI Institute of Liturgy: *Liturgical Guidelines on Church Architecture* (Pasay City 2000)

[21] Edward Foley, *From Age to Age* (Chicago: LTP, 1991).

[22] The author is indebted to H. Jedin's (ed.): *History of the Church*, Vol. 2 (New York 1993) for this and the following paragraph on Martin Luther's liturgical reform.

[23] Vatican II's Constitution on the Liturgy, art. 23, echoes this Lutheran principle: "There must be no innovations unless the good of the Church genuinely and certainly requires them, and care must be taken that any new forms adopted should in some way grow organically from forms already existing."

[24] H. Jedin (ed.): *History of the Church*, 416-418.

[25] Constitution on the Liturgy of Vatican II, art. 23: "In order that sound tradition be retained, and yet the way remain open to legitimate progress, a careful investigation – theological, historical, and pastoral – should always be made into each part of the liturgy, which is to be revised."

[26] "In essentials, unity; in matters of opinion, liberty; in all things, charity." On the authorship of this maxim by Rupertus Meldenius (c. 1627), see Philip Schaff, *History of the Christian Church* (Grand Rapids: Eerdmans, 1965), Vol. 7, 650-653. *Ed.*

# CONCLUSION

# Bath, Word, Prayer, Table:
# Reflections on Doing the Liturgical *Ordo* in a Postmodern Time

*Gordon W. Lathrop*

In 1985, a tragic church fire in northwestern Wisconsin destroyed an interesting old church bell. Sometimes directly, more often indirectly, that bell has drawn our attention here.

The title of this primer, its organization and some of its writing have drawn a certain inspiration from this bell. From the middle of the nineteenth century until 1985, first in Hutchinson, Minnesota, and then at West Denmark Lutheran Church in Luck, Wisconsin, the sound of the bell called together people of the surrounding communities. In the manner of much classic practice, however, the bell was *inscribed*, as if the first-person voice of the bell itself could be written down. In this case, the makers of the bell seem to have intended the inscription to articulate the meaning of the sounded invitation by expressing what was about to happen in the meeting. They made of the inscription a memorable little poem:

> To the bath and the table,
> To the prayer and the word,
> I call every seeking soul.[1]

The Hutchinson-Luck bell inscription has sometimes been taken as a more general symbol for the central matters of Christian worship. Even today, this present book seems to say, communities of needy people are summoned to participate in word and sacraments, themselves singing their way through that participation like a bell.[2] Even today, I say, the very matters listed on the bell are the most important things we have when we gather as Christians, and they are best set out with the centrality, the open clarity, the generosity of practice, and the absence of ecclesiastical pretension implied by the use of words like "bath" and "table."

The order of these things, as that order is written out upon the bell, is a *theological* not a liturgical order. Reflected there is the conviction of the nineteenth century Danish theologian N. F. S. Grundtvig (the Danish-American Christians of Hutchinson, Minnesota, and Luck, Wisconsin, were "Grundtvigians") that the "word" – that center of most nineteenth century protestant worship – is best understood through the meanings of baptism, holy communion and the Lord's Prayer. For Grundtvig, as for many Lutherans and other sacramentally formed Christians, these things function as the necessarily presupposed hermeneutical key for the existential meaning of the scriptures. Holy communion is itself a hermeneutic, a way of interpreting, as Dirk Lange has argued in this book. Or, as Grundtvig wrote, in an overstated polemical reaction to nineteenth century biblicism and fundamentalism, "Only at the bath and at the table, do we hear God's word to us."[3]

But the simple and humanly accessible names for these central things – bath, table, prayer, word – also reflect reformed liturgical practice, the kind of practice urged in this present primer: real water and a lot of it, welcoming us to life in the assembly of Christ; a shared meal, rather than a minimized memorial or a merely clerical event, feeding us with mercy now and welcoming us into the care of the earth and into a just economy for the marginalized; participatory prayer for all the needy world; beautiful and inclusive speech that accords with all of this and music that sings us through it; a word that arises from the meaning of the bath and stands clearly next to the meaning of the supper; and the whole event as intended for and available to questioning and suffering humanity.

These accessible names also imply a simple *liturgical* order. That order is the great outline of the ancient "mass" or divine liturgy or service of the Lord's Day. We gather, through the bath or its remembrance, to word and prayer set next to the table. If we add to this outline the current awareness that the open door to "every seeking soul" at the beginning implies also a sending out through that door at the end of the service, we have this resultant liturgical *ordo*, widespread in current ecumenical discussion and encouraged in and between many churches:[4] gathering through the bath; then word and prayer; then the meal; then the sending. We may call this simple and widely affirmed pattern "the ecumenical *ordo*." Such an *ordo* may be used as a tool to discover deep convergences and basic similarities between otherwise differing communities of Christians. Furthermore, granted some agreement in its simple list of central matters, this *ordo* may be used by us, in mutual affirmation and admonition, to encourage each other toward the clarity and largeness of bath and table, prayer and word in our communal ritual practice.

# Ordo: Bath, Word, Prayer, Table

POSTMODERN CHALLENGES TO AN ECUMENICAL *ORDO*

But in 1985 the parish church at Luck burned. In the fire, that bell was destroyed.

Even symbolically, does the Luck bell still ring? The understanding of Christian worship implicit in that old, now destroyed, inscription may be interesting historically. It may even be moving for us to notice, beyond the bell, the various nineteenth- and twentieth-century attempts of Protestant communities to balance their long-winded words with the renewed importance of ritual actions as well as the various attempts of Catholic communities to let their arcane ritual actions stand out in greater and more generous clarity, giving resonance to a newly important word. But are the matters set out as central by the Hutchinson-Luck inscription and the *ordo* implied by that centrality still relevant? Shall we still encourage each other in their use? Can this simple list still function to teach the meaning of worship and to establish an agenda for its reform, especially in a time marked by burgeoning diversity and by suspicion of anything that seems to pretend to universal validity, a time frequently called "postmodern"? Perhaps the very insistence on these things as *central* signals their immanent demise. Perhaps the ecumenical books and the denominational orders protest too much.

There are, after all, significant challenges to the idea of central matters in Christian worship, organized into an essential *ordo*, an idea for which the Hutchinson-Luck bell may stand as symbol. Those challenges may finally be even more serious than a church fire in reorganizing the thought about and the practice of Christian worship. Any primer in the liturgy, written in the twenty-first century, intending to enable an ecumenical and catholic discussion, has to take those challenges seriously in order to make clear what "liturgical *ordo*" ought and ought not mean.

For one thing, there is the question, "Whose *ordo*?"[5] That is, what communities in fact follow this pattern? But also, who gains power by the privileging of this pattern? These are significant questions. A phenomenological account of what actually occurs on Sunday morning in the diverse Christian gatherings in North America and in the world must grant the point that they do not all, by any means, easily fit into this description. Moreover, the description may be painted with too large a brush, leaving out too much that is actually and locally important, actually and locally owned. As Anscar Chupungco points out in this volume, more detailed consideration of the way patterns of worship are actually lived out may lead us to see that worship also divides as well as unites. Furthermore, even if one granted the usefulness of such a broad and simple outline, at least one other broad-brushed pattern could also be found. Many churches – in North America, but also around the world in places influenced by American practice – follow the so-called "frontier *ordo*": preliminary songs and readings and dramas prepare a gathering for a message and the message leads individuals in the community to decisions or conversions or opportunities for personal growth. So is the talk of the *ordo* intended to be a sort of liturgical imperialism? Does it privilege the Lutherans and Episcopalians and Roman Catholics? Does it marginalize communities which, as Melva Costen explores here, unfold their worship order out of the experience of praise? Or does it empower especially a certain kind of clergy who share a love of a certain kind of tradition? Such is the postmodern critique of the hidden dynamics of power – the power of the leader or the power of the supposedly objective scholar.

Perhaps yet more important is the challenge that can be made to the very idea of *ordo* by insisting that such an idea is a structuralist mistake. The *ordo* may not be merely a generally useful outline that is nonetheless painted with too broad a brush and applicable only in some places. It may be a mental construct forced upon the actual facts. Much more useful for the study of worship, by this conception, would be attention to local detail, to the many things that people really do when they gather for worship, to their own ideas of what they are doing, and to the local peculiarities and the locally thick and thin moments. *Ordo* may then be an unwarranted "meta-narrative," intending to indicate a widespread similarity of practice where none exists, ignoring local realities and actual communities, and hoping to impose a supposed universal agenda on this local reality. Such is the postmodern critique of overarching generalizations and "essentials."

So, does talk about *ordo* ignore or mask what actually is going on in worshiping communities? Does it mask the dynamics of power and its exercise? Is such talk trying to force alien meanings and a standard practice on quite diverse local phenomena?

But, even if we grant the importance of the idea of a shared simple outline of worship and shared central things, there might be yet another way to state the challenge. If the way the *ordo* means something at all, the way it creates meaning, has sometimes been explicated with the word "juxtaposition" – one thing next to another yields "meaning" as a third thing[6] – then what is the other thing that might be juxtaposed to *ordo* itself? How does *ordo* avoid becoming ideology? As Mark Taylor has written, "What second thing must be set next to the *ordo* as a whole for it, this *ordo*, to be fully what it is precisely in tension with this second thing, in difference from this second thing?"[7] Such is the postmodern challenge to ideology, to single and absolute meanings.

## Misuses of the *Ordo*[8]

It would seem that these challenges are decisive, convincing. The idea of pattern in worship, of certain shared central things, can indeed be used to compel change, insist on "my way" and not "yours," ignore local cultural realities, mask real and important differences, exclude others, even

## Ordo: Bath, Word, Prayer, Table

assert an ideology. "Do these things in this order," we can seem to be saying, as if liturgy were a matter of the mechanical application of formulae, "and you will have authentic Christian worship." More: this same assertion can be insisted upon. "You must do these things, in this order," says the denominational authority, the expert professor, the presiding pastor, the influential lay leader. Then, right away, in current North American context anyway, the conversation becomes a power struggle: "Who says? On what authority? What is your so-called authentic worship anyway?" Even in holy matters, ritual negotiations can wind up being about power, and even "word and sacraments" can be used as weapons in the hands of enforcers.

But does that misuse disqualify the idea of the ecumenical *ordo* altogether?

Unfortunately, power raises its head also in the insistent application of other patterns than the Gathering-Word-Meal-Sending pattern of the ecumenical *ordo*. Indeed, power – compulsion – seems never far away from the history of Christian ritual practice down through the ages. Liturgical unification, liturgical centralism, authorized liturgical formulae, enforced liturgical books have appeared again and again.

Also, let us be clear, the so-called frontier *ordo* has been imposed upon congregations. Furthermore, the evangelical Christianity to which this pattern is so strongly linked, is not a set of struggling marginal groups, in spite of that movement's long self-image of powerlessness, but the dominant religion of North America – and perhaps also of Africa – a religion currently linked to awesome political power. Moreover, this pattern of worship was originally designed to compel, to move the wavering individual toward conversion, to soak the Anxious Bench[9] with power for personal change. This pattern of worship endows the clerical leader with the central power in the room, a power to which the individuals of the assembly are subject.

But compulsion in worship always distorts the thing it seeks to reform. A primer on liturgical matters in the twenty-first century needs to state that clearly. One famous story might be helpful: In 1522, Martin Luther was away from Wittenberg, that university town at the heart of the sixteenth-century Reformation, and he was away from the congregation in that town that he served as pastor. He was resident in the Wartburg Castle, hidden and disguised, using the time to translate the Bible, since he was now excommunicated, under the ban of the emperor, and in mortal danger. His colleague in the university, Professor Andreas Karlstadt, knew that he and Luther and others had taught that the celebration of the mass should be reformed. It should be sung in the vernacular. It should center in the proclamation and praise of the triune God, not be overshadowed by the cult of the saints. The cup should be available to the laity. To us this sounds like a relatively modest list of changed practices. But

Karlstadt was deeply disappointed that these reforms had not yet occurred. So he acted. He persuaded the town council to pass laws requiring these changes immediately, as a matter of city law. He encouraged a large group of men – the group should probably be called a mob – to enforce these laws violently, to tear down statues in the church and force the use of the chalice. Luther heard, and, at significant risk to his own life, came back to town. As the pastor of the congregation, against these new laws of the town and out of concern for those who were being forced without understanding, he put the statues, the Latin mass, and communion in one kind back in place. He preached a series of seven sermons that called for the harder way of teaching and love, not the easy way of constraint, as the way of liturgical change. He resisted Karlstadt, the town council, and the mob primarily by simply preaching. Karlstadt left town, disappointed. Indeed, constraint is itself finally deeply disappointing, if the thing it wants to force is communally practiced and faithful liturgy. Liturgy is inevitably malformed by the constraint, tending then toward legalism and pretense. To do the right thing for the wrong reason is almost inevitably to do the wrong thing, at least in liturgy.

Luther was right. Teach and love, teach and love, and recognize that authentic change takes a long time. Nonetheless, it is important to note: Luther did not leave the congregation unchanged, mired in an incomprehensible rite, celebrated in a church filled with junk and with communion in only one kind. He did strongly lead, he did teach and love, and there was change. This story is not an argument for immobility or indolence, nor for a simply descriptive approach to what people do in liturgy. Luther did believe that there was an agenda for reform, an agenda that could be proposed as a gift, be welcomed in ways fitting with local gifts and local culture, and be accomplished without compulsion. The *ordo* of the Hutchinson-Luck bell inscription belongs to that tradition of liturgical change. It invites.

The postmodern challenges help us to see the importance of this assertion. Indeed, the postmodern challenges may help us to treasure the ecumenical *ordo* the more, especially when it is noted that an open meeting around a multivalent pool, around an interesting set of words and around an inviting supper is not, in the first place, designed to compel. Healthy liturgy, focused on strong central signs and not on individual personal decisions, makes a way of ever deeper significance available to its participants, but it also lets those participants be free.

## The *Ordo* as Ordinary Life, Ritualized to Bear the Gospel

Still, do not the postmodern challenges require of us that we give up altogether the idea of a shared agenda for liturgical renewal? Indeed, do these challenges not suggest that "renewal" itself masks an exercise of power on the part of the "renewers" and imposes a pretended universal ideology on the more primary local details of worship?

On the contrary, the invitation to let the communal practice of bath, word, prayer and table stand out in greater clarity is just that: an invitation. A critical invitation, an invitation with huge import, but still an invitation. Furthermore, its accent falls on matters that are, indeed, always local and ordinary: local waters; local bodies bathed in those waters; local words for telling living stories; local religious longings expressed in prayer; and local meals. While transcultural words can be used for these matters,[10] the reality is always concrete, participatory, and locally diverse. The classic Christian use of these matters roots both in their *local availability* and, at the same time, in the association of each of them with *Jesus*: with his reversals of religious meanings and his attack on religious boundaries, with his death and resurrection, with the Spirit poured out into the world from these events, and with the faith that Jesus Christ remains locally available, locally encounterable.

So, water flows locally. In the four gospels, water is a sign of the reign of God, now present in the world. Local words tell local stories. In the four gospels, traditional stories are given surprising, mercy-filled endings. In need, prayers arise from practically every set of local lips, to anything that might be regarded as being able to help. In the four gospels, the community is invited to pray for others and to pray in Jesus' name. Communal meals are a universally local phenomenon, in which our community assures its own survival and passes on its own culture. In the four gospels and the letters of Paul, commensality with Jesus is combined with an open door to the outsider and the sending of food to the poor. A liturgy that seeks to allow the centrality of bath, word, prayers and table, seeks to go the way of the four gospels, risks the way of the four gospels, commits to the way of the four gospels. Such a liturgy means to reorient local practice so as to invite us again and again to walk in the world in the way of faith. Such a liturgy means to care about this world, believing that to stand before the biblical God inevitably means to stand on the ground this God calls holy.[11]

Of course a community can choose to follow another *ordo*. In fact, even this "ecumenical *ordo*" can be followed in such a way that the faith-enabling and world-affirming surprises of its central symbols are not manifest. But a community can also be committed to the reception of these central things as gifts – gifts that align that community with the "sarcophilia," the flesh-loving character, of the gospels.[12]

Of course, there are *four* gospels. That very truth tends to the disallowance of ideology, of a single, universal truth, and a disallowance of a single formula in worship. All four give witness to the one God, and finally that one God is also a plural unity, a dance of three. But it is nonetheless astonishing to see how water, story, prayer and table, and the faith that is formed through them, recur in all four of the canonical gospels, in diverse permutations, with diverse accents, but still as the recognizable marks of communal life with Jesus.

The proposal that bath, word, prayer and table be allowed to be the center of local Christian liturgy, that they be continually refreshed to stand forth in clear and generous ways, is an invitation to let important materials of our local life be broken and ritualized to bear the surprising and life-giving gospel of Jesus Christ.[13] This practice ought not be the importation and imposition of alien materials, but the use of local materials to celebrate and proclaim a more-than-local meaning. Everyday stuff gets used on Sunday, if the liturgy is renewed. By this reading, "inculturation" is the most traditional of Christian liturgical themes, everywhere. Then, in Christ, our waters, our stories, our prayers, our meals, our spaces, our times, our religious longings themselves must no longer be used only for us, certainly not only for *me*. Time after surprising time, these things can become the materials of a new encounter with the death and resurrection of Jesus here, a new reception of the Spirit here, and so a faithful new reorientation to God's beloved world from here. They can become the means and tools of boundary-crossing communion and world-linking peace.

The invitation to let bath, word, prayer and table be continually refreshed at the heart of our assemblies, then, will be distorted if it is seen as some abstract, universal agenda. In the present time, it ought rather be seen as a thoroughly postmodern commitment to walk a way without assurances or universal meta-narratives, the way of faith.

In their conversations about the ecumenical *ordo*, participants in the Ditchingham meeting convened by the Faith and Order Commission of the World Council of Churches in 1994, agreed together about these things that are relevant to our question:

> This pattern of Christian worship . . . is to be spoken of as a gift of God, not as a demand nor as a tool for power over others. Liturgy is deeply malformed, even destroyed, when it occurs by compulsion—either by civil law, by the decisions of governments to impose ritual practice on all people, or by the forceful manipulation of ritual leaders who show little love for the people they are called to serve. At the heart of the worship of Christians stands the crucified Christ, who is one with the little and abused ones of the world. Liturgy done in his name cannot abuse. It must be renewed, rather, by love and invitation and the teaching of its sources and meaning. "And I, when I am lifted up from the earth, will draw all people to myself," says Jesus (John 12:32). The liturgy must draw with Christ, not compel.

# Ordo: Bath, Word, Prayer, Table

Furthermore, this pattern is to be celebrated as a most profound connection between faith and life, between gospel and creation, between Christ and culture, not as an act of unconnected ritualism nor anxious legalism. Every culture has some form of significant communal assembly, the use of water, speech which is accessible but strongly symbolic, and festive meals. These universal gifts of life, found in every place, have been received as the materials of Christian worship from the beginning. Because of this, we are invited to understand the Christian assembly for worship as a foretaste of the reconciliation of all creation and as a new way to see all the world.

But the patterns of word and table, of catechetical formation and baptism, of Sunday and the week, of Pascha and the year, and of assembly and ministry around these things – the principal pairs of Christian liturgy – do give us a basis for a mutually encouraging conversation between the churches. Churches may rightly ask each other about the local inculturation of this ordo. They may call each other toward a maturation in the use of this pattern or a renewed clarification of its central characteristics or, even, toward a conversion to its use. Stated in their simplest form, these things are the "rule of prayer" in the churches, and we need them for our own faith and life and for a clear witness to Christ in the world. We need each other to learn anew of the richness of these things. Churches may learn from each other as they seek for local renewal. One community has treasured preaching, another singing, another silence in the word, another sacramental formation, another the presence of Christ in the transfigured human person and in the witnesses of the faith who surround the assembly, another worship as solidarity with the poor. As churches seek to recover the great pairs of the ordo, they will be helped by remembering together with other Christians the particular charisms with which each community has unfolded the patterns of Christian worship, and by a mutual encouragement for each church to explore the particular gifts which it brings to enrich our koinonia in worship.[14]

## On Doing the *Ordo* in a Postmodern Time

But then what about the postmodern challenges? They need to be taken seriously. They will continue to be helpful to us in avoiding the misunderstanding and the misuse of the *ordo*. But they also require, now, a response.

To the question of "whose *ordo* this is," I answer that the ecumenical *ordo*, like all Christian worship matters, can be used badly, as a tool for the enhancement of disguised power. But when bath, word, prayer and table are indeed allowed to stand next to each other in strength, mutually reinterpreting each other, bearing witness to the God of the gospels like the beasts around the throne, then what is privileged will not be any clergy or any denomination. What is privileged will be rather the actual locality, the biblical Christ, and the call to faith, to worldly reorientation and to wider communion. The many cultures of humanity are welcome to sing their own songs, use their own local languages and signs, and find their own critical reorientations of this cultural material in doing this local *ordo*. Among those cultures will be the remarkably mixed cultures, the post-colonialist cultures, which mark so many of us in the current world. The Luck bell did not say, ahead of time, *why* every seeking soul was invited to these things. The reason – the new open door to God's beloved world through faith in Jesus Christ – could only be discovered in their actual practice.

To the charge of unwarranted structuralism, I respond that the discovery of these matters as alive in the four gospels and discoverable elsewhere in Christian liturgical history is not a timeless truth. It is indeed an articulation of the present time, arising out of present need, with a real human history. The ecumenical *ordo* is thus not *proven* by history, though it may involve a critical and interpretive re-reading of history, a re-reading claimed by the readers. The ecumenical *ordo* is rather one current, communal and faithful reading of the gospels, and it is a commitment to go the way of those gospels. Such commitment can be one of the great rediscoveries of a postmodern outlook. The invitation to the ecumenical *ordo* is not an invitation to submit to anyone's historical reconstruction. It is an invitation to find bath, word, prayer and table the places of Christ's local presence today and here. It is an invitation to say, with faith, these things are a gift from God.

Finally, to the inquiry about what is to be juxtaposed to the *ordo* itself, I respond that the ecumenical *ordo* of bath, word, prayer and table is, in its very structure, a continual, mutually critical conversation, word with sign, gathering with going away, here with there, inside with outside. Furthermore, every local place that practices the surprising bath of the Spirit, tells the surprising stories of grace, prays the prayer of faith, celebrates the reorienting table of Jesus, in its own local way, will itself be in dialogue with every other place, proposing yet more meaning than we had seen. Moreover, the catholic practice of this *ordo* will be challenged and enriched by its catholic exceptions:[15] by the Friends who call every meal the Lord's Supper; by the Salvation Army that estimates self-giving service to be the eucharistic act; by Baptists and Mennonites who invite their children into a long catechumenate; by evangelicals who have made the preparation for the sacrament to be the years-long focus of their meetings.[16] Similarly, these practitioners of the exceptions will be challenged and enriched by the presence of the *ordo* in other places – by the invitation to join, at least sometimes, in the ritual symbol that they want their lives to enact, by making the sacrament meeting, rather than the preparation for the sacrament, to be again the focus of the gathering. Of course, the ecumenical *ordo*, by this interpre-

# Ordo: Bath, Word, Prayer, Table

tation, is a commitment to go the way of the four gospels, including the way of their mutual critical juxtapositions with each other. There are other gospels. Their ritual implications are mostly other than the implications of the canonical four, with an accent on individual salvation and gnostic technique.[17] While they have no claim to be read in the Christian assembly committed to the way of the four gospels, let those gospels, indeed, be set in free dialogue with the practice of bath and word, prayer and table. The nature of the *ordo*'s commitment to faith amid the conditions of the flesh will only become clearer.

This present book has been written by a number of people who themselves represent the mutual re-interpretive dialogue that arises from the ecumenical *ordo*. They do not all say the same thing. But they do all reflect on the actual practice of bath, word, prayer and table, side by side with each other. They do give further thought to how we might do these things in the present time. They do think with us about how these things influence the place and time in which we gather. And they do especially think about how these things arise out of daily life and reorient us to faithful life in this world. I am deeply grateful to all of them. They are the best commentators on doing the ecumenical *ordo* in a postmodern time. They invite you and me to come along with them.

In 1949, Robert Frost set a lucid, generous little work called "The Pasture" at the head of his collected poems. It read, in part:

> I am going out to clean the pasture spring;
> I'll only stop to rake the leaves away
> (And wait to watch the water clear, I may):
> I sha'n't be gone long. — You come too.[18]

The invitation of the ecumenical *ordo* ought to be as simple as the invitation of the pasture spring. It is a gift. It flows with the living water of God. We did not make the water. But it does, periodically, need clearing out.

You come too.

## ENDNOTES

1. The actual inscription was "Til badet og bordet, til bønnen og ordet, jeg kalder hver søgende sjæl."

2. For an account of the bell, see Gordon Lathrop, "Strong Center, Open Door: A Vision of Continuing Liturgical Renewal," *Worship* 75:1 (January 2001), 37-38. In my further writing, the bell occurs in *Holy Things,* 89, 91, 103, 104, 110, 113, 122; *Holy Ground,* 224-225; "What are the essentials of Christian worship?," *Open Questions in Worship* I, 8; and, with Timothy J. Wengert, in *Christian Assembly,* 46-50.

3. "Kun ved badet og ved bordet, hører vi Guds ord til os." See further *Christian Assembly,* 43-44.

4. See, for example, Thomas F. Best and Dagmar Heller, eds., *So We Believe, So We Pray: Towards Koinonia in Worship* (Geneva: World Council of Churches, 1995), 6-7; Thomas F. Best and Dagmar Heller, eds., *Eucharistic Worship in Ecumenical Contexts* (Geneva: World Council of Churches, 1998), 29-35; *United Methodist Book of Worship* (Nashville: United Methodist Publishing House, 1992), 15; *Book of Common Worship* (Louisville: Westminster/John Knox, 1993), 33; *Common Worship* (London: Church House, 2000), 166, 228.

5. Some of the following questions have been asked by Michael Aune, "Ritual Practice: Into the world, into each human heart," in Thomas H. Schattauer, ed., *Inside Out: Worship in an Age of Mission* (Minneapolis: Fortress, 1999), 153; by James White, "How do we know it is us?" in E. Byron Anderson and Bruce T. Morrill, eds., *Liturgy and the Moral Self* (Collegeville: Liturgical Press, 1998), 56-57; and by Chris Ellis, "Reflections on James White, the Ordo, and 'Authentic Christian Worship,'" unpublished paper and personal communication. See also, especially, Maxwell Johnson, "Can We Avoid Relativism in Worship? Liturgical norms in the light of contemporary liturgical scholarship," *Worship* 74:2 (March 2000), 135-155.

6. *Holy Things,* 82; *Holy Ground,* 127.

7. Mark Lloyd Taylor, "A Response to Gordon Lathrop, 'Treasure in Earthen Vessels: On Liturgical Disappointment,'" unpublished paper from Summer Institute on Liturgy and Worship, Seattle University (July 6, 2004), 9.

8. My reflections on these misuses and on the positive re-framing of the idea of ordo are deeply indebted to the contributions made by Paula Lawrence Wehmiller, Melinda Quivik, Dirk Lange and Michael Burk to a symposium on the future of the ordo in postmodern and post-colonialist times, held at the Lutheran Theological Seminary at Philadelphia, on April 19, 2004.

9. The practice of an "anxious bench" for potential converts was widely used among those American revivalist congregations who followed what Charles Grandison Finney and others called "the new

measures." This practice was criticized by John W. Nevin in his classic study *The Anxious Bench* (second edition; Chambersburg, PA: 1844), in which he proposed instead "the way of the catechism."

[10] We call very diverse local practices by the word "meal" (or by similar words in other languages), for example. Nonetheless, the use of that word to link these diverse practices is not entirely without grounds. Otherwise we must despair of human language itself.

[11] See *Holy Ground*, 4.

[12] See *Holy Ground*, 129-135; and John Dominic Crossan, *The Birth of Christianity* (San Francisco: HarperCollins, 1998), 36-38.

[13] For more extensive reflection on this idea, see especially the contributions of Edward Schillebeeckx and Samuel Torvend in this volume.

[14]

[15] *So We Believe, So We Pray*, 7.

[16] See *Holy Things*, 157-158, and *Holy Ground*, 225-226.

[17] One can argue that the "revival" is an American development of the preparatory time of the old sacrament meeting. For this argument and its implications, see *Christian Assembly*, 121-131.

[18] See *Holy Ground*, 130.

[19] *Complete Poems of Robert Frost* (New York: Henry Holt, 1949). For the interesting application of this little poem to the theological and ecclesial tasks of the present time, I am especially indebted to John Vannorsdall.

# Contributors

Herbert Anderson, ELCA Theologian at Seattle University, Seattle, Washington, and Visiting Professor, Yale Divinity School (2004-2005)

Anscar J. Chupungco, OSB, Professor of Liturgical Inculturation and Liturgical Theology, San Beda College Graduate School of Liturgy, Manila, Philippines.

Melva Wilson Costen, Helmar Emil Nielsen Professor of Worship and Music, Interdenominational Theological Center, Atlanta, Georgia

Dirk G. Lange, Assistant Professor of Christian Assembly, The Lutheran Theological Seminary at Philadelphia, Pennsylvania

Gordon W. Lathrop, Charles A. Schieren Professor of Liturgy, Emeritus, The Lutheran Theological Seminary at Philadelphia, Pennsylvania

Cynthia D. Moe-Lobeda, Assistant Professor, Department of Theology and Religious Studies and School of Theology and Ministry, Seattle University, Seattle, Washington.

Gail Ramshaw, Professor of Religion, LaSalle University, Philadelphia, Pennsylvania

Don E. Saliers, OSL, Wm. R. Cannon Distinguished Professor of Theology and Worship, Candler School of Theology, Emory University, Atlanta, Georgia.

# Ordo: Bath, Word, Prayer, Table

Mag. dr. Edward C.F.A. Schillebeeckx, Professor emeritus for Systematic and Historical Theology,
    Radboud University Nijmegen, The Netherlands.

S. Anita Stauffer, former research secretary for worship, Lutheran World Federation,
    Geneva, Switzerland.

Samuel Torvend, Associate Professor of European Religious History,
    Pacific Lutheran University in Tacoma, Washington.

Dwight W. Vogel, OSL, Pilgrim Place, Claremont, California; Ernest and Bernice Styberg Professor
    Emeritus of Worship and Preaching, Garrett-Evangelical Theological Seminary,
    Evanston, Illinois

Gláucia Vasconcelos Wilkey, Assistant Professor, Liturgical Theology; Coordinator for Ecumenical
    Liturgies; Director, Summer Institute for Liturgy and Worship,
    School of Theology and Ministry, Seattle University.

# Publications of Gordon W. Lathrop

PRINCIPAL PUBLICATIONS:

BOOKS:

*Central Things: Worship in Word and Sacrament* (Minneapolis: Augsburg Fortress, 2005).

*Christian Assembly: Marks of the Church in a Pluralistic Age*, with Timothy J. Wengert (Minneapolis: Fortress, 2004).

*Holy Ground: A Liturgical Cosmology* (Minneapolis: Fortress, 2003).

*Holy People: A Liturgical Ecclesiology* (Minneapolis: Fortress, 1999)

*Holy Things: A Liturgical Theology* (Minneapolis: Fortress, 1993).

*New Proclamation, Year B 2000: Easter through Pentecost*, with Linda Maloney, Neil Elliott, Frank Senn (Minneapolis: Fortress, 2000).

*Readings for the Assembly*, three volumes, Cycles A, B, C, with Gail Ramshaw (Minneapolis: Augsburg Fortress, 1995, 1996, 1997).

*Proclamation 6: Easter A* (Minneapolis: Fortress, 1996).

"What are the essentials of Christian worship?", vol. 1 in the series *Open Questions in Worship* (Minneapolis: Augsburg Fortress, 1994).
*Psalter for the Christian People*, with Gail Ramshaw (Collegeville: Liturgical Press, 1994). This psalter also appears in the *Book of Common Worship* (Louisville: Westminster/John Knox, 1993).

*Living Witnesses, The Adult Catechumenate: Congregational Prayers to Accompany the Catechumenal Process* (Winnipeg: Evangelical Lutheran Church in Canada, 1992).

*Proclamation 4: Advent and Christmas B* (Minneapolis: Fortress, 1990).

*Lectionary for the Christian People*, three volumes, with Gail Ramshaw (New York and Philadelphia: Pueblo and Fortress, 1986, 1987, 1988).

*An Easter Sourcebook: the Fifty Days*, with Gabe Huck and Gail Ramshaw (Chicago: Liturgy Training Publications, 1988).

Translation of Herman Wegman, *Christian Worship in East and West: a Study Guide to Liturgical History* (New York: Pueblo, 1986).

*Paschal Mission* (Chicago: Liturgy Training Publications, 1983, 1984).

*Lectionary Themes* (Minneapolis: Augsburg, 1976).

*The Joyful Fast: Lenten Meditations for Students* (Chicago: National Lutheran Council, 1965).

SERIES EDITED:

*Open Questions in Worship* (Minneapolis: Augsburg Fortress).
    2. What is "contemporary" worship? (1995).
    3. How does worship evangelize? (1995).
    4. What is changing in baptismal practice? (1995).
    5. What is changing in eucharistic practice? (1995).
    6. What are the ethical implications of worship? (1996).
    7. What does "multicultural" worship look like? (1996).
    8. How does the liturgy speak of God? (1996).

ARTICLES IN BOOKS AND JOURNALS:

"A Sermon for Sunday 15 in Year A," forthcoming in *Cross Accent*.

Review of Siobhán Garrigan, *Beyond Ritual*, forthcoming in *Worship*.

"Conservation and critique: principles in Lutheran liturgical renewal as proposals toward the unity of the churches," in James Puglisi, ed., *Liturgical Renewal as a Way to Christian Unity* (Collegeville: Liturgical Press, 2005).

"Conservazione e critica; principe del rinnovamento liturgico luterano: quali proposte per l'unità delle Chiese," in Giacomo Puglisi, ed., *Il Rinnovamento Liturgico come Via all'Unità Christiana* (Rome: Centro pro Unione, 2004), 92-104.

Review of Alan Lewis, *Between Cross and Resurrection: A Theology of Holy Saturday* in *Interpretation* 58:1 (January 2004), 82-83.

"Texts in Tension: Translations for Contemporary Worship," in Harold W. Attridge and Margot E. Fassler, eds., *Psalms in Community: Jewish and Christian Textual, Liturgical, and Artistic Traditions* (Atlanta: Society of Biblical Literature, 2003), 373-378.

"Sunday, Assembly, Sky: How Does Liturgical Time Locate Us?" *Liturgical Ministry* 12 (Spring 2003), 75-83.

"Thanksgiving and Beseeching: A Liturgical Spirituality of Reorientation in the World," in W. Emilsen and J. Squires, eds., *Prayer and Thanksgiving: Essays in Honour of Graham Hughes* (UTC Publications, Sydney, Australia: 2003).

"Gottesdienst im lutherischen Kontext," *Handbuch der Liturgik* 3 (Vandenhoeck & Ruprecht, 2003).

"Holy Ground: Biblical and Liturgical Reorientation in the World," *Worship* 77:1 (January 2003), 2-22.

"Bible, Use of in Worship;" "Daily Prayer 5: Lutheran;" "Eucharist 8: Lutheran;" and "Word, Services of the, 8: Lutheran," in Paul Bradshaw, ed., *The New Westminster Dictionary of Liturgy and Worship* (Westminster John Knox: 2002).

"A Lutheran Professor Looks at the *Book of Common Worship*," *Presbyterian Outlook* (September 30, 2002), 8.

"The Enduring Legacy of Robert Hovda," *Worship* 76:4 (July 2002), 338-344.

"Eucaristia con crianHas," *TEAR: Liturgia em Revista* 5 (August 2001).

"Chistian Worship and Christian Unity," *Benedictine Bridge* 6 (Ordinary Time 2001).

"Come to the Waters: Communal Liturgy and Spiritual Formation in North American Theological Education," *Tro & Tanke* 2001:7.

"Strong Center, Open Door: A Vision of Continuing Liturgical Renewal," *Worship* 75:1 (January 2001), 35-45.

# Ordo: Bath, Word, Prayer, Table

"At the Intersection of Eucharist and Capital: A Response to Rodney Clapp," *Proceedings of the North American Academy of Liturgy* (2000), 51-54.

"'The Bath and the Table, the Prayer and the Word:' N. F. S. Grundtvig and the Lutheran Contribution to Ecumenical Liturgical Renewal," in *Grundtvig Studier 2000* (Danske Boghandleres Kommisionsanstalt: Copenhagen, 2000).

"Aidan Kavanagh: an introduction," in Dwight Vogel, editor, *Reader in Liturgical Theology* (Collegeville: Liturgical Press, 2000).

"A Contemporary Lutheran Looks at the 1549 *Book of Common Prayer*," Virginia Seminary Journal (January 2000), 35-43; reprinted in *The Anglican* 30:1 (January 2001), 5-9.

"The Revised Sacramentary in Ecumenical Affirmation and Admonition," in Mark R. Francis and Keith F. Pecklers, eds., *Liturgy for the New Millennium: A Commentary on the Revised Sacramentary: Essays in Honor of Anscar J. Chupungco, OSB* (Collegeville: Liturgical Press, 2000), 129-141.

"The Water that Speaks: the *Ordo* of Baptism and its Ecumenical Implications," in Thomas F. Best and Dagmar Heller, eds., *Becoming a Christian: The Ecumenical Implications of Our Common Baptism*, Faith and Order Paper 184 (Geneva: World Council of Churches, 1999), 13-29.

"Worship in the Twenty-first Century: Contextually Relevant and Catholic," *Currents in Theology and Mission* 26:4 (August 1999), 283-313.

"Liturgy and Mission in the North American Context," in Thomas H. Schattauer, ed., *Inside Out: Worship in an Age of Mission* (Minneapolis: Augsburg Fortress, 1999), 201-212.

"Baptismal Ordo and Rites of Passage in the Church," and "Preaching in the Dialogue of Worship with Culture" in S. Anita Stauffer, ed., *Baptism, Rites of Passage and Culture* (Geneva: Lutheran World Federation, 1999), 27-46, 245-258. Parts of this volume, including the article on baptismal ordo, have been translated into Spanish and French.

"New Pentecost or Joseph's Britches: Reflections on the history and meaning of the worship ordo in the megachurches," *Worship* 72:6 (November 1998), 521-538.

"How Awesome is this Place! The LBW and the Encounter with God," in R. R. Van Loon, ed., *Encountering God: The Legacy of the Lutheran Book of Worship for the 21st Century* (Minneapolis: Kirk House, 1998), 40-51.

"Bibel. V. Praktisch-theologisch. 1. Christlicher Gottesdienst," and "Jesus Christus. II. Jesus Christus in der Geschichte des Christentums. 2. Liturgiegeschichte," in *Religion in Geschichte und Gegenwart, Vierte Auflage,* (Tübingen: Mohr Siebeck, 1998).

"God's Time and Our Times: Christian worship and local cultures in dialogue," *Australian Journal of Liturgy* 6:3 (May 1998), 117-130.

"'O Taste and See': The Geography of Liturgical Ethics," in E. Byron Anderson and Bruce T. Morrill, eds., *Liturgy and the Moral Self* (Collegeville: Liturgical Press, 1998).

"What is the Shape of Worship as the New Millenium Approaches?" *Parish Practice Notebook* (Spring 1998).

"North American Lutheran Worship at the Close of the Century," *CrossAccent* (January 1998), 3-5.

"The Bodies on Nevado Ampato: A Further Note on Offering and Offertory," *Worship* (71:6, 1997), 546-554.

"How does the Lutheran tradition illuminate the catechumenal process?" in Samuel Torvend amd Lani Willis, eds., *Welcome to Christ: A Lutheran Introduction to the Catechumenate* (Minneapolis: Augsburg Fortress, 1997), 48-56; reprinted in *Parish Practice Notebook* (Winter 2001), 1-5.

"The Worship Books in Mutual Affirmation and Admonition: Liturgy as a Source for Lutheran-Reformed Unity," *Reformed Liturgy and Music* (21:2, 1997), 88-92.

"Extreme Symbolism: Word as Sacrament, Sacrament as Word," *Parish Practice Notebook* (Spring, 1997).

"Transforming Offering: a response to Carter Lindberg and Paul Rorem," in *Dialog* 35 (Fall, 1996), 258-262.

"Worship: Local yet Universal," in *Christian Worship: Unity in Cultural Diversity* (Geneva: Lutheran World Federation, 1996), 47-66. This volume has also been translated into German, Spanish and French.

"The Shape of the Liturgy: A Framework for Contextualization," in *Christian Worship: Unity in Cultural Diversity* (Geneva: Lutheran World Federation, 1996), 67-75.

"Koinonia and the Shape of the Liturgy," *Studia Liturgica* 26 (1996), 65-81, also published as "La Koinonia et la Forme de la Liturgie," *La Maison Dieu* 204 (1995:4), 83-106.

"The Lectionary in Year B," in *Sundays and Seasons: Worship Planning Guide, 1996-1997* (Minneapolis: Augsburg Fortress, 1996), 5-8.

# Ordo: Bath, Word, Prayer, Table

"The Lima Liturgy and Beyond: moving forward ecumenically," *The Ecumenical Review* 48:1 (Jan. 1996), 62-68; reprinted in Thomas F. Best and Dagmar Heller, eds., *Eucharistic Worship in Ecumenical Contexts* (Geneva: World Council of Churches, 1998), 22-28.

"On the Practical Use of the 'Shape of the Liturgy'," *Parish Practice Notebook* (Summer, 1995).

"Knowing Something a Little: On the Role of the *Lex Orandi* in the Search for Christian Unity," in Thomas F. Best and Dagmar Heller, eds., *So We Believe, So We Pray: Towards Koinonia in Worship*, Faith and Order Paper 171 (Geneva: World Council of Churches, 1995), 38-48.

"The Origin and Early Meanings of Christian Baptism," *Worship* 68:6 (November 1994), 504-522.

"Give the Word to Eat and Drink; Let the Bread and Cup Be Heard," *Pastoral Music* 19:1 (October-November, 1994), 41-44.

"On baptizing adults: the catechumenate among Lutherans," *Parish Practice Notebook* (Summer, 1994).

"Luther: *Formula Missae*," "A Lutheran Theology of Worship," and "Lutheran Worship," in Robert E. Webber, ed., *The Complete Library of Christian Worship* (Nashville: Star Song, 1994), vol. 2, 188-195, 286-288, and vol. 3, 165-172.

"Baptism in the New Testament and its Cultural Settings," in *Worship and Culture in Dialogue* (Geneva: Lutheran World Federation, 1994), 17-38. This volume has also been translated into Spanish, French and German.

"Eucharist in the New Testament and its Cultural Settings," in *Worship and Culture in Dialogue* (Geneva: Lutheran World Federation, 1994), 67-82.

"Worship and Culture in the Lutheran Reformation," in *Worship and Culture in Dialogue* (Geneva: Lutheran World Federation, 1994), 121-128.

"A Contemporary Lutheran Approach to Worship and Culture: Sorting Out the Critical Principles," in *Worship and Culture in Dialogue* (Geneva: Lutheran World Federation, 1994), 137-151.

"At Least Two Words: the Liturgy as Proclamation," in *Liturgy: We Proclaim* (The Liturgical Conference, Summer, 1993), 1-3, reprinted in Blair Gilmer Meeks, ed., *The Landscape of Praise: Readings in Liturgical Renewal* (Valley Forge: Trinity, 1996), 183-185.

Review of William Willimon, *Peculiar Speech: Preaching to the Baptized* in *Liturgy 90* (May/June 1993), 14-15.

"A Sense of the Season," in *Liturgy: From Ashes to Fire A* (The Liturgical Conference, Summer, 1992), 1-4.

"At the beginning of the Service: Moments which welcome a stranger to the Gospel," *Parish Practice Notebook* (Spring, 1992).

"Paying attention: the practice of homily preparation," *Liturgy 90* (April 1992), 4-6.

"Christian Leadership and Liturgical Community," *Worship* 66:2 (March 1992), 98-125.

"Hvad er liturgisk teologi, og hvorfor er den vigtig? Kommentar til den nordamerikanske debat," *Kritisk forum for praktisk teologi* 46 (Denmark: 1991), 40-52.

"The Philadelphia Seminary and the Liturgy," in 125th anniversary volume of the Philadelphia Lutheran Seminary (Philadelphia: 1991).

"Holy Things: Foundations for Liturgical Theology," in R. Lee and D. Truemper, eds., *Institute of Liturgical Studies Occasional Papers*, 7 (Valparaiso, Indiana: 1991), 6-53.

Translation of Herman Wegman, "*Successio Sanctorum*" in J. Neil Alexander, *Time and Community: Essays in Honor of Thomas Julian Talley* (Washington, Pastoral Press: 1990).

"At the Table," nine articles on communion practice in *The Lutheran*, 3:3-11 (February - August, 1990).

Foreword to Thomas G. Christensen, *An African Tree of Life* (Maryknoll, Orbis: 1990).

"Justin, Eucharist and `Sacrifice,'" *Worship* 64:1 (January, 1990).

Review of R. W. Franklin, *Nineteenth Century Churches, Worship* (May, 1989).

"How Symbols Speak," *Liturgy* (January, 1988). Reprinted in *Sisters Today* 65: 326-332 (September 1993).

"AIDS and the Cup: Notes for Parish Use," *Parish Practice Notebook* (Fall, 1987). Reprinted in *Worship* and *Liturgy 80*.

"The Institution Narrative," in Frank Senn, ed., *New Eucharistic Prayers* (New York, Paulist: 1987).

"Burial, Lutheran" and "Marriage, Lutheran," in J. G. Davies, ed., *A New Dictionary of Liturgy and Worship* (London, SCM: 1986).

# Ordo: Bath, Word, Prayer, Table

Review of J. Reumann, *The Supper of the Lord, Worship* (November, 1985).

"What are we hoping for?" *Accent on Worship* 3:4 (1985).

"Improving Our Tradition," *The Lutheran* 23:13 (1985).

"A Rebirth of Images: on the Use of the Bible in the Liturgy," *Worship* (July, 1984); reprinted in Dwight Vogel, *Reader in Liturgical Theology* (Collegeville: Liturgical Press, 2000).

"Yielding to Polycarp: Concelebration Reconsidered," *Lutheran Forum* 17:3 (1983).

"Words at the Solstice: Four Theses and Eight Christmas Greetings," *Dialog* (Christmas, 1982).

"Scripture in the Assembly: the Ancient and Lively Tension," *Liturgy* (Summer, 1982).

"Tree of Death, Tree of Life," *Liturgy* (September, 1980).

"Pastoral Liturgical Theology and the *Lutheran Book of Worship*," *Dialog* (Spring, 1979).

"The Lord's Supper on the Lord's Day," *Lutheran Forum* 12:3 (1978).

Translation of the eucharistic prayer of Hippolytus of Rome in *Lutheran Book of Worship* (Minneapolis, Augsburg: 1978).

"Liturgy: Pattern and Image for Ministry," *Liturgy* 22:7 (1977).

"Liturgy and Ministry: the Availability of the Holy," *Liturgy* 22:4 (1977).

"The Eucharist as a 'Hungry Feast' and the Appropriateness of Our Want," *Living Worship* 13:4 (1977).

"The Prayers of Jesus and the Great Prayer of the Church," *Lutheran Quarterly* 26:2 (1974).

"Liturgy of the Hours," in Gabe Huck and Virginia Sloyan, eds., *Parishes and Families* (Washington, The Liturgical Conference: 1973).

"On Bringing the Ark from Ashdod to Jerusalem: Reflections on the Use of the Eucharistic Prayer in Lutheran Celebrations," *Response* 13:2 (1973).